AIMING HIGH

AIMING HIGH

*Masayoshi Son, SoftBank Group
and Disrupting Silicon Valley*

ATSUO INOUE

HODDER &
STOUGHTON

First published in Great Britain in 2021 by Hodder & Stoughton
An Hachette UK company

3

KOKORAZASHI TAKAKU: SON MASAYOSHI SEIDEN
Copyright © 2021 Atsuo Inoue

Original Japanese edition published by Jitsugyo no Nihon Sha, Ltd., Tokyo
This English edition is published by arrangement with Jitsugyo no
Nihon Sha, Ltd., Tokyo c/o Tuttle-Mori Agency, Inc., Tokyo.

The right of Atsuo Inoue to be identified as the Author of the Work has been
asserted by him in accordance with the Copyright, Designs and Patents Act 1988.

Translation from Japanese in association with First
Edition Translations Ltd, Cambridge, UK.

A CIP catalogue record for this title is available from the British Library

Hardback ISBN 9781529338577
Trade Paperback ISBN 9781529338584

Typeset in Caslon 540 by Hewer Text UK Ltd, Edinburgh
Printed and bound in India by Manipal Technologies Limited, Manipal

MIX
Paper from
responsible sources
FSC™ C104740

Hodder & Stoughton Ltd
Carmelite House
50 Victoria Embankment
London EC4Y 0DZ

www.hodder.co.uk

Prologue   An unregistered plot of land

Even now Son Masayoshi's earliest memory comes back to him in his dreams. In it, he is a child running through a subway built under the railway near where he used to live. He recalls, 'Dark subways and tunnels were always terrifying for me as a child, so whenever we had to pass through one to get to wherever we were going I would always start crying.' Sobbing loudly and running fast, the end of the subway begins to fill with light at the point his voice is about to give out, the tunnel opening up to a bright, sunlit world.

Son would revisit the old haunts where he was born – in Saga Prefecture on the far western island of Kyushu in the Japanese archipelago – and that subway he used to timidly dash through with his cousins and older brothers as a young boy was still there. A lot of time had passed since his childhood and the entrance and exit of the subway was narrower than he remembered – an average car, for example, would not get in.

It was also considerably longer than he recalled and somehow, even with the passing of time, the memories of traversing the tunnel in tears and the sense of fear were still palpable. Son would feel his heart start beating faster and his chest growing just a little bit tighter, although he would then comment, 'However, once I'd got out of the subway I was so overjoyed, it was like seeing the world through completely new eyes.'

The story of Son Masayoshi begins on an unregistered plot of land near Goken Road in Tosu Municipality, Saga Prefecture.

'The land belonged to the Japanese National Railways. Both of my grandparents had come over from South Korea, hiding in the hull of a small fishing vessel,' Son recalls.

They had nothing to eat, no place to stay and could not speak the Japanese language. You could not even say they were starting from square one, such was their situation. They were facing an uphill struggle just to *reach* zero. 'The grounds were completely off-grid. It was the sort of place only homeless people would go to.' Son's grandfather, and others like him who had come over from South Korea, collected bits of galvanised iron sheets and built a shelter as protection against the elements, and in doing so formed a small colony.

As the plot of land was not registered it was illegal to live there and Japanese National Railways employees would routinely burn the place down as if they were carrying out just another controlled burn of company lands. The next day, however, the structure would be rebuilt, restored to its previous state, just with new bits of discarded galvanised metal. The whole charade repeated itself, over and over. They could burn the structure down as often as they liked but it would still be rebuilt by the next day.

Son recalls: 'They had settled there illegally, and so they were resolute, they had no other options. This was a matter of survival for them and you could kick them, you could try to stamp them out, but with each blow, each setback, their will to live only grew stronger.'

Even though the message being sent was that they were better off dead, they had to live. Son has thought about this. 'My dad's generation possessed the same resilience and determination. I'm like the sequel to my dad – if everyone calls me an entrepreneur then I've got to say for the record it was my dad who was the original entrepreneur in the family. I like to look at it from the angle that my dad was the original *Godfather* and I'm the *Godfather Part 2* – the story of the father and the son is one and the same.'

Fast-forward to 14 November 2020 and both Son and his father – Mitsunori and Masayoshi – were watching the Pacific Baseball League Climax Series together at the Fukuoka PayPay Dome when Mitsunori surprised his son with an off-the-cuff comment. 'Masayoshi, recently you've become more and more like a whale – you're only feasting on sardines, you're not really bothered with the smaller fish. Except in your case the sardines are platform providers.' Masayoshi was caught off guard by the fact his dad knew the term 'platform provider' and the fact he knew that in recent times NASDAQ had taken to referring to the SoftBank Group as a whale.

The surprises did not stop there, however, as Mitsunori continued with comments on his son's company's performance. 'Nvidia are a solid acquisition but getting them into cahoots with Arm is a stroke of genius – there's the possibility there they'll become a huge platform provider.' Aged 85, Son Mitsunori was at the cutting edge in terms of the latest technical advances on the market and no one knew this better than his own son, Masayoshi commenting, 'I had the best teacher around in yourself, Dad.'

When Son was in his first year of primary, aged six or seven, Mitsunori gave his wife a strict order: she was not to drop suffixes used to address people in Japanese (such as -san, -chan or -kun: it is common for parents to do this with their children as they are higher up the pecking order of respect) with him, but rather to call him Masayoshi-san. 'From the age of six or so she's actually always called me "Masayoshi-san". I think what my mum and dad thought was that by always addressing me with a respectful suffix I would grow up to achieve a position worthy of such respect.' It was part of his father's bringing him up as though he were raising a prince to become king one day, and another part of that was instilling in him a mentality to live for other people and their well-being.

At the same time – his first year in primary – Masayoshi had decided that when he grew up he wanted to be in a position of responsibility, with a whole legion of employees working under him, which would explain why when it was time to select the class president his was the first hand to shoot up for the candidacy. He was always at the head of the class and even at this young age had tremendous mettle, the result of the rules his father had set concerning his upbringing. Masayoshi comments on his father's approach: 'Rather than be told exactly what to think I was taught about ways of thinking about things, and so for that reason I only ever received praise from my father. I think that's the best way to raise a child'.

As a boy, the most frequent reason why Son would have to walk the dreaded subway was because on the other side of it was the River Daigi, which is where his Uncle Shigenori lived. Masayoshi's cousins were close in age to him, so they were more like brothers. They would play and go fishing in the Daigi together. For Son and his siblings and cousins this was their playground in the summer months.

Son would watch as the other boys in his family would catch fish using broad nets, but by the time he was 10 he was joining in casting nets from the river's edge and splashing about to scare the fish into them. Crayfish and loaches would find their way into the nets as well, but the boys were only really ever after sleek and nimble minnows.

Son Jong-kyong, Masayoshi's grandfather, loved fishing in rivers and his wife would prepare *tsukudani* or boiled fish from his catches.

If Son Jong-kyong's main reason for catching fish was to have something to eat, for Masayoshi it was a source of pleasure: fishing was not a daily activity, and the contents of his stomach did not depend upon a successful catch at the river that day.

Whilst Masayoshi was still in primary school his family moved away from the settlement, but on weekends and days off Mitsunori still regularly met up with his parents and brothers and sisters for a mass family meal, which entailed trips to the Daigi every weekend and during summer holidays.

'I learnt a lot about catching fish during those trips. It was best to go around nine or ten o'clock at night as that's when the fish get sleepy, and if you scare them the right way into the nets you can catch loads more than you would do than in the daytime. The scenery of a mountain river at sunset in the middle of summer – like the folding screens painted by Senju Hiroshi – is seared into my memory, conjuring all manner of remembrances of the good times, which is why even now I still love going to rivers.'

Every day was a new adventure for the young Masayoshi, especially going through the subway tunnel. 'Now I'm investing in unicorn start-ups and trying to suss out what the landscape will be like in ten years' time, but really that is an extension of the feeling I had coming out of that awful tunnel and heading out to catch some fish. The sense of excitement I felt when we were living on that unregistered plot in Tosu is exactly the same.'

The first time Masayoshi would ever see a copy of his family register was when he was in high school and had to apply for a passport so he could attend a short-term study-abroad programme in the United States. In the field where his address would have been were the words 'unregistered plot'. He thought it was odd and wondered why the land would not be registered. Son remembered thinking, 'I'm a nobody – the land I was born on isn't even on the books.'

When he came to leave the country on the school trip to California, Son noticed the passport another student was holding had a red cover – the colour of a Japanese passport. What Son had was a signed entry permit – he was considered a foreigner. Going through passport control meant he had to stand in the foreigners' queue, and it was then that the penny dropped: he was a foreigner living on an unregistered plot of land.

Up until this point Son had gone by the surname of Yasumoto (a Japanese surname), had spoken to his classmates in Japanese, and had for all intents and purposes lived his life as a Japanese student. Being singled out and forced into another queue made his heart sink; the sense of alienation was unbearable. The other students looked perplexed – surely, he was in the wrong queue. Son offered no explanations as his heart sank even further.

Once Stateside in California his disposition brightened and he quickly forgot about the whole ordeal, recalling, 'When I looked up and saw that blue sky leaving San Francisco airport and those massive motorways unlike anything in Japan, with six lanes – and that's just the one direction – it was extraordinary, I felt amazing.'

There were people of all races there but they all spoke the same language and somehow all managed to peacefully coexist as American citizens, and seeing this made Son realise that his own problems were trivial by comparison. That 'unregistered plot of land' mindset could do one.

Along with the vast, sunny American sky, Son would also take tremendous inspiration from the figure of Sakamoto Ryoma described in *Ryoma Goes His Way*, and when he returned to Japan he would begin going by the surname of his ancestors: Son. His reasoning was simple: he wanted to express his true feelings and offer inspiration to those like himself who were concerned about their place of birth or surname. Everyone had the right to dream, after all. He also wanted people to take inspiration to do the impossible and challenge their limits.

'The cards I was dealt meant I started at a deficit compared to everyone else, but in the end that proved an extraordinary source of inspiration and energy to go on and do the impossible. I am beyond thankful to God for that gift.'

Regardless of the fact he had started from less than zero his childhood was still fun, enjoying himself with the other children and going fishing – it's not like he could catch fish on his own. There had to be someone to handle the net, then someone else making an almighty din and rustling through the aquatic plant growth and then someone else to direct the fish into the net. As long as everyone did their bit they could bring in a decent haul. Son comments, 'Everyone had a shared goal and we worked together as a team, which was what made it so much fun when we caught loads of fish.'

Son does not and did not particularly enjoy going fishing on his own, with a rod and line, having to set the line and then sit still until a fish came along. There was effectively nothing to do, no strategy or line of attack. 'Whenever you go out fishing with a trap or a net you need a plan first. You've got to know where the fish are so you can place the net in the right place. You've got to survey the waters, check the direction and speed of the current, prepare your tools and then make sure everyone is on the same page about who's doing what. Then you decide on your tactics – things like how to literally catch the fish whilst they're napping.

'And you check the holes in the mesh of your net – if too small then the net is likely to clump up and get tangled and then you only end up with minuscule fish, but if the holes are slightly larger then you'll catch the larger fish and the small fish can glide on through. And that's how you bag the big ones. It's the exact same principle the SoftBank Vision Fund operates on.'

In the nearby reservoirs or elsewhere on the Daigi people would be fishing with a line and rod, but Son and his friends were always quick to disparage them – what good was spending all day on that approach? When do you call it quits? 'If I'm 10 years old and going to trap fish in the river then I want to catch every last one, and you can only do that with a broad enough net. In the end we caught infinitely more fish this way than if we'd gone with the line and rod approach, to the point my granddad couldn't finish his plate we'd caught so much. That's the sort of growth I'm after.'

The lasting memories from his childhood in Tosu inevitably involve the subway, the river and having to start from a deficit. And the games of hide-and-seek. Together with the other children Masayoshi would play hide-and-seek in the middle of the night, sneaking into pigsties and hiding behind the animals themselves or on the roof. To keep the livestock from getting out, the pens were lined with barbed wire and on one occasion Masayoshi, running away from his pursuer in the dark, caught a faceful of barbed wire. It was a painful lesson that some hiding places were better than others.

'It was exciting because you weren't allowed to go into the pigsty, which of course made it the ideal hiding spot. You could ride on the rafters of the sty, behind one of the columns supporting the structure, underneath the eaves – and then if all of a sudden a hand reaches out in the darkness and you've been caught by whoever's "it", it's a thrill unlike any other. I always loved that element of risk and excitement whenever playing with the other kids, that sense of always being alert, always being "on". I always had to win.'

Indeed for Son it is never enough to simply try his hand at something or dabble in it – he will be in it to win, studying the ins and outs for any foothold that may gave him an advantage. The inherent risk involved is an infinite source of excitement and joy as well.

Masayoshi may have grown up in a poor family, but life was always fun. The the Korean settlement was built in a ditch next to a railway line and so the rhythmic pulse of the trains and their whistles going past became his lullabies, Son commenting, 'This probably sounds a bit sad but the sounds of the trains going past were exciting, they instilled a certain energy and vitality in me. Trains were another source of thrills as a boy.' A steady rhythm would announce the arrival of a train speeding past their home, its destination the future, Son calling it 'the sound of hope'.

His father's business steadily got bigger and bigger and so the family were able to escape poverty, to the point where Mitsunori became wealthy enough to be the first person in Tosu to purchase his own personal car. 'I was able to watch him make his money and climb the ladder, shadow him almost, and as he climbed higher and higher I felt prouder and prouder. Even though it was just a small business I was party to the whole process of him becoming an independent success. I'm so glad he was my dad.'

The Sons would eventually leave Tosu, with Masayoshi enrolling in Hikino Primary School in Kitakyushu (Fukuoka). Whilst he frequently got top marks in his year, his textbooks never actually left the school grounds – they never even saw the inside of his school bag, which only ever contained his packed lunch and another bag with his gym shoes in.

Outside of class he was the leader of the gang, often heading up expeditions into the local mountains or losing himself for hours playing football with the rest of the neighbourhood kids. And then suddenly, in his second year of primary school, not once did he go outside to play. Instead, he threw himself completely into his studies.

A number of graphs done by the pupils as an assignment hung on one of the walls in Masayoshi's classroom, amongst which was one page torn out of a notebook, full of self-study notes and bearing the cherry-blossom-shaped stamp of the teacher's approval. Up until that point Masayoshi had hardly ever received the teacher's cherry blossom seal but one day, he thought to himself, one day he would have the most and that classroom wall would be covered with them.

He began revising frantically, knowing that, regardless of the subject, if he studied hard his work would be acknowledged.

At no point in time did either of his parents have to tell him to 'hit the books'. In fact, it was quite the opposite: 'Study in moderation – if all you're going to do is revise you'll never become a decent human being!'

In the event that a family outing or such was announced, Masayoshi would inevitably stay behind to work. His family started to worry, wondering what exactly had got into him.

The reason was a simple one though: he wanted the seal of approval and was going to learn the material properly, having no time for rote memorisation. Arts and crafts were inherently enjoyable and Son was also greatly drawn to how a painter could take a blank canvas and then fill it with pictures.

Seeing his son engage in such creative endeavours filled Mitsunori with tremendous pride and he would tell his son, 'When I look at you . . . I'm at a loss for words, I don't know what to say.'

'What do you mean?'

'There's a good chance you're a genius,' his father replied. 'The brightest in all of Japan, and I know you're going to go out there and make a name for yourself.'

Masayoshi was already well beyond what would be expected of a child his age and his doting parents were over the moon, praises coming thick and fast. These were genuine, however, and as a result Masayoshi began to take their words to heart, recalling, 'I started to believe that if I set my mind to something, I could achieve it. I really became obsessed by the idea that I couldn't let myself be satisfied with "just average" – maybe I really was a genius.'

As this thought took hold, the side of his personality capable of pushing onwards no matter what began to develop exponentially, although at the time all he had was a hazy dream and self-belief. Ultimately, he was Korean, and there were serious questions concerning whether he would be accepted by Japanese society at large.

Masayoshi's time in secondary school was ordinary, attending the Kurume University Preparatory High School, which was second only to La Salle High School in the prestigious high school rankings for Kyushu. During his first year in high school and prior to his trip to America he asked his grandmother to take him with her on a trip back to Korea: he abhorred the fact it was a taboo subject in his household and wanted to see the country of his ancestors before he set off Stateside.

The trip lasted just under a fortnight and what Son found was a country of unspoilt land with apple orchards lining the roads. Arriving at his grandmother's village, all of his extended family there had come to welcome them; whilst they were not financially well off by any stretch of the imagination – the village did not even have electricity – what they did have an abundance of was good cheer and concern for each other.

Son felt blessed and incredibly thankful for the care and affection they showed him during his stay. There was no social hierarchy in the village, just the simple townsfolk, and Son swore to himself that one day he would bring them joy and prove himself a true asset to society.

PART ONE

Chapter 1　　**On his way**

The date is 27 January 1973. The United States, North Vietnam, South Vietnam and the Provisional Revolutionary Government of the Republic of South Vietnam have signed the Paris Peace Accords. What was supposed to have been an honourable exit for the Americans was later annulled and the Vietnam War raged for another two years. In the summer of that year, a boy from Kyushu would travel to the United States for the first time, having enrolled on a language course there.

The excitement and anticipation of visiting such an unknown and far-off place were soon punctured on arrival at the Tokyo Haneda Airport international departures gate. He now had to split off from his friends and head to the designated foreigners' gate. 'What's so different about you?' asked a friend, although Masayoshi pretended not to hear him. Back in those days, Japanese and foreigners were separated at the international departures gate.

Up until then Masayoshi had led a regular life as a Korean national in Japan with no real concerns – this was his first brush with the reality of the matter. The experience was not a pleasant one, his grand departure for America deflated by the banal reality of it all.

Upon boarding the aircraft, and while his friends were still bubbling with excitement, Masayoshi quietly fell sound asleep. It seemed nothing could faze him.

The aeroplane landed in San Francisco without incident. The California sky was endless, blue, clear – quite different to the sky in Japan. Masayoshi inhaled deeply and the brain fog caused by travel and jet lag completely disappeared. He forgot all about the humiliation he had experienced at Haneda Airport.

Classes for the language training course were to be held in classrooms belonging to the University of California, Berkeley. It was still hard for Masayoshi to distinguish between the 'L' and 'R' consonant sounds, even for common vocabulary words, despite being able to read them perfectly well from his English lessons in Japan. Take, for example, 'McDonald's'. In Japanese this is pronounced *MOCK-dough-NAH-roo-dough*, but in American English it is something completely different altogether.

Later in life, and due to speaking commitments at conventions in both the States and around the world in front of large audiences, Son would develop considerably more confidence in his handling of the English language. His first trip abroad, though, was spent coming to grips with the pronunciation.

Outside of his studies he was also able to take in some of the sights of the American West: the city of San Francisco itself, Yosemite National Park and the Grand Canyon National Park. More than tourism, however, shopping and the vast American motorway network would have a greater impact on Masayoshi.

Everything was huge and his own problems seemed insignificant in comparison.

Berkeley in the 1970s was an interesting place to be due to the number of anti-war protests held concerning what the Americans were getting up to in Vietnam. From an academic standpoint, too,

American universities were gaining global prominence, having produced multiple Nobel Prize winners.

Once the day's lessons were over, Masayoshi would frequently walk around the campus with his classmates. During these walks he would regularly chance upon students enjoying college life each in their own way: one giving a passionate speech, another banging a Taiko drum, a bare-chested female student lying on the grass reading a book.

Berkeley was filled with all kinds of people: people with a different colour skin or age group compared to his own. America was a melting pot of races. Masayoshi had read about this in his textbooks, although seeing it with his own eyes could be overwhelming at times.

Whilst America may have been experiencing a period of upheaval due to the Vietnam War, Masayoshi was glad he had made the journey. Returning home to Japan, all smiles and bronzed after his four weeks abroad, he had an announcement to make to his parents:

'I'm going to leave school.'

Naturally, this declaration was met with strong opposition from his family. All his relatives warned him that it was much too soon – he'd only just started secondary, why couldn't he wait until he had graduated? And was schooling really the issue at hand here?

Masayoshi's own reasoning was that even if he went through the trouble of finishing university he would not be accepted into Japanese society because of his nationality. The gears were turning inside his head, however: if he graduated from an American university they would have to rate him back in Japan, and so he set about looking for a way to make this happen. Life was too short and if he didn't act now he would regret it later.

Masayoshi was acutely aware that life is measured in decades, years, months, weeks, days, hours, minutes, seconds – all of them counting down. He was determined to live every second to the fullest. *How far could he go at Berkeley under that vast blue sky?* Masayoshi had made up his mind and was unyielding in his convictions, although he never at any point stopped worrying about his family. To further complicate matters, soon afterwards Masayoshi's father began coughing up blood.

'You think it's all right to leave your poorly father behind whilst you go off and do your own thing?'

'You know your mother is going to miss you.'

'At a time like this when your family are really struggling to keep things together, you're going to go gallivanting off to America?'

Masayoshi found himself in the same predicament as Sakamoto Ryoma, the man who ushered in the modern era of Japan. Sakamoto had deserted the conservative Tosa clan and become a *ronin*, a lordless samurai. In that era, desertion was a serious crime and affected not just the deserter, but also his family members and relatives.

Even so, Masayoshi's mind was made up – this was something he had to do for himself. If he put off his second American trip now, that door may not open again. Following one's principles would occasionally mean having to step on a few toes, or so Masayoshi reasoned.

Besides, he knew there would come a day when he would be able to return the favour to his family – the task at hand was to stay focused on his trip to the New World and to plough ahead.

His relatives could protest all they liked about his plans, but the first person to give Masayoshi his blessing was his father, bedridden in hospital due to problems with his small intestine. His only condition, issued to Masayoshi at his bedside, was that he come home once a year to visit.

* * *

Prior to his departure in February 1974 for California, Masayoshi's Kurume High classmates organised a farewell do for him at the Ishibashi Sport Centre in Fukuoka, where they wished him every success in future over fizzy drinks and sweets, all joining in to sing the theme song from the popular television drama *The Young Ones*. The lyrics were prescient, particularly the line stating 'You're going to go off and do it'. Masayoshi wasn't above shedding a tear or two at the party.

His family saw him off at Fukuoka Airport. His mother, patting his back, her voice trembling from the tears, made him promise her to come back to visit them. Masayoshi's response, whilst in the affirmative, was purposely curt. As the plane flew towards its destination, memories would float into Masayoshi's mind only to vanish and then reappear again. This rare indulgence in sentimentality was only temporary, however.

Masayoshi was enrolled on a course in the English Language School at the Holy Names College (now Holy Names University), located in the San Francisco suburbs. The university itself was a private Roman Catholic school founded in 1868, well known for its nursing and economics programmes. Masayoshi plunged into his English language studies with aplomb.

'You Japanese?'

His interlocutor may have been asking in Japanese, but Masayoshi would respond in English: he was hell-bent on only speaking in his second language and this stubbornness served him well, as he very quickly got better and better in the language.

On the university grounds there was a long flight of stone steps, at the top of which was the chapel balcony, which on a sunny day had a tremendous view of the Richmond–San Rafael, Golden Gate, Bay and San Mateo bridges. Perhaps more relevantly – although Masayoshi could not yet know that his fate would be decided there

– Silicon Valley and its high concentration of high-tech companies could also be seen, albeit further off in the distance.

More distant still was the Pacific Ocean, and on the other side of the Pacific Ocean, Japan, where his dream of becoming an entrepreneur had been born and had sustained him this far.

Chapter 2   **Skipping high school**

It may have been exactly at this point in Masayoshi's life that fate came calling, or rather the door to a brighter future began to slowly open. On 9 August 1974, Richard Nixon resigned from the American presidency as a result of the Watergate scandal. On 14 October of the same year, Nagashima Shigeo, famous Yomiuri Giants baseball player, retired from the sport, signing off with his immortal phrase, 'The Giants are eternal, are indestructible.'

The new academic term in America that year began in September. The California sun was less intense than usual in Daly City, just south of San Francisco, where, after completing his language course at Holy Names, Masayoshi's new school, Serramonte High (public), was located (incidentally, in 1994 the school would be closed, later being reopened as a training school for computer engineers and a school for adults).

Back in 1974 a nervous-looking young man in a short-sleeved polo shirt, jeans and long hair knocked on the door of the principal's office.

Anthony Trujillo gave the young man a friendly smile and asked him to sit down. Trujillo – a man of sturdy build and deep voice – had been a famous American football player in his university days. He was now quite popular amongst the student body as he was hardly ever seen without an infectious smile on his face.

He beckoned to Masayoshi.

'My teacher told me you wanted to see me.'

While in the US Son had taken on the forename of John, under which he had enrolled as a second-year student at Serramonte High. It had only been one week since he had started school – what could have gone wrong?

In the classroom every last one of his classmates looked like they could have been film stars. There were no problems with any of them – all of them were approachable and Masayoshi was likewise friendly in his dealings with them. It truly was like he was living out the film he had written for himself in his mind, although recently he had started to feel as if things were slightly different from what he had expected. He felt like he was on a completely different level, and not in the sense that he was lagging behind everyone else – quite the opposite.

'What do you say to moving you up to the third-year class, straight away?' The principal's eyes flashed behind his glasses. He suddenly got very serious. 'I've just had a look into your records . . . It doesn't look like you actually graduated from high school in Japan.'

'Yes – I wanted to study abroad in America.'

'Even though' – Trujillo looked suitably astounded – 'you never completed the first-year curriculum.'

Under the four-year system in place at Serramonte, Son graduating from middle school in Japan was the equivalent of having finished the first year in the States, so he had enrolled as a second-year high school student.

'But, I just want to get into university as soon as possible.'

Trujillo was stunned by the pure naivety of the student's words. Son's attitude was not exactly what was Trujillo was expecting from someone from the Far East – the avoidance of confrontation at all costs. Quite the opposite, if anything; Son was proactive.

The next day, however, he was in class with the third-year students.

For the next five days – during mealtimes, in the bathroom, whenever he had a free moment – Son's nose was buried in a textbook.

Trujillo saw the effort he was putting in and decided Son should be treated as a special case, firstly being promoted to the third year and then the fourth year, blowing through any obstacles placed in his path. The only thing left was to sit the standardised tests for admittance to university.

In America at least it is not uncommon for people who have not finished secondary school to be admitted to university. That being said, however, a pupil finishing the high school curriculum in only three weeks and then going on to achieve a good result in the brutally difficult standardised tests was almost unheard of.

If Son could pull this off, though, he would receive a certificate stating he had completed high school – despite not having turned 18 yet – and would be able to sit university entrance examinations. The stakes were high: he would have to pass in maths, physics, chemistry, history, geography and English. Failing even one would mean he would have to sit the whole thing over again. Trujillo – having never once pulled rank or said 'no' to Son, sticking by him no matter what – helped him by looking into every possibility and even writing him a letter of recommendation.

The standardised tests were spread out over three days, with each day covering two subjects. Examination started at nine o'clock in the morning.

Son opened the first test booklet, took one look at the questions asked and was immediately frightened out of his wits.

This was a completely different beast to any examination he had ever sat in Japan – the questions seemed to leer at him from the examination paper on his desk. A normal student might have given up at this point based on the sheer number of questions alone – the test booklets consisted of dozens of pages.

Son let out a low groan, mentally weighing up his options.

Anyone else would have cursed their own recklessness at having got so far out of their depth. If Son failed this year's examination, he would have to wait until next year to do a resit, and in his own mind he couldn't afford that kind of luxury.

He set about his task straight away. Son was only going to live once and he wanted to leave his mark on human history. Doing the same thing as everyone else would never get him anywhere near the history books. For once in his life, Son felt the urge to pray, but not to God. In this case the Fates were good enough for him. His resolve steeled, the first thing Son did was ask the invigilator if he could use a dictionary; then he requested a time extension. Unfortunately an exception could not be made for him.

Son's countenance sharply changed, and who can say what tenacity welled up inside of him to drive him on to finish. Son cannot remember the exact words he used, but he mentioned something to the effect of wanting to make a direct appeal, then got up and left the examination room and headed for the staff room.

Things had definitely got more serious but Son did not lose composure, not for an instant. He had been born with a steely resolve. The teachers in the staff room had started to gather around him, eyeing him curiously.

The tense mood in the room suddenly began to lift as they rang up the state Board of Education. In a typically American act of candour and earnestness, the superintendent on the other end of the line was less bothered about the rightness or wrongness of Son's appeal but rather struck by his enthusiasm. Appeal upheld. Looking back now, Son can only laugh at how the whole scene played out, but at the time he was desperate.

No matter the cost, Son had to overcome this obstacle – his American dream was riding on his standardised test results.

His request for a time extension was granted, although he was not told when exactly he had to finish. Son interpreted this as being whenever he felt like it. He got stuck into the examination and his concentration did not let up until he had solved every last problem. Naturally, the examination had been designed with American students sitting it in mind, where encountering and dealing with advanced vocabulary is part and parcel of the experience.

This was where the real fight started.

If Son had been American, upon reading the questions he would have quickly been able to work out what the question was asking. In Son's case this preliminary task was quite time-consuming. Once he understood what the question was asking, he then had to try and give his answer in good, proper English . . . but failing that, anything was better than nothing.

Still, the way the questions were written obscured their meaning and doubts began to creep in as to whether or not he was answering them correctly. Squinting, deep in concentration, he read through the questions again and again. It was now three in the afternoon. The invigilator called time. The other students sitting the examination stood up and filed out of the classroom whilst Son bloody-mindedly carried on grappling with the questions in front of him. The hands on the clock in the examination room were pointing at 11pm when Son finished on that first day.

The invigilator was clearly exhausted as well, only managing a haggard 'Well done'. Son smiled and offered a meek 'thanks' in response. He walked back to his lodgings in a daze then plopped down on his bed and put the Beach Boys' greatest hits on.

The second day of the examination included American history. Son went with his gut feeling for virtually all of the answers, again not finishing until late a night.

The third and final day was physics, and Son was at the limits of exhaustion.

It was after midnight – technically a different day – when he handed his papers back.

Two weeks later, Son received a letter from the California State Board of Education. The results were in – Son opened the letter, his heart pounding. The maths result was close to perfect. Physics had gone reasonably well. Scores for English, chemistry, history and geography were all poor, but then he caught sight of the one word that almost made his eyes pop out of his head: PASS. He let out a cry of joy – he had done it.

During the past two weeks Son had frequently thought of throwing in the towel if all that effort had amounted to him having to re-sit the examination the following year. He hated making up excuses to himself, though, and his relief was tangible at the gamble to stick with his convictions paying off.

And so Son completed four years of American high school in only three weeks and became eligible for enrolment at university. The academic transcript on file at Serramonte High reads as follows: 'On 23 October 1974 Jung-Eui Son (his Korean name) withdrew his enrolment from our school.'

One of the administrative workers in the academic office commented on Son's time at Serramonte: 'Even though he technically didn't graduate from our school, all of us here are proud of the fact someone like Mr Son came to study here in the first place.'

Chapter 3   Life-changing encounters

Several weeks after having enrolled on the ELS course at Holy Names College, Son had a chance encounter with Ono Masami, a beautiful, slender, long-haired girl. It was love at first sight and by the second date, Son had made up his mind: he wanted Masami to be his wife. Despite the fact the two hadn't even held hands yet he intuitively knew she would be one day.

What was most attractive about her in Son's mind was her strong character and grace. He couldn't believe his luck in meeting such a wonderful woman and his heart would skip a beat as soon as he would see her in the school halls. The two started off by studying together in the library, spending half the time getting to know each other and the other half hitting the books. They would eat together in the cafeteria as well.

Masami can recall her first impression of Son, stating she wasn't exactly sure how old he was and also how odd he was. After his half-year at the English Language School, Son enrolled at Serramonte whilst Masami entered Holy Names College proper, so it looked like the two wouldn't be together for another three years.

It's safe to say Son's desire to study together with Masami again was another factor driving his desire to get high school over with as soon as possible; looking back, this was actually a defining moment that would chart his course for later in life. Son stuttered and his voice cracked with excitement as he told Masami after passing his standardised tests that he was going to enrol at Holy Names too.

And there was another life-changing encounter in store for Son, a chance meeting of the most serendipitous kind.

Whilst out doing the big shop at his local Safeway, Son happened to be flicking through a copy of *Popular Electronics* magazine when a close-up of the recently announced Intel 8080 computer chip (a microprocessor capable of processing eight-digit numbers consisting of 0s and 1s, which would give birth to the personal computer as we know it today) caught his eye. Son had never been so impressed in his entire life.

There seemed to be some sort of awesome energy emanating from the photo out of the page, beckoning him. He was intrigued by how something so small could possibly alter the course of human history. He explains it like this: 'It was like when you watch a really powerful scene in a film or get caught up in a piece of music and you start tingling all over. It was the exact same feeling. I was tingling all over and warm tears started falling down my face.'

It was a road to Damascus moment, light reflecting off the geometrical shape of the chip. Son viewed computers as an intellectual life form that would go on to surpass humanity.

'Out of all of the human inventions to date this was the biggest and the best. The light it radiated was incredibly beautiful. Maybe humans had finally developed something with the capacity to transcend intelligent production activities.'

Masayoshi bought the magazine, cut the page out and placed it in a clear file, which he then put in the rucksack he always carried with him. (In fact, Son and his rucksack were almost inseparable – it went with him to the toilet and at night he slept with it under his pillow.

After six months of so much tender love and care, it had been completely worn out.) It began to dawn on him that he could be involved in computing in some shape or another and that is what he set his heart on.

As an aside, there was another young man who'd had an identical Damascene moment just like Son when he discovered the existence of the single-chip microcontroller. That young American was none other than Bill Gates, founder of Microsoft. Similar to Son, Gates would recall that in 1974, during his second year in university, he picked up a copy of *Popular Electronics* and was completely blown away by what he was reading. In an interview for this book, Gates described his own life-changing encounter as follows:

'I was genuinely moved. In my opinion, *Popular Electronics* completely changed the relationship between humans and computers.'

The article in question would have appeared quite small and inconsequential to your average reader, announcing the launch of the $350 Altair computer kit manufactured by MITS, a company based in Albuquerque, New Mexico. Gates got in touch with Paul Allen, his friend and fellow computer genius, straight away. Allen had met Gates when they were students at Lakeside High School in Seattle after they started using a PDP-10 teletype unit the school had bought to access a time-shared computer. The two were fascinated.

Their reaction was: 'The time's come for us to port BASIC (a programming language for beginners) to microcomputers and there's not a moment to lose!'

It was the start of an arms race within the nascent computer industry and the two had just developed a way for BASIC to run on an Altair. Gates was only 19 at the time whilst Allen was 22. Allen quit his job at Honeywell and Gates dropped out of Harvard to move to Albuquerque and start Microsoft. Steve Jobs and Steve Wozniak were also at the forefront of the emerging computer industry (they would go on to found Apple Computer Company in 1976), while Scott McNealy (Sun Microsystems) and Larry Ellison (Oracle) could also be said to be Son's contemporaries.

The digital information revolution was calling and all of these individual Damascus moments would lay the groundwork for it to become a reality.

In September 1975, Son enrolled at Holy Names College, telling himself he had to really knuckle under and study.

Son was not the type to do things half-heartedly, so the first thing he set about doing was getting his hands on a decent quality door. For Son, American-style doors were quite large – virtually reaching the ceiling – and he bought one such specimen (without a handle) at a local furniture shop. He carried the door back to his room and placed it on top of two steel cabinets, thereby creating a work desk large enough to accommodate all of his textbooks, dictionaries and reference materials. Anything and everything he needed, it was all there within his grasp. He had three light sources as well.

Mealtime, bath time, driving to wherever – any time was a good time to study. Son would tape his lecturers' talks and then listen to them back on his headphones. If he got stuck at a red light, he'd feel like he was wasting too much time so would have a look at the textbook inevitably propped up on the steering wheel, with one eye on the material and the other on the road. Without fail, the car behind Son's would sound its klaxon once the light turned green, knocking him out of his study-induced trance. He would hastily put his foot down on the accelerator and speed off.

Walking around the university campus, Son was quite well known for his odd fashion sense, with his yellow rucksack filled to bursting with textbooks, and trousers Son had customised himself with large sewn-on pockets to accommodate a handful of pens, his ruler and calculator, all of which would noisily bang together in time with his steps as he walked from one lesson to the next, attracting colourful comments from passers-by. The bizarrely dressed young man raced around the campus, his encounter with the previously unknown world of single-chip microcontrollers spurring him on in his studies.

Chapter 4   **Non-conformist**

On 1 October 1975, Muhammad Ali, the world heavyweight boxing champion, would defend his title against Joe Frazier, Ali battering the challenger with jackhammer punches in the 14th round, effectively ending the match.

Whilst in terms of sporting ability there is little sense in comparing the boxer with Son Masayoshi, the two certainly shared a similarly superhuman drive, the latter devouring textbook after textbook after textbook. On average, he would only sleep three hours a night – five hours if he fancied a lie-in. Looking back, Son recalls feeling just like Ninomiya Sontoku, the 19th-century Japanese economist and philosopher, pouring every last ounce of his energy into swotting up. The comparison is certainly apt.

Just prior to sitting his first examinations at Holy Names College, however, Son caught a very nasty strain of flu and was all but completely bedridden with a soaring fever. His appetite completely disappeared and he was – physically speaking at least – in the worst shape of his life on the day the examination date rolled around. Mentally speaking, though, he was jumping for joy, contrary to what most students would feel before having to sit an exam. He could barely contain himself. Masami had the same bout of flu, but was looking after Son as he tossed and turned in his fever dreams.

The exam results were the best Son had managed so far – all As. As he still wasn't feeling any better once the examination cycle had finished, and his fever wouldn't subside, Son was rushed to hospital. His examining doctor wore a very dark expression on his face as he walked into the room to give his diagnosis. 'Did you yourself not even realise how unwell you are?' he asked him.

Academically, Son continued to be unrivalled, making the dean's list alongside several other top-ranking students. It was his first real victory as a student studying abroad.

Kawamukai Masa'aki, business producer, lecturer at the Kyoto University of Art and Design and fellow Holy Names College alumnus, gives his impression of the school, having studied there in the 1990s. 'It was a good university with a strong liberal bent. You had people of all races mixing together and everyone got on really well with each other.' Studies were divided up into 15 specialist courses or majors, covering topics such as economics, history and political science, with the nursing programme being particularly popular with Japanese students.

Whilst now no longer a faculty member, Sister Marguerite Kirk still remembers Son, who sat her Monday-Wednesday-Friday eight o'clock accounting class. She remembers seeing him dashing down the long stone steps running beside the chapel in his rubber *zori* (sandals) and hand-made trousers, bursting into the classroom and grabbing the seat closest to the blackboard.

'Oh, he certainly stood out. He would look at you with such bright and shining eyes.'

The other students in the class were a mix of nationalities, from places as far-flung as Japan and Indonesia to closer to home, from Mexico and the United States. In a class of 20 Son was sure to stand out on looks alone, but what Sister Kirk recalls as most impressive was his tendency to stick around after her lectures had finished so he could pick her brain more. His goal was to start a business.

Sister Kirk was in her late thirties and was only a part-time lecturer, but was left astonished by her strong-willed student. Son was of a mind that things taught in lessons should inevitably be put into practice, and Sister Kirk – duly impressed by his determination – was intrigued as to what exactly he had in mind: 'I want to start up a video game business.'

Naturally, Sister Kirk did not think Son was going to spark a home video-game craze. Later on, though, Son would run a business importing Space Invader cabinets from Japan; this is quite revelatory as, despite his career not even having started yet, he already had the ideas in place.

In front of the cafeteria on campus was a space for the students living in the residence halls to relax and unwind. There was a small kitchen area there which barely saw any use, which Son and a friend saw as an opportunity to start a business. Son laid out his plan to the university administrative office to use the kitchen to make cheap and healthy dinners for students. Permission granted, he then set about handing out flyers and finalising preparations.

The location of the kitchen couldn't have been better. There were always two students working the kitchen, which was open for two hours every day. Yakisoba, stir-fried noodles and wonton soup were all on the menu; the prices were cheap and the taste wasn't half-bad either. Including clean-up and preparation times, the kitchen was in operation for four hours every day, with an hourly wage of $2.50 being paid out.

It was a smashing success, but then unexpected issues started to crop up, mainly due to Son's friend and business partner getting creative mathematically with the books. Being betrayed by someone he trusted came as a complete shock to him and Son learnt the hard way that money and friendship do not mix well. After only six months 'Son's Diner' was closed. All things considered, however, it had been a good experience and ultimately gave rise to the first principle of Son's own business philosophy: you can't do business on your own, so you've got to be careful who you pick to be your partner.

Son would finish at Holy Names College in less than two years, and had decided he next wanted to attend the University of California, Berkeley, where he had studied during his first trip abroad during high school. In lieu of a traditional entrance examination, Berkeley would only allow third-year university students to transfer in. To get the ball rolling, Son rang up the Department of Economics and spoke with the secretary there. The matter was addressed at the next faculty assembly meeting and Son got his response: he would be allowed to enrol. There was some paperwork to deal with, but it was no big issue – he was in.

Only 10 per cent of Holy Names College students had ever successfully transferred to Berkeley. Son wanted to study there no matter what it took, and in 1977 joined the Department of Economics at the University of California, Berkeley, one of the top universities in the United States. And to make things even better, Masami would also be admitted to Berkeley's Department of Astrophysics the same year.

Chapter 5   # Master inventor

The Californian sun makes for rich, mellow wine. It is also fertile ground for geniuses. Heading out of San Francisco and over the Bay Bridge, the city of Berkeley and the University of California campus of the same name lie on the opposite shore. Founded in 1868, it has since become the top public university in America and is divided up into 14 different faculties and vocational schools. Students from over 100 different countries have flocked to study at the picturesque 500-hectare campus overlooking the San Francisco Bay.

The natural scenery is not the only sight to behold, though – the facilities are also of an impressive scale. Each faculty and school has its own dedicated library housing a world-class collection of books and reference materials. Son had been interested in several American universities, but Berkeley had won out not just because of the fact it was an elite university, having produced a large number of Nobel Prize winners, but also because of the freer, less restricted atmosphere about the place.

The surrounding areas are filled with shops selling psychedelic shirts and incense and generally full of life. Son recalls one fellow male student of suspect sartorial taste as well: he had let his hair and beard grow out on the right side of his face then completely skinned – beard, eyebrows, hair, the works – the left side. Not that it mattered, as his marks in maths were consistently top of the class and he could even spot errors in the formulae he was given to solve. His lecturers were more than a little intimated by him. Son was also quick to point out misprints or wrong equations in his textbooks, but this other fellow was on a completely different level. There was another time he witnessed a male student dressed up like Spiderman spend all day climbing up the side of a building.

What most excited Son about Berkeley, however, were the computer facilities on offer. Everything on campus was open for use by students 24 hours a day and there were terminals in every building, hundreds of them all lined up in a row – a truly glorious sight for Son to behold. Never one to squander an opportunity, he made sure to put them to good use during his time at university.

The subjects Son put the most effort into studying were maths, physics, computer science and economics, scoring all As – the highest mark only awarded to the top 5 per cent of the class. In languages, despite having a natural handicap, Son also managed to rank higher than everyone else.

Son was supported in all things at Berkeley by Masami, his girlfriend, and after one conversation in particular things suddenly became much more serious between them.

'Tell your parents to stop sending money over,' he said to her one day. 'I'll tell mine to do the same.'

Masami looked at him with eyes full of amazement, and hope. Did he mean what she thought he meant with those words? The passion welled up inside of her as she contemplated spending the rest of her life with him. Son was sincere.

'If we get married, then I'm going to do the providing.'

He knew what he was after, though: as soon as he had finished university, he wanted to start working as an entrepreneur straight away. Finding work straight out of university wasn't always a given for students, but Son was confident he could manage it.

There had to be a way and he was determined to start laying the groundwork for that future as a student. The harsh reality of the fact that he would have to start earning enough to pay for his own expenses each month was also looming on the horizon.

Before he moved to America to finish high school and enter university, Mitsunori, Son's father, had been admitted to hospital, and both his father's condition and how his family back home were managing weighed heavily on his mind. Even so, he wondered whether he would actually be able to survive without the money his family was sending over, as he was still enrolled at Berkeley and his future was still up in the air. A part-time job was out of the question.

At the time, Son was receiving 200,000 yen a month in remittances from his family, but it had become a considerable burden for them. Son was at a loss as to what to do: in his own mind, he could only afford five minutes of free time a day – the rest of the time was to be dedicated to studying.

As Son settled into a routine at Berkeley, he found he had a bit of time to dedicate to other pursuits. He wondered aloud whether or not there were any jobs going requiring only five minutes' work a day where he could pull in over $10,000 a month. His friends thought he had lost his mind.

The only work available to Japanese foreign-exchange students was manual labour – pot washing in restaurants or street cleaning. With manual labour putting a strain on your body, intellectual work was the only option for Son. Son, however, didn't have any money or the connections to get that kind of work. There was one and only one thing he could do, he decided. He would come up with inventions, patent the ideas, then sell them on.

Matsushita Konosuke, the 'God of Management' and founder of Panasonic, had got his start at a small factory. Another business forebear Son looked up to, his first steps towards becoming a global electronics magnate had been the invention of the two-way socket and the bullet-shaped bicycle lamp. Son now had his precedent – it was time to start inventing things. It was a far-fetched plan, but this was no time to hesitate and he set to work immediately.

As you would expect, there were a number of first-class bookshops at Berkeley as well as others dealing in second-hand books sold off by students who no longer needed them: the ideal scenario for Son, who ran around town buying up every book he could find on patents.

It goes without saying Son had no experience of inventing anything. Coming up with an invention was incredibly hard. He would have to look into the guidelines and procedures about how patents were actually granted for things and then put all of his knowledge into practice. It was a mammoth task.

None of this was a joke to Son, though, it was just one more step along the route of his life's plan and he would see it through to the end. Son wondered whether or not Thomas Edison had been able to come up with an invention a day – managing such a feat would be nothing short of miraculous.

In place of a diary, Son had a notebook he kept in English (his 'Idea Bank') where he recorded, in detail, over 250 different ideas for inventions. Whilst in the end he fell short of his goal of an invention a day, there were some truly great ideas – unique and typically Son – gestating inside the Idea Bank.

Son's confidence had grown by leaps and bounds over the course of the year from simply sitting down, setting his cheap alarm clock to five minutes later and then trying to come up with something smart.

Over time, Son realised there were three main approaches to inventing things: the first was searching for solutions to problems. Whenever a problem or hardship cropped up in life, Son looked for a way to resolve the issue. Necessity is the mother of invention, as they say. Pencils with a completely rounded body would tend to roll off the table when set down – much to his annoyance – so the workaround solution to this would be to make pencils with a square-shaped or hexagonal body instead. Then, after identifying the problem, he applied deductive reasoning to come up with a solution.

The second approach was lateral thinking, or looking at things from the opposite perspective. Take something which is traditionally round and make it square. Turn something that has always been red, white. Take something big and make it small. Son applied this approach to his idea for a new type of traffic light. It would use the same design and colours everyone was used to, but throw geometrical shapes into the mix, with circles, triangles and squares used for the various signals. In this way colour-blind people would be able to tell which phase the light was in.

The third approach was combining pre-existing things. Take a radio and a tape recorder, combine them and *voilà*: the radio cassette player. Most of the inventions Son came up with in America fell under this third category, as he could systematically come up with things this way.

Chapter 6 **Unprecedented**

S on was 19, in his third year at university and in the prime of his youth. Most university students would be busy with their studies, sport or going out on dates. Within the broader scope of a person's whole life, however, what exactly does it mean to be 19? Son's guiding principles would be unimaginable for the ordinary person: he already had a 50-year life plan he was intent on following.

- Phase 1 was to set up a company in his twenties – the exact industry didn't matter at all. It was all about creating an identity and if he could manage this then all of his youthful ambition would have paid off.
- Phase 2 was far more outlandish – delusional even – and that was to amass a war chest of 100 billion yen.
- Phase 3 – his forties – would involve challenging a big company for market dominance.
- Phases 4 and 5 – his fifties and sixties – were to be spent ensuring the success of his business and then passing it on to the next chief executive.

A 19-year-old with this sort of foresight and life plan was truly unprecedented and typical of his anything-but-average youth, which would explain his drive and obsession to get things done, and now.

'For every new day, a new invention.'

Surprisingly, Son had managed to pull his invention scheme off, thanks largely to combining pre-existing things into something new. To facilitate this, he had written down random nouns in English – 'tangerine', 'spike', 'memory' – on cards. Once he had amassed a deck of around 300 cards, he would pull three out of the stack, turn them over, and then see whether or not the words he had chosen could be combined into a new product. The three words could be completely nonsensical together, but could still produce good ideas, no matter how eccentric.

For a historical precedent, the 19th-century poet Comte de Lautréamont (a contemporary of Rimbaud's) would take two things which at first glance had nothing in common – say, a sewing machine and an umbrella – and then combine them to create a unique idea, effectively kick-starting the surrealist movement.

Whilst manually turning the cards over, the thought occurred to Son that there should be a more systematic way of performing such a task – or better yet a way of getting a computer to do it. A computer would certainly be able to come up with inventions more easily and efficiently. In the 1970s, however, not just anyone could program a computer – if they even had access to one – and at any rate, they would need to know the ins and outs of the machine for his plan to work.

The first issue – accessing a computer – was easy enough at Berkeley, so he stepped into the 24-hour computer lab and started feeling out the possibilities. It was common for students in the computer lab to chat to each other with any questions or sticking points they came across, as well as swapping information. They kept their stomachs full on milk and bread, and if they got tired would have a quick kip in a sleeping bag they'd brought.

What was unique about Son's approach to utilising a computer was the fact he was using it to generate ideas as opposed to using it as a glorified calculator. First, he would create a computer program where he could input the cost of the individual 'parts' – the concepts he had written on his cards. Additionally, he would rate each part for newness out of 10, for size out of 5, and then rate his own knowledge of the part out of 30, before keying these figures in. Or perhaps he would set a figure for how relevant this was to the invention – ultimately, he ended up with around 40 elements to enter into the computer. The lab supervisor was intrigued by what Son was getting up to – it was the first time he had ever seen a student use a computer for creative purposes.

He submitted his computer program as part of a free project required as part of his computer science class and received an A. The program would be pulling three 'cards' out of a pool of 300 – how many hundreds of thousands of possibilities would come out? Then for each card, the computer would calculate a score using each rating as entered, lastly providing a list of the elements with the highest scores presented first.

This was only possible because Son knew his own program and knew what he wanted to get out of it. And yet the five-minute time-limit rule was still in strict effect: he could only dedicate five minutes of his time to reviewing the results with a high score.

Using his own subjective judgement, Son sifted through the list of results that had the highest probability ratings. The results were just as good as those from the old-fashioned method of cards and a notebook, but Son's unique genius shone through once again in his decision-making method: it was time to narrow results down to one.

Out of the 250 ideas in the Idea Bank, he selected one concept: a talking electronic translator. It would combine a speech synthesiser, dictionary and liquid crystal display and would later be marketed by Sharp as the original pocket translator.

However, based on his own calculations, making a prototype on his own and getting a computer to fully voice the unit would take 10 to 20 years – completely skewering his 50-year life plan.

Although still a university student, he viewed himself as a businessman to the bitter end and couldn't help but wonder if there was some sort of secret recipe he could rely on. It would be more efficient to partner with the heads of the various fields he was interested in. Life is short; he had to use the time he was given effectively. Son got to work on his plan.

He first got his hands on a copy of the list of researchers at the university, then used the pay phone at the Martin Luther King Jr Student Union to ring up all of the physics and computer science lecturers and assistants on his list.

Everyone he contacted mentioned the same name in relation to speech synthesis: Dr Forrest Mozer, of Berkeley's famed Space Sciences Laboratory, was the leading authority on the subject. Son went to see him straight away.

Despite not having made an appointment, Mozer signalled for 'John' – Son's English name of preference – to come in and have a seat. Without pausing even once, Son explained in fluent English the ins and outs of the talking electronic translator he envisaged.

He spoke passionately of his plans to firstly develop a synthesiser capable of translating words into and out of nine different languages, and then incorporate a speech synthesiser for the voice function.

When interviewed for this book, Mozer expressed his delight at Son's tremendous idea, jokingly suggesting they should perhaps change the name of the Space Sciences Lab to the Son Masayoshi Building. 'His idea for the pocket translator in itself wasn't particularly novel, but then he told me he had plans to sell it in airports and in kiosks, which was really quite unique.'

Mozer was 48 and already a leading authority in his field when he first met Son, but still took the time to hear the young man's grandiose plans out. He was somewhat taken aback by Son's offer to co-operate with him out of the blue, but unfortunately had entirely too much on his plate already.

Forehead sweating and tugging at the unfamiliar tie hanging round his neck, Son pleaded desperately, 'I want to use your speech synthesiser. There's no way I can do this without you.' Mozer listened intently.

Son didn't have any money, but asked whether or not a fee-for-service payment based on the end result would be satisfactory. If he could come up with the money for a prototype and sell that on to a company, then he would draw up a formal agreement concerning payment. The terms offered were frankly outrageous – surely Mozer would object to such a preposterous offer.

He did not, though. Instead the internationally renowned researcher decided to take a gamble on the enthusiasm and zeal of a young stranger; and Son's life may have turned out quite differently had it not been for Mozer.

Chapter 7

Treasure every encounter

'**M**r Lu, there's a customer kicking off about his order!'
There had been no problems in his establishment when the young, white waitress barged through the doors of the diner back office, looking on the verge of tears. Hong Lu, a student who had started off as a dishwasher to pay his way through university, was working as the night-shift manager.

The popular ice cream parlour, the rather perfunctorily named Ice Creamery, had 22 tables – enough to seat 100 people – and with sandwiches and sides also on the menu and the fact it closed at one o'clock in the morning at weekends, it had become a popular meeting place for young people.

'The customer says we didn't make it like he ordered it so he isn't going to pay.' Hong was 1.85m (6ft 1in) tall, and well-built. The customer who was complaining about his ice cream apparently wasn't content to leave it be.

'Which one is it?'

'The one speaking Japanese, the Japanese-looking youth . . .'

Upon hearing the word 'Japanese', Hong's ears perked up – out of all the students who frequently visited the Ice Creamery, Japanese ones were few and far between. It must be one of those jumped-up

Japanese tourists who've recently started swarming the West Coast who's placed some sort of extraordinarily fussy order, he thought to himself. Regardless of how he felt, however, Hong was in the services industry and was quite proud of the fact he was the manager of one of the best-known ice cream places in Oakland. He steeled himself as he went to speak with the customer, knowing that no matter how outrageous the claim he'd have to placate them then and there.

Hong quickly realised this particular customer wasn't about to go down without a fight. The young man was quite clearly from the Far East, and his complaint was he had ordered a milkshake – not what he had been served.

Hong replied that it wasn't a problem, he'd make another and make sure it was up to his standards. If he still didn't like it they wouldn't charge him, but Hong did ask him not to bother coming back.

Hong made the next milkshake to specifications then gave it to the waitress to deliver, but kept his eye on the customer as he tried it. He was not about to overlook any little change in the customer's facial expression that he could use in his defence.

Hong, dressed in a neck tie and apron, wandered over and bent in a slight bow as he politely addressed his customer in Japanese.

'How is it?'

'Oh, wow, this is really nice.'

The customer – Son Masayoshi – was beaming. Masami, sitting next to him, gave Hong an apologetic grimace.

This was how Son would meet Hong Lu, his first business partner.

Hong was born on 3 November 1954 in Taipei, Taiwan. He eventually became the chief executive of UTStarcom, a start-up that received a lot of attention in both the United States and China. He stepped back from that role in 2006. Having someone he could speak to in Japanese held a special meaning for Hong, as his mother was an overseas Chinese born in Japan and aged six he had moved to Japan with his parents.

After graduating from Tokyo Metropolitan Area Jonan High School, Hong had immigrated to America through a relative living there and enrolled in Berkeley's Department of Civil and Environmental Engineering. He too had an American dream he was chasing after. As he had been educated in Japan his Japanese was perfect, the trade-off being his mastery of the English language wasn't what it could have been.

His encounter with the eccentric Son at the Ice Creamery had been the first time he'd met a fellow Japanese speaker in the States.

Several months later, Hong's eyes caught sight of a young man in *zori* with a rucksack, navigating the usual throng of students at Berkeley with his nose stuck in a book. It was his problematic customer from the Ice Creamery and Hong instinctively called out to him.

'Hang on, you're . . .'

'Oh, right, you're the manager from the ice cream place!' The two exchanged pleasantries and formally introduced themselves.

'You study here?'

'Yeah, which means you study here too?'

The two carried on speaking in Japanese. Despite being two years ahead of Son in his studies, as soon as the two found out they were both studying at the same school, they became fast friends.

Son started taking Masami to Hong's workplace regularly for ice cream dates. Towards the end of 1977, Son approached Hong during one of his shifts.

'You ever thought about going into business together?'

'Doing what?'

'I've got a good idea for a business so I'm starting a company.'

Hong couldn't believe his ears.

Hong muttered something non-committal, but internally he still couldn't believe what he was hearing and thought Son was just talking a load of nonsense. His boldness was certainly beyond his years – Hong wondered what Son was thinking, casually suggesting going into business together. It was probably something on the level of starting up an ice cream parlour together.

He couldn't shake Son's words, though, and after hearing him out understood he was planning something monumental. The fact remained that Son was two years his junior and wasn't even close to graduating. Son knew he wanted to do something he himself had yet to think of: it had to be a fresh idea and it had to do good business.

Hong slowly began to realise Son was serious about his proposition and the more he heard his Japanese friend speak about his ideas, the more he thought he might actually be on to something. Eventually he performed an about-face to his initial response.

Hong was deeply intrigued by both Son's enthusiasm as well as the new ideas he was coming up with. Ultimately, if it was all some sort of elaborate ruse, he could always start over again. He decided he'd give Son two years.

The first company Son Masayoshi ever incorporated was called M Speech System Inc., the M standing for Mozer. Son was the youngest person in the entire company.

Mozer was, in his position as the leading authority on speech synthesis, the keystone around whom Son would build a team to integrate this functionality into the electronic translation device. For Hong, even at this early stage, seeing Son work was a mind-blowing experience. His enthusiasm was contagious and Hong started feeling like he was being pulled into Son's dream.

It was time to take a gamble and start up the venture. The annual income Son was offering was $20,000, a competitive wage for a recent graduate at the time.

'Can you actually pay me that amount though?' asked Hong.

Son, wearing a broad grin, nodded nobly.

The first company meeting was held in the rented flat Son lived in on Whitmore Street, in Oakland. Son had drawn up a rather vividly illustrated organisational flow chart for company operations. Hong had been assigned the task of 'Miscellaneous matters'.

'What exactly is "miscellaneous matters" supposed to be?' he inquired.

'It means you'll be doing anything and everything,' Son smoothly replied.

Up until now, Son had only explained his plan for the company in general terms; Hong's first task would be drawing up a three-year plan for the company. The request blindsided him, but he was prepared to give it everything he had and promptly put all of his effort into coming up with the plan. The business climate would be impossible to predict. And the exact features of the translation device had yet to be determined as well.

Hong flashes a wry smile as he reflects back on the task. 'I'd been racking my brains over the three-year plan. It was my job, after all. However, I had completely forgotten to take those sorts of things into consideration.'

It was his first attempt at trying to pre-empt future trends and from that day onwards, Hong started commuting to Son's apartment to work every day. Gradually, however, he was starting to grow uneasy – was Son going to actually pay his wages?

Chapter 8 **A day to remember**

Son was seemingly capable of being in all places at all times.
Naturally, he didn't dare miss his classes, but whenever he had a break between them he would pop into Mozer's office for a visit, often heading straight to meetings with the project-team members he'd recruited after that. With his drive and passion, the project slowly started to get off the ground.

All the same, Son always being in lectures or meetings meant Hong couldn't make any headway on the project. Finally reaching the end of his tether, he asked Son whether or not they wouldn't be better off making his new house their office.

At the time, Hong had just made a down payment on a house in Tulip Avenue in Oakland. Whilst he did have some savings, he also had to borrow money from the bank to make up the rest of it. Hong was reliable and sensible, letting out the spare room and then using the rent money to pay off his mortgage. The living room became M Speech System Inc.'s headquarters.

On his first payday, Hong received a cheque for $1,800 from Son and promptly went to cash it.

The cheque bounced. Son didn't have enough money in his account, so Hong couldn't get paid. Most people would describe this situation as being far from ideal – Hong, however, knew Son wasn't the sort to purposely issue bad cheques. He had faith in Son.

When the next payday rolled around, that cheque bounced as well. That was twice, now.

The corners of Hong's lips curled up into a bitter smile as he considered the situation. Typical Son, of course. It wasn't that he was consciously swindling Hong, but rather the fact he probably never thought to check how much money he had in his bank account as he was too busy frantically running around doing other things.

It's still not uncommon for him to leave home without any money – taking his wallet wherever he goes was never a habit of his – for a strut around town. Since his Berkeley days, Son has done extraordinarily well for himself in terms of the big numbers, but even when starting out he never had any interest in small figures. This is another area where Son's mindset was completely different to ordinary people, and this attitude has apparently changed very little since.

At the time, the talking electronic translator had yet to be completed, and getting the exclusive sales rights for the speech synthesiser parts as a single unit would be the first practical step Son would take to reaching his goal.

All sorts of things would become possible with the integration of a speech synthesiser with other machinery, such as having the unit activate in time with customers entering and leaving a shop, saying things like 'Welcome!' or 'Thank you for your custom!'

San Francisco had its own Japantown – where Japanese emigrés had settled – so Hong hurried as quickly as he could to find someone to do business-oriented translations of a steady stream of documents he would then send off to Japan.

Responses and inquiries came back promptly and in rapid succession from around 20 to 30 major manufacturers, quoting between

$200 and $300 per chip. Son was elated: the response had exceeded their expectations and they had the luxury of choice. Hong told Son to head off to Japan to start sealing deals and signing contracts; Son, ever proactive, did not squander a second and booked a seat on the next available flight.

He wouldn't come back for another three or four weeks and Hong was swamped in work the whole time, even attending his boss's lessons without asking so he could answer the roll call in his name.

Hong knew he had been right to go along with Son's plans and Son knew he had a right-hand man he could trust to take care of anything and everything.

The time right after start-up is always the most difficult phase for a business, but things were comfortably starting to fall into place at M Speech System Inc. That being said, they were soon about to face a new pitfall lying in wait for them, with the multinational company National Semiconductor informing Son they would have to renege on sales rights in Japan. If National Semiconductor Japan – their Japanese subsidiary – did not give the deal the green light, they would block all sales.

They were clearly lying, having had second thoughts about the deal. They were trying to keep Son's business in check and weren't above resorting to foul play or cunning.

Son was still new to the world of business so was ripe for taking advantage of. He had no idea about agreements – he was still a university student, after all – and naive to much of the more practical goings-on of the business world, much less the arsenal of tricks and traps more experienced negotiators would employ.

Son asserted the legitimacy of the agreement in place with National Semiconductor Japan and negotiations stalled. Despite having received the exclusive sales rights, there was no formal agreement in place and ultimately no such agreement could be reached.

Son was incensed and gave a rare stinging rebuke, saying they should just leave National Semiconductor to their own devices.

He backed down from the sales of the speech synthesiser, having learnt his lesson about the importance of contracts.

Reaching this point, the team realised they had to complete their talking electronic translator and fast, and some members had grown exasperated from the ordeal with National Semiconductor. There was one team member, however, who did not view the ordeal as a setback and was willing to bet it all on Son and his pocket translator. Chuck Carlson had been added to the team on the advice of Mozer, advice that Son duly heeded.

Carlson was a hardware design engineer and lecturer at UC Berkeley who had worked on the team responsible for installing a microcomputer in the *Apollo* spacecraft. He sat down with Son, listened to his ideas, then four months later had finished the hardware.

The speech synthesisers of the day were quite large, so weren't fit for the purpose Son had in mind – they needed to be smaller, portable. Furthermore, Son's basic concept envisioned use of the device by a large number of people in places such as airports. This last point was what was unique and appealing about the project for Carlson.

On 23 September 1978, Son was racing towards the Berkeley Space Sciences Lab in his beloved second-hand Porsche 914. He was calling on Mozer, who upon his arrival gave him a gentle smile and signalled to the next room, where Carlson was frantically grappling with his kit.

Today was the final deadline for getting the German-language prototype up and running – hence Son being there in person – but they had fallen behind schedule. Son called out to Carlson, who replied: 'I've done it – it's working.'

The prototype – a black box – had a keyboard attached to it which Carlson started tapping on. The liquid crystal display showed the English greeting. Next Carlson pressed the button marked 'Translate' and the screen changed from English into the German equivalent. Son jumped for joy – Carlson had done it. He gave him a hearty slap on the back. It truly was a day to remember.

However, there was one more reason why it was going to be a day to remember for Son: he announced to the room that he was on his way to his wedding to Masami.

Son looked at his watch – he was supposed to have been there at two, but it was already well past that time.

Chapter 9   # Wedding bells

Masami had been waiting at the courthouse since two o'clock. In lieu of tumbleweed, fallen leaves blew past. It was September 1978 and the Californian autumn was in full swing. The rolling hills, a lush green in the summer, were starting to turn muted shades of red and orange.

Son was pushing his Porsche 914 to its limits as he sped towards the courthouse. At the bottom of the hill, he turned right onto Stadium Rim Way then shot past the North Gate as he tore off towards the city centre, ignoring however many red lights. The Berkeley courthouse was a short distance away from the university – only 15 minutes – but to Son, it felt like it was taking an eternity to get there.

Masami was uneasy, reasoning he must have got caught up in a traffic jam or there had been an accident along the way. She was relieved when she finally caught sight of Son making haste in her direction, then was overcome with emotion: it was their special day, after all.

'Just where have you been!?' Masami cried. Emotionally she was walking a fine line between relief at the fact he was safe and utter exasperation at him having made her wait on their wedding day.

Son bowed his head, apologising unreservedly and giving his excuses: they had just finished the prototype and he had lost track of time.

Masami rolled her eyes and gave him a look but left it at that – she knew Son better than anyone else and how he was completely oblivious to the outside world when he got stuck into his work. His ability to block out the outside world and concentrate when studying was superhuman. That was the Son she knew and loved, the Son who would get so caught up in his thoughts he would inadvertently run into telephone poles whilst walking down the road.

Son hurried to the entrance door of the courthouse and tried to push it open. To no avail: it was just past five in the afternoon and the doors were already locked.

Son shouted for help.

From out of nowhere a large black security guard with a gun at his waist appeared. 'We were due to have a wedding here today, can you ask the judge to open up for us?' Son was desperate.

'The judge left a long time ago, son. You'll have to come again another time.'

Son, shoulders slumped, was beside himself. He couldn't apologise enough to Masami. They rescheduled the wedding for a week later at three in the afternoon.

On the day of the wedding Son once again planned on visiting the Space Sciences Lab, but this time swore to himself he wouldn't be late. He checked his watch.

The prototype electronic translator was done, but Son still wasn't satisfied. Looking at things from a practical standpoint, he wondered whether or not a big black box was going to set the world on fire in terms of sales. He asked a staff member who was milling around for their opinion on the matter, they started bouncing ideas back and forth, and before Son knew it, it was just past three.

What would it take to get Masami to forgive him again this time? She was once again standing outside the courthouse, waiting.

'You got lost in your work again, didn't you?'

The two entered the courthouse and spoke to the receptionist. 'We're a little late for our appointment, but is there any way we could see the judge?'

The receptionist was stunned – who would be late for their own wedding day? Or rather, in this case, who would be late for their own wedding day . . . twice? One would normally advise against missing an appointment made with a judge. And yet the receptionist seemed moved by Son's earnestness and rang up the judge in his chambers.

Son was frantically looking around the room.

He spotted the guard who had brusquely refused to let them in last time and, after making eye contact, the guard gave him a polite, acknowledging smile. Son reckoned he would know just how desperate he and Masami were to get married.

The receptionist came back. The judge would see them.

Chapter 10   **Contract signed and dated**

In the summer of 1977 Son had written to 50 Japanese home appliance manufacturers detailing his intent to develop a talking electronic translator, making plans to visit the 10 or so who replied in person, amongst which were Canon, Omron, Casio, Matsushita Electric Industrial (now Panasonic) and Sharp.

He took advantage of the summer holidays and travelled back to Japan with Mozer in tow.

Son's younger brother Taizo – who at the time was yet to enter primary school – can still vividly recall his older brother coming home, the whole family gathering around as Son and Mozer gave a demonstration of their prototype talking translator. 'I remember Masayoshi keying in *Konnichi-wa* in the machine and it saying "Hello" back. It was really uncanny, I'd never seen anything like it – Dad was completely gobsmacked as well.'

Son had invented the very first electronic translation device with voice function, capable of translating into and out of Japanese and English. Whilst the concept itself was revolutionary in its current state, the device could not be readily marketed – there was still the matter of putting it into practical use. To achieve this a company would firstly need to have the technology to make the translator smaller, lighter and more affordable from a manufacturing perspective.

At this point in time Sharp, Casio, Sony and Matsushita all possessed considerable technological prowess due to the success of their calculators, and Son strongly believed that one of these companies would be capable of making his invention a viable product. Out of the companies that had written back Sharp was Son's preferred option, as they had been the first Japanese company to develop their own calculator. As pioneers within the electronics industry they were the first choice. The favourite.

This posed a problem for Son as he – not subscribing to a conventional approach to negotiations – didn't know whether he should target them first.

Perhaps before trying to land the big fish straight away they should first try negotiating with several other smaller companies as a way of seeing whether or not their invention had legs. But that approach was unsatisfactory as well – whilst certainly bold, going that far may be over-thinking things. In the end, he decided to do a little warming up before going to see Sharp.

The first and second companies they went to see said exactly the same thing: they'd definitely think about it if the device was a little bit smaller.

The next company they visited was Canon, who when they saw Mozer in attendance felt more confident about the proposal, and even more so when they actually saw the prototype in action.

Next up were negotiations with a section head and acting section head from Casio. They had no interest whatsoever.

Looking back at this meeting – how insultingly brusque the manager was and the shock of being turned down by one of his favourites – Son now believes it was almost as if the bitter disappointment was something he had to experience. After the meeting Son would never approach Casio for any future dealings ever again.

The next day Son headed to Abeno in Osaka, where Sharp had its industrial machinery division.

Hiding his nerves, Son calmly unwrapped the prototype unit and presented it to the division manager and several of his subordinates he had brought along. 'If you could manage to turn it into a nicer product, then yes – we'd be interested in it.'

The manager wasn't one to mince words. Son, on the other hand, was at a loss for words for a moment. Obviously if the prototype were developed to the product stage it would still be an unknown quantity, which is exactly why Son was exploring his options at the present time – to see whether that was viable.

Unlike all the other companies, Sharp had not necessarily refused his idea outright. After many negotiations Son had finally found someone who understood his way of thinking. If he dedicated time to the relationship, he thought he could get them to come around to his point of view.

The next thing Son did was typical of his character and also in line with one of the core tenets of his management philosophy.

There is a Japanese proverb that goes, 'If you want to shoot the general, shoot his horse first', meaning if you want to quickly achieve a goal you need immobilise your opponent first and aim to get the people on your side by undermining your opponent. This is a very Japanese way of thinking and an idea most Japanese would subscribe to – Son, on the other hand, wanted to go after the general first. He found a public phone and rang up the Osaka branch of the Japanese Patent Attorneys Association, getting them to provide him with the details of the patent offices who knew a lot about Sharp.

Son was willing to ride every ounce of good luck he had been born with. After being told to ring up one person after another, Son finally managed to get the details of the eponymous Nishida of Nishida Patent Office, who had previously done work for Sharp's Patent Division.

Armed with his address, Son headed to his office straight away to seek advice on whether or not his invention was worth patenting and – on top of that – to get Nishida to introduce him to the key cogs in the Sharp machine so he could negotiate directly with them.

In response to Son's rather blunt request Nishida gave him the name of the then head of the Technology R&D Division, Sasaki Tadashi; Son then asked Nishida if he would ring Sasaki up for an introduction.

At the time Sasaki was the head of the company's central Research & Development & Innovation (R&D&I) laboratory, having overseen the development of the calculator, liquid crystal display and photovoltaic cell, being viewed by many as the man who revolutionised the electronics industry in Japan – for Son personally he would become one of several great benefactors.

Nishida, confirming his electronic translator could be patented, was not in a position to turn down Son's request. Son's strategy was paying off and his heart skipped a beat when Nishida told him Sasaki would see him the next day. Finally he was going to meet the man who would be able to make his ideas a reality.

Son, cool and persistent as ever, did not let the occasion get to his head, not forgetting to ask Nishida about the patent filing procedures for his translator.

The next day Mitsunori got on the train from Kyushu to Osaka, meeting up with his son at Sharp's central R&D&I lab in Tenri, in Nara Prefecture, and was the one to present the prototype to Sasaki.

Sasaki saw tremendous potential in the device and may or may not have spotted something in Son as well. There was a keen glimmer in Sasaki's eyes as he pronounced the prototype to be quite interesting. Sasaki was well versed in computer software and he appeared blown away by the device, despite Son explaining there were still some modifications he needed to make.

To Sasaki, a man in his sixties, Son appeared much too young to know as much as he did about the device, but he also sensed that on the inside Son was driven by an indomitable will. His way of thinking didn't seem to be like that of any other young people his age in its conviction and vigour. Sasaki would remember the young man's earnest face and serious gaze.

'He had pitched the prototype to a number of companies but none of them could be bothered with it. He was down about it at first but after giving a demonstration of what the unit could do his demeanour completely changed. I've never seen a person so possessed of self-belief. I knew they weren't there on a get-rich-quick scheme.'

Sasaki believed a young person like Son was truly a rare find, so he should do everything he could to help develop his talent. He was deeply impressed and willing to take a risk on the young man, so much so that he arranged for Son to immediately be paid 40 million yen for the patent contracts. He also asked Son to begin development on French and German versions of the software, bringing the total contract money to roughly 100 million yen. Son would call this his 'million-dollar contract'.

It was the very first time Son had signed an agreement and when Son saw the proud look on his father's face his own joy increased that much more.

Son had taken on big business on his own terms and won, and moreover he had done it in Japan, his country of birth. His million-dollar contract was the perfect crystallisation of all of the hard work, acquired knowledge and sheer endeavour of his youth.

Chapter 11   **Dreamer**

How did Hong Lu, Son's friend and business partner, view the man?

When interviewed for this book, Hong responded by calling Son 'a gambler and a dreamer who doesn't play to lose'.

The American high-tech magazine *The Industry Standard* described Son in similar terms – 'gambling man' – on the cover of its 4 September 2000 edition. Indeed, it is a well-known fact that Son bet everything he had on the internet, but regardless, his friends never saw him as an ordinary businessman.

As for anyone and everyone with a dream they hold on to, actually making that dream a reality requires a lot of talent and dogged tenacity, as well as the willingness to face up to and overcome obstacles.

Having found success with his talking electronic translator, Son relocated (both home and office) to a new site on the second floor of a three-storey building near the Oakland airport, changing the company name from M Speech System Inc. to Unison World in the process. The name was impressive and anyone who heard it would remember it straight away.

On the whole, the company was starting to take the appearance of a successful one.

One day Son walked in, handed Hong an envelope and thanked him for having worked so hard. Hong opened the envelope up to find it was filled with share certificates – or rather papers with the appearance of share certificates, as they weren't exactly the real thing. Whilst Unison World was certainly a promising young company, they weren't anywhere close to being listed on a stock exchange. Taking things to the extreme, Son may as well have handed Hong an envelope with a bunch of blank paper in it, but Son wasn't the sort to joke about or wind Hong up, not when it involved something like share certificates.

The meaning behind the envelope was that he was giving Hong 10 per cent of the company, which would later increase to 20 per cent.

Son was truly chasing after his dream at this point, and now another major business opportunity was to come his way. One day the smallest titbit of news caught Son's eye – it had to do with Japanese arcade games.

During his multiple trips to Japan and back, Son had caught wind of a boom occurring in this market in Japan, with Space Invaders becoming incredibly popular between the months of March and August 1979.

Space Invaders had been developed and released by Taito, a Japanese game designer, the previous year and marked a sea change, being drastically different to the video games that had come before it. Like a science-fiction book come to life, the game featured an alien army swarming the player's base on earth. Players would control their own gun battery, manoeuvring it to shoot down the space invaders. It was a completely novel idea and simplicity itself, although unprecedented at the time.

Son was obsessed with the game, although not as a player – it had caught his eye for business instead. His conclusion was the whole thing was too simple and straightforward: the video game boom was only temporary. One cabinet cost 1 million yen (approximately $10,000), but once the boom was over, you'd be stuck with the cabinet and little else.

As Son predicted, the boom ended as quickly as it appeared. His foresight was astounding enough, but what was more astounding was what he did next.

Son first asked himself why the Japanese had become so enthralled with Space Invaders in the first place. It was here that his unique interpretation of human behaviour would begin to take over and provide an answer.

The Japanese get passionate about things, but that passion cools just as quickly as it appears. Americans, however, are different. Son sprang into action, flying off to Japan to buy a Space Invaders cabinet.

He arranged a meeting with a Taito manufacturer and started negotiations regarding buying a cabinet. Son started off by offering $500 for one cabinet, knowing full well they normally went for the equivalent of $10,000. A wickedly cold smile spread across the representative's face.

Son wasn't the sort to back down at this point and when his counterpart did all but sneer at him, he may as well have conceded defeat. Son could see right through him and asked him how much it would cost them to store all of their unsold cabinets. He'd pay them in cash in 90 days. Ten cabinets at $500 apiece.

The representative gave a bitter laugh: 'OK, you've got me.'

It bears noting that Son was only 22 at this point, and yet he was getting up to things quite far removed from your average young person.

Son ended up dispatching the cabinets back to the US not by ship, but by air, another case of his unique genius at play. The cabinets were left over from the *démodé* Space Invader boom in Japan, so your average company would have sent them by sea; in Son's case, he deliberately chose the more expensive air freight. Taking into account customs procedures, it would take about three days for them to arrive, but had they been sent by ship, it would have taken three months – by which time he would have had to pay for them. Anyone else doing this would have fallen at the first hurdle, but Son's business sense was too sharp and his thinking as far removed from ordinary as possible, whilst still keeping a cool, lucid, budget-minded outlook.

When Son got back from Japan, Hong looked surprised at his latest venture.

After all of the hard effort he had put into graduating from a first-rate university, he was going to be shifting video-game cabinets? He was beside himself.

Son and Hong couldn't find any shops who would let them set up a Space Invaders cabinet on the premises so the two decided to go to a restaurant for their lunch, then they rang up the manager of the restaurant afterwards.

They wanted to set up one of their cabinets there.

The manager responded by saying the whole thing sounded dodgy, but Son pressed him slowly, explaining how popular it had been in Japan. As the manager started to show some interest, Son went in for the kill.

'We'll split the profits fifty-fifty. If you still think it sounds dodgy, at the very least would you give us a three-day trial run?'

Son would later recall this negotiation: 'If the person you're dealing with stands to profit from the deal, then they'll start to see you as an ally. After that, it gets easier to talk to them and eventually they'll even start coming back to you for things.'

In this way, if Son were to lend a business a helping hand, no one would turn him down.

Changing his tactics, Son started looking at restaurants catering to the lunch crowd as sites where he could set up his Space Invader cabinets. One of the sites selected was Yoshi's, a thriving Japanese restaurant and nightclub located near UC Berkeley at the intersection of College Avenue and Claremont Avenue.

The manager was a bit taken aback when an erstwhile patron and university student told him he wanted to set up a cabinet in there, but he was eventually won over by Son and took two.

Chapter 12   # Springtime in Berkeley

Even though Son Masayoshi had already distinguished himself as a top-class businessman in 1979, he was only starting his fourth year at Berkeley's Department of Economics. He was still to graduate.

At the time, he was importing Space Invader cabinets, which seemed like the most natural business opportunity in the world. However, for a university student who had come from Japan to study abroad in America in the 1970s, it was completely unheard of.

There were restaurants and clubs who didn't want cabinets, but Son had the courage and tenacity to overcome this resistance so was on his way to ensuring success – it wasn't in his character to take 'no' for an answer. Occasionally he would press proprietors for direct, face-to-face negotiations, which was too aggressive for some of his counterparts.

He may have only wanted to do business with them, but restaurant managers were concerned that having the games cabinets there would ruin the atmosphere of their establishments.

Son's response to this was that his counterpart must not be interested in generating business, which was inevitably met with protest and disbelief. Son would continue, explaining that he had done a deal with Victoria Station – a popular steak house at the time – to let him set up Space Invaders cabinets in their waiting areas. Most restaurant managers eventually gave in to his tenacity at this point.

An unexpected phone call came one day, however.

A year previously, Hong Lu had still been working as the manager of the Ice Creamery, the ice cream parlour where he'd met Son. Now they wanted him to come out because the cabinet he and Son had set up there had apparently broken down and customers were complaining.

Son rushed out to the Ice Creamery, hastily greeting the managers and then hurrying over to the machine to have a look. He tried starting the game up, to no joy. Son was beside himself in disbelief – he was certain the machine was brand new – and started troubleshooting in his head. Could it have sustained damage during transport? Son opened up the cabinet and neither he nor the people who had been queuing up to play the game could believe their eyes at the sight in front of them: the coin box was overflowing with quarters.

There wasn't anything wrong with the game per se – the coin box simply hadn't been emptied so the game couldn't start.

Son solemnly and majestically scooped up the quarters in both hands and then presented them to the restaurant manager, who couldn't have been happier. At times like this, Americans weren't afraid to show their true or frank emotion, and the manager asked Son point blank if he would bring another cabinet over.

Ultimately Son had gone from being a university student with zero capital to recouping what he'd spent purchasing the machines and having them flown over in roughly two weeks.

Half a year on, he had imported 350 cabinets and had turned a profit of over a million dollars. Again, he had started with nothing, and this sort of success would inevitably catch the attention of other American businesses, with Unison World just managing to sneak into the top 100 of profitable companies in northern California.

Son wouldn't rest until he was the best in the world, however. Common sense would dictate that what he had sought to do would be impossible, that there was no way.

Ted Dolotta, who worked as executive director of SoftBank USA, gives some insight into Son's habits in this respect.

'Son was the sort of person who would attend a lunch appointment with someone here in San Francisco and then after that immediately fly out to New York for a meeting with someone else. That's unheard of, it's next to impossible. For Son, however, when it comes to business, the words "unheard of" or "impossible" just don't enter into his vocabulary – he's a truly extraordinary person. Most people just wouldn't naturally think of scheduling meetings over lunch in San Francisco and New York on the same day.'

According to Dolotta – incidentally, one of the few Americans to actually know Son well and who the latter would call his 'American dad' – there were two specific things about Son which made him stand out.

The first was his uncanny ability to get to the very root of problems whenever they emerged, meaning he could then address them very quickly. The second was that he – quite simply – worked stupidly hard. In addition, he was able to synthesise a number of different viewpoints, one after the other after the other.

A good demonstration of Son combining these talents would be in his takeover of a video game arcade near the Berkeley campus, proving the perfect place for students to escape the rigours of university life for a minute. It was in the same area as book and music shops – a prime location for an arcade – and the location is still a favourite haunt of students.

Students are notorious for being skint and yet Son managed to purchase the site for $9,000 – with a little help from the bank and Hong Lu mortgaging his house. The bank, in fact, were so impressed with Son's detailed business plan and sheer enthusiasm that they gave him a prime rate: truly exceptional conditions for a loan for a university student.

The purchase of the arcade meant Son had just concluded his first business takeover and he was sure of its success, his self-confidence once again defying all odds and normal expectations, which according to Dolotta was one of his master strategies.

Within three months business profit had tripled and Son had thoroughly streamlined operations, having analysed what each machine was pulling in. Detailed, in-depth research was important to Son and he was able to identify various trends amongst the games on offer, such as those which punters didn't care much for in the first place, or those which had been popular at the start, but people had since cooled on.

Every single day, Son was looking at each machine, seeing what it was pulling in. This was his first business strategy.

He prepared detailed graphs for each cabinet so he could tell at a glance the exact day each machine hit the break-even point, with cash flow being a constant priority. He set a target for each unit and then worked steadily towards achieving each one. This first strategy would evolve over the years and ultimately end up a pillar of Son's business philosophy: the 'daily settlement of accounts'.

His dedication to constant, steady effort is one of the things which makes him extraordinary, showing that – to riff on a phrase – geniuses are not a built in a day.

The games line-up at the Berkeley arcade consisted almost entirely of tabletop-style 'cocktail' units, making it hard to introduce new games. Son dreamt of a time when he could just replace the circuit boards inside the units to change the games. Boards were small, so dispatch costs were in turn considerably lower.

As the 1970s became the 80s, Son would release the latest popular titles from Japan – Pacman, Galaxia and Scramble – in the States, one after the other.

It was Son's way to see things through to full completion once he had made a start, and he expected no less of his employees.

When recruiting part-time staff at the arcade, Son would only hire Americans, as they were the target audience for his business from the very start. It was the 1970s in California and hippie culture was in full effect, with a considerable number of the potential employee pool being given to selling weed and taking on other similar dodgy odd jobs.

At the start Son was quite indiscriminate in his hiring policy, resulting in a number of people displaying utter incompetence and total slackers ending up on the books.

Son would observe all of his employees on their third day at work. The first day on the job was just that and some people who would otherwise do good work just couldn't get to grips with the task at hand straight away – an inevitability and completely understandable. On the second day, the average person would normally have got used to what they were supposed to be doing and would start slotting into the team. However, if an employee's attitude and general competence hadn't improved by the third day, then they would promptly be given the pink slip.

Son set his sights on students who needed a part-time job and liked computer games: the sort who you wouldn't have to keep an eye on and would do their job properly. Pursuing these strategies, the arcade Son had bought out recorded three times the profit every month, the end result of his remarkable business mind.

At the time, however, Son was still thinking about what he wanted to do next.

He had named his company Unison World, which held a number of different meanings – such as including part of 'Unix', the operating system developed at Berkeley.

Unix had originally been invented by AT&T at the Bell labs, with the Berkeley computers licensing an early version of Unix propriety extensions to develop would become known as the BSD (Berkeley Software Distribution) OS; incidentally, Unix could be used with servers connected to the internet.

Son combined the 'Uni' from Unix with his own surname, the meaning of 'unison' on its own (as in 'together') not being lost on him. The 'World' part came from his own ambitions of being a company that did business on a global scale.

On the second anniversary of the company's founding Son – for whom consistency was an important element in all things – had a surprise in store for Hong: he was appointing him vice-president of the company. Hong's hard work had paid off and he was glad Son had noticed this, but he wanted to know when exactly he'd be taking over the new role. Never one to put things off when they could be done now, Son told him he'd be starting immediately.

From 1979 and throughout 1980, Unison World's profits grew steadily, at which point Son once again blindsided poor Hong by announcing he was going back to Japan.

Hong was at a loss for words and couldn't understand what had sparked this decision: everything was going well with the business and, furthermore, knowing Son and what he was like, there was no doubt he stood a better chance of success in America compared to Japan.

Son set out his reasoning.

'Business is going well, so all of you are going to say I'm a supreme idiot for leaving now, but I've always viewed Unison World as a dry run for setting up another company in the future. From the very start my plan was to go back to Japan once I'd finished university.'

There was another side to Son's logic as well, something much more personal.

'I made a promise to my mother to come back home and, come what may, I intend on keeping that promise.'

For Son, his mother's love was far more important than any business or profits.

Speaking about this incident later, Son smiled as he said the following:

'By way of an example, if you were to throw a friend under the bus for 100 million dollars . . . you'd still be scum. Friendship has got to be worth more than that.'

It's a philosophy that cuts right through Son's life.

In March 1980, Son graduated from Berkeley. More than a school, it was a place where he'd learnt almost everything he needed to know about life, and marked a starting point for him.

In the 1980s, Berkeley had already set up its own computer network, although on a small scale. Son had also been a frequent presence in the Evans Hall computer room, which is to say that in a certain sense he was a product of Evans Hall, the statistics, economics and mathematics building at Berkeley.

Despite pangs of sentimentality and nostalgia, Son was looking ahead to a bright new hope.

'There was definitely a side of me that wanted to stay in America and carry on with my business, but I was determined to start all over again in Japan and make a roaring success of it, making a company where my trading partner was the world.'

His time in America had been formative and profoundly influential, but in March of that year, Son went home to Japan. His goal now was to be the best in all of Japan, the only outstanding matter being which exact field he would set out to dominate. His determination and goals were set; it was just a question of filling in the finer details.

PART TWO

Chapter 13   **A young Don Quixote**

If one were to make a list of the highest-ranking universities in the United States, it would include Harvard, Yale and Berkeley.

It was a given that anyone who wanted to be admitted to Berkeley would have to be incredibly diligent and studious, but around the time Son was due to graduate, Harvard had been in touch about pursuing a postgraduate degree with them. They weren't the only ones either – MIT (Massachusetts Institute of Technology), the best school for sciences in America, also desperately wanted Son to come and study with them. Berkeley's postgraduate studies department had also approached him with an extraordinary offer involving waiving his tuition fees.

Son had initially transferred to Berkeley as a third-year under-graduate and then after a further three years had graduated. Taking this statement at face value – Son needing five years to graduate instead of four – some people may think that his marks were poor, hence the later graduation. This was anything but the case, as Son had had to take a year off to get his business up and running as well as being able to fully dedicate himself to developing the prototype for his talking translator.

Son had done well for himself as a student businessman, but he was no slouch – not by any stretch of the imagination – when it came to studying and he didn't neglect his studies during his gap year either. No one could have known this at the time except for Masami, who was privy to his swotting up behind the scenes.

If Son had decided to pursue postgraduate studies, he undoubtedly would have been welcomed with open arms in any university and, regardless of the field of study, would have made a fine researcher.

Rather unfortunately for academia, however, Son Masayoshi's passion was not for research. Son himself explains this. 'No matter how you look at the times I happened to grow up in, they were times with a one-in-a-million potential. In a manner of speaking, the world was my oyster.'

Doing business was fun and Son was burning up inside to show the world exactly what he was capable of. He wasn't so naive to believe he would be able to completely steamroll the business world, however – it simply wasn't that sort of place. Son's judgement was capable of seeing his ambition through.

In Son's mind, there was another urgent reason driving all of this – Masami. The two had been together since meeting at the English Language School and had got married in his third year of university; it was Son's belief that great men were capable of making their wives happy.

In March 1980 – still having yet to be issued his diploma – Son graduated from UC Berkeley. One week before the ceremony, however, he returned home to Japan. He wasn't bothered with the paperwork, telling his family he hadn't gone to university just for the diploma at the end.

Some eight years later, Son – thinking ahead to when his daughter would be at the age when children are at their most inquisitive, and to pre-empt any questions about whether or not he actually went to university in America – would make it a point to go back to

Berkeley, when he was in the States during the contract signing with Interactive, and request a copy of his BA.

At the registrar's office, the girl working there was dumbfounded by his request, but quickly did a search in the school's computer database and was able to identify Son. Still bemused by the situation, the registrar asked him where he'd been all of these years – she couldn't believe a student wouldn't want their diploma.

As for Son, he was just as surprised the school still actually had it.

And so, having finished six years of living and studying abroad, Son returned home to Japan. His first order of business was to incorporate a company on the south side of Fukuoka with its premises near Ohashi Rail on the Nishitetsu-Omuta Line.

One year later – in March 1981 – Son would move his business to the local government and business hub area of Fukuoka, Hakata, changing the company name to Unison World, with a focus on market research.

When completing the registration formalities and filling in the 'company representative' field, Son gave his name as Son Masayoshi. He wanted to be explicit about his heritage, although his use of his Korean surname would rankle with his relatives, putting him on the receiving end of comments saying he had no idea what he was doing openly admitting to being a Zainichi Korean (long-term Korean residents of Japan).

'My relatives tried to persuade me that [by using my Korean surname] I wouldn't be able to attract employees or get any money from the bank. Dad didn't take one side or the other, he kept schtum. All of them only had painful memories in this respect so they could only understand the hurt of it all. However, I wanted to be completely honest about things and use my birth name, and furthermore I wasn't about to deal with employees and banks who wouldn't accept me for who I was. There was no way I was going to turn my back on it all.'

Within Japanese society discrimination was superficially denied as being non-existent although, in truth, it had just manifested in less obvious ways; intentionally and openly using a Korean surname would prove disadvantageous from the start, if not an outright hindrance within the business world. His family only wanted their young son coming back from years away in America to fully grasp the actual reality of Japan, the more insular of the two countries.

Son would not be dissuaded from his approach, however. In America – the country where he had effectively grown up – no one was bothered about anyone else's nationality and Son had no time for Zainichi Koreans being overly self-conscious about their bloodlines. He was not afraid; having tasted the freedoms afforded him in America, he was going to carry on living as such. He was a Korean, living in Japanese society.

Later on, Son would admit to having problems accessing a Japanese passport as a Korean citizen, leading him to fully naturalise. 'A nationality is just a mark or a brand. I pay taxes here in Japan and as a citizen I have rights too.'

Acquiring Japanese nationality, however, is not a simple process and the Ministry of Justice initially refused Son's application, on the basis that Son was not a Japanese surname. There was no precedent and Son was told in no uncertain terms that if he wanted to naturalise, he would have to change his name.

Son – somewhat anticipating this – put his secret plan into action. In Korea, a wife does not take her husband's surname (as is traditionally the case in Japan) and Masami's surname was still Ono – her maiden name – at this time. Son had her go to the courts and apply for a change of name, taking on his own surname. On his second application, Son went back to the Ministry of Justice and asked them to look into whether or not there was anyone of Japanese nationality with the surname Son. If there was in fact a precedent, then his application would be accepted. Having conducted his search, the official responded stating they had indeed found someone – his wife. From that point onwards, Son Masayoshi would live his life as a Japanese national.

In the 1980s in Japan, start-up companies were unheard of and there were questions running round Son's head concerning how exactly he was going to develop his company.

He had founded a company, but it was really only a company in name only – something for Son to bide his time with until he could make up his mind about which of the number of markets in Japan he wanted to sink his teeth into. Company results were next to nil.

In Son's mind, since he was doing business in Japan, there was no point in bothering unless he was going to be a market leader. He set about gathering up data whilst making his plans, immediately coming up with over 20 business ideas. Researching whether each was a viable option would take time, so Son employed one full-time staff member as well as one part-timer.

The company office was located on the first floor of a two-storey office building. Despite being of poor build and the roof being made out of tin, there were no leaks when it rained; the office space itself was at best 15 square metres (165 square feet) and the stairs creaked whenever anyone walked up or down them.

There was no air conditioning either, so if anyone turned the fan off during one of Japan's sweltering summers, whoever was in the office would start sweating rather quickly. The trouble with that, however, was having the fan on would mean stacks of papers would inevitably get blown every which way and it was up to Son to pick them up and collect them.

It was around this time that Son's first of two daughters was born; he can still recall the overwhelming emotion he felt when he saw Masami lovingly cradling his daughter for the first time. Tremendous joy welled up inside of him thinking back to the woman he married at Berkeley and now with their very first child.

Finishing work in the evening and coming home late at night, Son would frequently come home to his daughter crying as only babies can do . . . and he did have to change the odd nappy as well.

Son – if nothing else – was a bundle of energy and every morning would drive to his office and make plans. He knew he wanted to do something, but couldn't identify one thing in particular and was starting to grow impatient with the situation.

At the time Son had zero income: he had precisely nothing coming in and felt like he was traversing a tunnel with no actual exit. He was growing anxious. Once he had settled on what he wanted to do, there'd be no turning back or even changing lanes later.

He'd choose his market and then aim straight for the top. The trouble was, Son was completely obsessed by the first hurdle, but wasn't entirely certain about which angle to approach that hurdle from.

'Due to inertia I was at a point where I didn't want to decide my own fate – but doing things half-heartedly was not an option.' Son was faced with choices. Even if he could immediately hit upon a market he was interested in trading in, after 10 years he was certain he'd hit a plateau, at which point he'd have to change sectors, and that wasn't what he wanted to do.

Son pulled one of his notebooks from university out – it contained methods and principles he'd learnt along the way. He decided to write down whatever popped into his head: making a list of his thoughts – or rather absolute conditions – for selecting a market to get into.

- There's no point in doing business if you're not taking a gamble on something.
- Has the sector got room for growth in future?
- In 50 years' time will this be something I would want to completely lose myself in?
- It shouldn't require obscene amounts of start-up capital.
- I'm young, so whatever it is I can do it.
- In future I'm going to be the core that a business group revolves around.
- I want to do something completely unique that no one else in business has ever thought of before.
- Even if it's slow going for the next 10 years, I want to be the best in my sector in Japan.
- The key to business success is believing you're making people happy.
- In the latter half of the 20th century, the world will change by leaps and bounds.

There were 25 such statements on his list.

Taken at face value, they would constitute a completely obvious business management philosophy, but where Son stands apart here is how – for the purpose of making his decision – he assigned each statement its own index number. For each individual line of business he created a stack of papers over 30cm tall, and with 40 different lines if you piled them one on top of the other, they would have stood a dozen metres tall.

Son was prepared to devote his entire life to the one scoring highest, going by the system he devised.

Standing on top of a makeshift podium made out of tangerine boxes and under the tin roof of his office, Son began pontificating to an audience of his one full-time employee and his one part-time worker. 'Profits will have to be ten billion yen in five years, then fifty billion yen in ten years. Eventually I want to be able to count profit in trillions of yen.'

His two employees listened to him carry on in silence, but having to listen to Son babble on about his ambitions on a daily basis like a man possessed soon became intolerable and the two would quit. If a comparison could be drawn with Son at this point, it would be with the character of Don Quixote. With one difference however: Don Quixote was a knackered old man gallivanting about La Mancha whilst Son had only just turned 24. Something fierce was welling up inside of him.

Chapter 14   **The giant and the genius**

The reason Bill Gates gave for dropping out of Harvard was that the time he spent developing computer programs was much more important to him than anything he could have studied.

Son was in awe of Gates's vision for the times they lived in. Like Gates, Son had his gaze focused squarely on what was to come, acting as his source of confidence and pride.

Approximately a year and a half after moving back to Japan, Son finally struck on the industry he wanted to dedicate his life to: computers. Having crunched the numbers, he was positive of the fact computers would take on an increasingly major role within society and – on top of that – the digital information revolution was on its way to becoming a reality.

In 1981, Son's eagle-eyed gaze was already fixed on the goings-on of the times he lived in and in September of that year he founded SoftBank Japan in Onojo, a southern suburb of Fukuoka.

The company would focus on distributing software. Son was going into wholesale. The name of the company itself was an accurate description of business activities ('soft' being an abbreviation of 'software'), but also hearkened back to Son's student days and his Idea Bank – his notebook full of invention ideas. Son had always liked the implications of the name as a treasure vault full of knowledge and ideas.

The company wouldn't deal in operating systems (OSs) – they would be trading in application software or bust.

Son's chance of a lifetime had finally arrived and the timing couldn't have been better, as every October the international home appliance and electronics industry held its annual trade show, and that year, the host city was going to be Osaka.

Out of the 10 million yen start-up capital, Son invested 8 million on the trade show – quite a considerable amount, so what was the plan? 'If we didn't have loads of software to hand then we wouldn't be able to open up any sales channels, and as we didn't have the sales channels, we were in a position where we'd inevitably have to purchase software. In any event, I wanted to seize the opportunity afforded me by the trade show and use it as a springboard.'

After having his participation in the show confirmed, and despite not being in the same league, Son did something completely unheard of: he hired out a larger booth that wouldn't have been out of place for a company the size of Sony or Panasonic. Common sense would dictate here that using 80 per cent of your start-up capital for such a purpose would be ill-advised, at best.

Son set about contacting every software company he could find, all of whom were bemused by his proposal. Son would pay for the venue fee – against all better judgement, he would take on all of the trade show expenses personally – and kitting-out costs for the booth, and all the companies had to do was provide him with the software to show. The proposal was met with puzzled looks – it all sounded too good to be true.

Son would reply that it was all geared towards gaining mass exposure quickly for his company. 'The whole point is for SoftBank to have a large booth where we present ourselves alongside software from each of the individual companies. That's all.'

Not surprisingly, hardly any companies were initially interested in partnering with him on the idea. From their point of view, Son had either money to burn or he was mad for software. And yet, Son's booth turned out to be a greater success than anticipated, consistently full of sales representatives, people working for electronics companies and distributors. The total value of transactions performed at the trade show was only 300,000 yen, but in terms of the number of visitors, it was one of the top two booths.

After the expo had ended, customers would enter into direct dealings with each individual software maker presented, and that was enough for Son. The fact that SoftBank Japan was starting to make a name for itself meant the show could be considered a smashing success. Soon, Son would be in constant meetings with software companies on a daily basis, from sun-up to sundown, to such an extent that from the outside looking in, he may as well have been an employee of these companies.

It was 1981 and Son had finally got his business up and running in Japan – the same year Bill Gates felt assured of his success with Microsoft. The events ushering in the information age of the 1980s would take place simultaneously in both the United States and Japan.

In the summer of 1980, Gates and Microsoft – then still a small company – would enter into important business negotiations. The CP/M operating system (an 8-bit OS) was capable of running all manner of 8-bit software, drawing the attention of IBM, who approached the manufacturers of CP/M with an offer. They weren't interested.

IBM then thought of going one better and creating an OS for 16-bit computers; as part of this plan they approached Gates. At the time, IBM were the colossus of the hardware industry, holding over an 80 per cent market share in the large-scale computer sector. For all intents and purposes, IBM were their own empire, although they weren't without an Achilles heel – the truth was they were falling by the wayside in the small-scale computer market so were aiming to develop and release their own personal computer within the space of one year.

The competition was extremely fierce, to the point where as soon as one type of unit appeared on the market, a newer, more impressive unit would be released afterwards, meaning development teams would have to respond in kind and more than promptly. In terms of strategy, IBM had come to accept they would no longer be able to do things as they traditionally had done – developing everything in-house – so they licensed Microsoft to develop the OS for their personal computer.

Their initial proposal to Gates involved a hardware system based around a 16-bit microprocessing chip. Gates did not have an OS to hand he could mount onto the hardware, having purchased BASIC from its manufacturing company and then making improvements to it. The jump from 8-bit to 16-bit systems was an attempt to pre-empt the epoch-making advances of the time and was based on changing people's minds about what a personal computer could actually be, from a toy to a viable business tool. Gates's own visionary insight was that the personal computer had a much broader audience than any oversized machinery would.

With third parties adopting an open-architecture model that could be freely copied, IBM seized the opportunity to establish a global standard, with Gates and Microsoft making contributions in this respect. The improvements made to the OS would come to be known as the Microsoft Disk Operating System (MS-DOS for short), which is the groundwork on which the Windows we use today is predicated. The first MS-DOS licensee would be IBM, who would rename the system PC DOS for their own hardware. The personal computer arrived in 1981, and with it Bill Gates had taken his first step towards the future.

There may have been an ocean separating the two but, in Son's mind, there was no doubt a rival had appeared on the scene.

Chapter 15 **Getting things done**

Tokyo was alive and buzzing with the hustle and bustle of New Year's Eve. Somewhere, amidst all the din of the metropolis, a phone was ringing in a certain cramped office, the new premises of SoftBank Japan, Son having relocated from Fukuoka.

Calling it a proper office would be generous when the premises were simply two tables tucked away in a corner of the Senshokaikan multi-use building near Ichigaya Rail. It was evening and Son had just got back in. He rushed to answer the phone.

Son was busy trying to raise funds, as he had invested 8 million yen out of his 10 million start-up capital in attending the Osaka Electronics Show, only making 300,000 yen from the show itself. In an effort to secure funding to see the year through, Son had been pounding the pavement.

The voice on the other end of the line was Fujiwara Mutsuro's, asking in a broad Kansai accent whether or not he had heard of the company Joshin Denki. Son replied he had not. Fujiwara sounded somewhat disappointed with Son's response, but nevertheless began explaining what exactly his company dealt in.

Joshin Denki had, on 24 October of that year, opened J&P Technoland – the largest specialist personal computer shop in Japan

– in the Nipponbashi electronics quarter of Osaka. To celebrate the occasion, they had held a massive opening sale.

The reason Fujiwara had opened a computer shop was an off-hand comment he had heard from the science-fiction novelist Komatsu Sakyo complaining that computers were doing good business in Tokyo – so why wasn't anyone selling them in Osaka? Under Fujiwara's leadership, the sale had recorded a whopping 64 million yen in turnover in just 11 days, leading to massive media coverage. The best-selling pieces of hardware were the PC-8001 from NEC, the MZ-B from Sharp and the FM-8 from Fujitsu, amongst others.

Despite Tokyo and Osaka being worlds apart at times, anyone – Son included – working within the field of computers would have heard the news. So Fujiwara was both surprised and discouraged that Son hadn't heard of Joshin Denki.

J&P Technoland measured just shy of 1,000 square metres – by comparison, the average size of a computer shop at the time would have been just over 30 square metres at best. J&P were completely covered on the hardware front but, going forward, Fujiwara wanted to focus more on software. Their selection at the time was not what it could have been and he was contacting software companies who could act as potential suppliers.

Son, although somewhat bewildered by the explanation, was nevertheless in awe of what he was hearing. A computer shop of that size sounded too good to be true – it was most likely just your typical Osakan businessman talking big.

Fujiwara explained how Ike Kozo, an acquaintance of his, had told him how Son wanted to start up a software supply company, but was having a rough time of it because he did not have any trading partners. Ike worked as a consultant for a software company and had first heard of Son from his Osaka Electronics Show exhibition – their meeting must have been kismet.

Fujiwara had searched high and low for Son's contact details and, once in hand, had rung him up. His proposal was a simple one: he wanted Son to pop down to Osaka and have a look around J&P. The offer was a bolt out of the blue and Son's voice cracked as he stated his interest, albeit with a caveat. As much as he wanted to go to Osaka, there were reasons why he couldn't give a definite answer straight away. He had used up almost all of his money on the trade show earlier that year and paying rent and other such necessary expenses meant he had hit rock bottom. It was the end of the year; this could be his first deal.

Frankly, Son was just short of having what it would cost to get to Osaka and back, so he gave the excuse of his diary being chock-a-block. On the other end of the line, Fujiwara sounded dejected, but Son added that he would head down to Osaka in the New Year; and with that, the phone call ended.

Fujiwara Mutsuro had started working in an electronics store in Nipponbashi, in Osaka, immediately after finishing high school in Hiroshima, instead of going on to study at university. In terms of relevant experience for the position, he had been an amateur radio enthusiast. At the time the chief executive of Joshin Denki was Jogu Hiromitsu, overseeing a workforce of 60 employees with an annual turnover of 600 million yen.

Jogu left his seventh-floor office for the day, stopping off at the fifth floor to knock on Fujiwara's door on the way out as was his custom to see how they'd done in sales that day. Fujiwara was upbeat; they'd done well. He had just got off the phone with Son.

'I've just had a very interesting conversation with a young businessman in Tokyo.'

Fujiwara knew what Jogu's response would be just from the look in his eyes. If Fujiwara was interested enough in something to raise the matter with Jogu, then it must have been something special. 'It's nothing yet, but we'd do well to get this fella on board.'

Son's line of reasoning when talking to Fujiwara – amassing all of the software developed around the country into one single place – had been unequivocal. Never one to shy away from blowing his own trumpet, he would go on to mention the added value he would bring to the table working together with J&P. Fujiwara was hooked, telling Son that if he was willing to talk that big, then Joshin Denki were willing to take a chance on him.

Son – despite being so happy he could cry – had had to reply that unfortunately there was no way he could make it down to Osaka.

The next day, Fujiwara rang Son up.

'Hiya, Son, I've got some good news for you. Jogu, our chief executive, is heading up to Tokyo and really wants to see you.'

Son made up his mind about Jogu the second he saw him. Standing before him was the head of a major company, who yet did not have any time for any trappings or frivolities. Son was going to have to be persistent, winning him over by setting out his stall and being completely honest and sincere. He started out by speaking about computers and all the possibilities they offered, but how all he had were his dreams and his enthusiasm.

Son reminded Jogu of himself when he was younger, stating that he understood his position and extending an offer to him to come down to Osaka to see J&P. He was confident Son could go a long way with that much heart and passion.

Seeing J&P in the flesh was an equally staggering and intoxicating experience for Son – it was huge, much larger than he had envisioned – and this made him rise to the occasion, drawing out the best in him.

Fujiwara made his offer: he wanted an exclusive deal with SoftBank Japan. Son had no qualms, although he did have his conditions, chief amongst which was having software from every manufacturer in the country available. Fujiwara told him that was fine, but he'd need everything sorted by 31 January – effectively one month's time.

It was a big ask, but Son said he felt up to it and would do everything he could to make it happen.

Once the New Year's festivities had ended, Son found himself travelling back and forth from one end of the country to the other, from Hokkaido to Kyushu, as at the time there were a number of excellent software companies based in both locations. With characteristic proactivity, Son met the deadline he was set, purchasing every type of software available – from games to utility software – from around 100 different companies, coming to approximately 10,000 titles at a total cost of 64 million yen.

The first time video-game fever really caught on amongst Japanese children was the latter half of the 1970s. It reached its peak in 1979 with Space Invaders, after which a number of games would be developed throughout the 1980s.

At the centre of the video-game explosion was Hudson Soft, a Hokkaido-based developer headed up by Kudo Yuji. Kudo, despite having turned down Son's request to exhibit Hudson titles at the Osaka Electronics Show, was nevertheless intrigued by his character and sent Hiroshi, his younger brother and Hudson's deputy general director, to meet him.

At this point in Son's life, these extraordinary encounters were starting to stack up, one on top of the other; looking back, this could only be attributed to fantastically good luck. He was beginning to question whether his winning streak would ever end.

In autumn 1981, Son met Kudo in Hudson's Tokyo office in Akasaka. Sitting down for their first meeting, Son immediately began speaking. 'I realise this is probably much too soon, but I want to enter into an exclusivity agreement with Hudson.'

Son's proposal was simple and clear: he wanted an arrangement whereby Hudson titles would only be available to retailers by going through SoftBank Japan, despite the two just having met for the first time. Anyone would naturally be taken aback if, having only just introduced themselves, their counterpart was immediately trying to pressurise them into an exclusivity agreement. Kudo Hiroshi had been born in Hokkaido and, like Son, possessed burning ambition. He wasn't about to just idly go along with Son's proposal.

Upon hearing Hiroshi's refusal, Son calmly replied that SoftBank Japan wasn't the sort of company to do things halfway and that Hudson would get ten times more than their current figures. It is hard to know what exactly Kudo Hiroshi would have thought when Son said these words. Was he dumbfounded? Did he think Son was suffering delusions of grandeur? Hiroshi sat in silence as Son carried on speaking.

'I am a genius.'

In the future, as Son came back for more and more meetings, he started to seem more and more like a genius to Hiroshi – at any rate, he had never met anyone who could so naturally and shamelessly proclaim themselves such – but this statement at this stage must have taken his breath away.

'I want to make SoftBank Japan the top distribution company in Japan.'

Despite having fielded the call from Joshin Denki, Son still had no proven track record – or funds, for that matter. All he had were his enthusiasm and a dream. However, becoming the number one distribution company in Japan, whilst certainly a lofty goal, was no delusion and the chief tools at his disposal for making the dream a possibility were his negotiating skills and indefatigable proactivity. A sense of wonder was beginning to bubble up inside of Hiroshi, a sense of awe that there were entrepreneurs like this in Tokyo.

Son having said his bit, Hiroshi replied stating Hudson would require a 30m-yen deposit – the equivalent of a month's sales – for an exclusivity agreement. Undaunted by the amount, Son stated his acceptance and then hastily went around to everyone he knew trying to raise funds for the deal.

His first meeting with Hiroshi had been in autumn, with Hiroshi setting the 30m-yen deposit for exclusivity rights to be paid at the start of winter. It was now December and the deadline was looming, but Son's working-capital account had dried up.

Chapter 16   **Prescience**

There exists in the Japanese language a word, *toshukuuken* – clutching at air. It means you have no track record of results. It means you have no social standing or reputation. It means you started out with no money – nothing at all, really.

Within Greek mythology, there exist the contrasting figures of Prometheus, the Titan who thinks before taking action, and his brother Epimetheus, who acts first and then thinks later. Without any doubt whatsoever, Son was more inclined towards Prometheus's life outlook, taking action having absolute faith in his own abilities and furthermore being blessed with outrageously good fortune.

Whenever his back was against the wall, he was always bailed out by someone he came into contact with who was touched by his proactivity and enthusiasm and wanted to support him.

After great pains, Son had managed to scrape together the 30 million yen he needed for the deposit with Hudson, but he was scraping the bottom of the barrel with his operating capital. The road to becoming the top software distributor in Japan was going to be a long one. At all the major banks no one was interested in a young dreamer brimming with enthusiasm – all they saw was that he had no track record of results, or really anything for that matter. *Toshukuuken*.

At the start of 1982, Son finally got his lucky break with the banks, landing an appointment with Gokitani Masayuki, manager of the Dai-Ichi Kangyo Bank (now Mizuho Bank) in Kojimachi, Chiyoda (Tokyo).

Son had turned up in his most chic American wear and, after exchanging pleasantries calmly and politely, got down to business. He spoke about how he had studied at Berkeley and lived in America, founded his own business there, and since coming back to Japan had set up a software distribution company, mentioning the Joshin Denki and Hudson deals he had in the offing.

His voice began to rise in volume as he spoke about the coming information age and how this was bound to happen in Japan as well, with SoftBank Japan having been founded on three principles:

1) The company would specialise in the digital information sector.
2) The company would work closely with infrastructures.
3) The company wouldn't pursue individual goods but rather large swathes of the market and sectors.

Gokitani may have had no idea about computers, but he was immediately able to grasp the core message behind Son's pitch. At the time, Son was mainly dealing in video game titles but, looking ahead, he wanted to increase the number of titles that were more geared towards business.

Half an hour passed as Son carried on speaking about his dreams and aspirations, with Gokitani eventually being swayed by the enthusiasm of the young man sat in front of him and telling him that if there was anything he could do, he would like to support him in it. Hearing those words Son broached the subject of taking out a loan – he needed the money, but if the deals he was negotiating went through, he would be golden.

The volume of his voice further increased as Son declared he needed 100 million yen. Gokitani's subordinates, who were also sat round the table with him, picked up that he was seriously considering giving Son the green light and began taking notes. In the event Son was given a loan, and they would have to file a report with the investigations department at the head office.

'Have you got annual reports, balance sheets and statements of profits and losses for the past three years?' Gokitani asked Son. Son, of course, in all seriousness responded by saying that he didn't have anything, but no one could beat him when it came to passion, zeal and enthusiasm.

'I haven't got anything I can give as securities either, I don't like asking people for things.' In his time as a banker Gokitani had never heard of a loan being given without any securities pledged in return. Son continued: 'Even though I've not got any securities to pledge is there any way you could give me the loan at a prime rate?' Son's asking for loans at prime rates was something he had been inculcated with since his time at Berkeley.

Gokitani had never met anyone who had made such demands during their first meeting – Son was effectively asking the impossible here – and could be forgiven for feeling a bit uncomfortable with the situation. His intuition told him that each individual venture-investment case that came across his desk was by nature unique, and he had become something of a lending specialist for ventures and areas that were somewhat removed from the ordinary. He was extraordinarily proud of the sixth sense he had developed as a banker for these sorts of projects and, whilst Son's request may have been almost extortionate, there was something different about him; listening to him speak reminded Gokitani of himself.

A competent banker will – simply by virtue of having to deal with however many people a day for days on end – develop amazing powers of observation to the point where they are capable of perceiving whether their counterpart will act in good or bad faith or are serious about their business propositions or unscrupulous. A branch manager will possess the self-belief and insight required to say they have not made an error in judgement when making financial decisions. It is, by nature, an heuristic business. Gokitani was still struggling to come up with a fixed idea of what exactly Son was all about when one of his subordinates stated they had gone over time and he had other commitments to see to.

Gokitani asked Son whether he could run a credit check on him and whether he could give anyone as references, to which he gave his contacts at Joshin Denki and Sasaki Tadashi at Sharp.

Generally speaking, the amount of money a branch manager could personally approve for loans was in the order of 10 million yen – 100 million was well outside the scope of Gokitani's remit. In the case of funding for entrepreneurs, more due diligence than normal is required; at this stage, passion and dreams aren't enough, and Son's project now had to face the scrutiny of Dai-Ichi Kangyo Bank's credit and business departments.

The credit department was tasked with dealing with major companies who they'd worked with in the past, whilst the business department oversaw ventures such as SoftBank Japan.

Gokitani got in touch with the head of the business department, telling him he had found himself in a quandary. The business department supervisor's brow furrowed – there wasn't an easy answer to this in terms of future prospects for the sector. The supervisor suggested striking up casual conversation with colleagues about computers and what sort of future they thought they had, as none of the in-house experts really knew.

Gokitani himself had never actually used a computer before but, according to Arahata Yoshimitsu, one of his young and competent subordinates, the computer sector was quietly going through a boom phase and there was potential for it going forwards. This was more than enough for Gokitani.

Chapter 17   # The cry of the wild and savage soul

A fter getting approval for the loan from the bank, all seemed to be going well at SoftBank Japan, the company going from strength to strength.

The company had been founded in Fukuoka with only three employees, but by 1982 this figure had increased to 30 and turnover was in the order of 2 billion yen. Looking at the figures for 1983 reveals a massive leap ahead, with 125 employees working at the company and profit in the amount of 4.5 billion yen.

Son's daily life was a whirl of business activities, working Saturdays and Sundays and sleeping as little as he could to keep up with running his company. His employees likewise were kept very busy, to the extent that if they couldn't finish their tasks during working hours, it wasn't uncommon for them to spend the night there, collapsing on a sofa or huddling up in a sleeping bag for a quick snooze.

Perhaps it was the constant skimping on sleep, but recently Son had started to feel a bit sluggish – and that was inevitable with so much work to be done. Or at least that's what he wrote the general malaise off as. In response to this, Son had implemented a regular health screening programme, his own results coming back one week after his check-up.

'Further testing required'. The blood started to drain from his face.

Son knew he felt unwell, but had just chalked it up to overwork – his test results told a different story, however. Exhaustion from overwork was one thing, but this was generalised weakness and the doctor told him that the constant exhaustion was due to poor liver function – his hepatitis B antigens (HBeAg – proteins released into the bloodstream to combat hepatitis B) were outside of the normal range.

If a patient tested strongly for HBeAg, it would indicate their body was fighting off an active virus. Son wasted no time in getting over to the nearest university hospital and remained stoic as the doctor gave him his diagnosis: chronic hepatitis.

Son was told to call off all work and check himself into hospital for treatment; if he refused to do so the doctor couldn't guarantee he would live. Son could only respond by shakily asking how long treatment would take. The expression on the doctor's face darkened. At the time, chronic hepatitis was a fatal disease and there was no known way of completely curing it. The doctor replied by stating that if the chronic hepatitis progressed and developed into cirrhosis of the liver, the next stage after that was cancer.

Son was beside himself and could only repeat his question from earlier, about how long treatment would take. The doctor couldn't say. What he could say for certain is that Son's chances of developing cirrhosis within the next five years were quite high. Son duly checked himself into hospital.

When his old friend Hong Lu heard the news, he flew out to Japan from California to be beside him. He was accompanied by Masami for the visit and when Son saw the two, he immediately burst into tears.

Masami in particular could not get her head around the situation, but if there was any relief to be had, no matter how small, it was that Son did not appear to be chronically ill at all. He began speaking with Hong about what he'd been thinking about doing, starting with liquidating Unison World in the United States and selling it on to Hong, at a price of around 2 billion yen.

Hong looked away – he didn't have access to that sort of money. Son told him he would introduce him to a lender and he could repay whatever he had to borrow by setting a small portion of turnover aside for this purpose each month.

Users were fickle in the video-game business, always excited for the next new release, but as soon as one was out they were straight on to the next big thing. Hong, having become the company owner, had got out of the video-game business after careful consideration, being more interested in development software that could be more useful to a larger number of people, such as titles that could create greeting cards and timetables. These would develop into top sellers in their own right, even 10 years after their release. It was quite a canny business move on Hong's part – his foresight was greatly respected in the business – and a playbook Son would later crib from.

It is safe to say here that the underlying motive for selling Hong management control over the company was also – friendship aside – a cool-headed business decision, opening up room for Son to plough ahead with new ideas.

At the time, Son kept his own employees in the dark about his hospitalisation – SoftBank Japan *was* Son Masayoshi, after all – and the official company line was the chief executive was away on a busi- ness trip in America, although his long-term absence would affect the company.

A small number of executives, and virtually all of his employees, thought he actually was away in the States. Tateishi Katsuyoshi was one of the few executives – he would later become one of Son's trusted lieutenants – who knew what the truth was. Tateishi started working for SoftBank Japan in 1982, supporting Son in each individual area of the company, from operations to funding to procurement.

At the time, Son was frequently flying back and forth between Japan and the United States, so SoftBank Japan's business partners were as in the dark about the reality on the ground as (most of) his employees. Tateishi was Son's right-hand man, so if he told everyone he was off in America on a business trip, no one had any reason to doubt him.

In the meantime, however, Son did manage to break out of hospital and sneak into his own head office on occasion, grinning from ear to ear and enjoying every second of being back home. A makeshift bed was set up behind his desk for whenever he needed a lie-down.

All things considered, Son was frantically doing his best to carry on as usual whilst coping with a chronic illness all by himself. This pained Tateishi, who nevertheless thought that if anyone could overcome hepatitis, it would be his superior. The feelings Tateishi had inside were not driven by acceptance and empathy, but rather faith and a belief things would get better.

He had finally got his company up and running and was doing well for himself, but now he had to accept the reality that he possibly only had five more years left to live. His daughter was only 18 months old and Masami was pregnant again – he had a lot to live for. For the time being, however, he was bedridden with nothing but his drip for company, waiting stoically for death to come for him, whenever that would be. There was no way he could anticipate his next relapse – he would just have to grin and bear the uncertainty of it all and live as best he could whilst wasting away.

What was life, after all? Who was he living for? Himself? His family? His employees, his customers? Never mind himself or his family, did this mean he wouldn't be able to carrying on living and trying to benefit society?

In the end, you only get the one shot at living.

Laid up in his hospital bed, Son became a seeker, desperately questioning the meaning of life, and would later confide in interviews for this book about the feelings he had to face at the time.

'At night I would cry on my own in the hospital room – the treatment was really horrible. My daughter was still really young and I'd only just got the company off the ground. I kept on asking myself why I had to die at a time like this. If word got out about me being poorly, the bank would pull funding, which is why I'd sneak out of hospital and turn up to meetings – we had to keep the façade up at all costs. I often asked myself for what reason I was working so hard . . . And the conclusion I reached was it was because I wanted to do a job that would make people happy.'

Despite being bedridden, Son couldn't take his mind off work. He had always been chasing up Sasaki at Sharp to get him to introduce him to people who were good at finance and marketing.

The chance had come up for Sasaki to have a business meal with Omori Yasuhiko, the deputy general director of Nihon Keibi Hosho (Japan Security Services, who have since changed their name to Secom), so he invited Son along as well. The two met for the first time in Elmy, the members' salon restaurant of the New Otani Hotel, Son speaking to Omori about his grand dream.

Omori was equally impressed and flattered. Son's response to anything work-related was always well thought out, with an abundance of caution. He kept a cool enough head to do well in business, but if he felt like someone he was meeting for the first time was a kindred spirit, he had a tendency to place too much faith in them. Whilst this may have actually been one of his merits, it was also occasionally a weakness. 'Business owners who like to do a lot of start-ups tend to like new things and are just as quick to get really excited about things as they are to cool on those same ideas. I've come to realise that this was my own weak point.'

Given the above, Son most likely expected Omori to have skills he himself did not possess. When Omori went to visit Son in hospital, the latter asked him if he wouldn't be interested in helping out with the running of the company.

Omori was 52, 27 years Son's senior, a graduate of Keio University's School of Economics, whose first job had been at Nomura Securities. The highest position he reached there was head of the International Division before moving to Japan Security Services to work as an adviser, later being promoted to deputy general director. He had a vast experience of dealing with shares and marketing, amongst other areas.

After giving the matter deep consideration, Son asked Omori to take over as SoftBank Japan's acting chief executive until he got out of hospital. Son would be the chief executive, Omori would be the company director and SoftBank Japan would become a metaphorical tandem bicycle. Omori was officially unveiled as company director in April 1983; at his welcoming party, he stood side by side with Son, both all smiles.

Despite all appearances to the contrary, Son's long, hard battle against his condition had only just begun.

Chapter 18   **The bellow of the ailing tiger**

ate can be cruel sometimes. Whilst Son was laid up in hospital, a business rival would appear on the scene in the form of ASCII's Nishi Kazuhiko, who was more than willing to take the fight to SoftBank Japan. The two had been destined to clash and – two months after Omori Yasuhiko had taken over as company director – Nishi versus Son kicked off in earnest, a lake of smouldering magma erupting between the two sides.

On 16 June 1983, Nishi, flanked by Bill Gates from Microsoft and representatives from the 14 largest computer and home-appliance manufacturers in Japan, held a rather triumphant press conference where he announced ASCII had got on board with the MSX standardised home computer architecture.

Up until this point in time, each different type of computer used its own central processing unit (CPU), meaning the programming language was different for each, which in practical terms meant different versions of a single software title would have to be developed separately for each individual system it was intended to be released on. All of which is to say that 'compatibility' as a concept hadn't been invented yet. Further complicating the matter was the fact that even if one manufacturer's various computers used the same programming language, they all had their own particularities, meaning there was no compatibility between the various models from the same line of computers.

For compatibility to work, the CPU, programming language and development tools would all have to be the same, and if this could be achieved then a single instance of software could run on different hardware environments. The compatibility issue was one that would carry on up until companies adopted the DOS/V standard specifications in the early 1990s; travelling back in time to the 1980s, now Nishi was putting MSX forward as the common OS of choice.

Looking at the situation more objectively, however, it was grounded in ASCII's desire to achieve hegemony over the market.

Son was in hospital when he heard the news, flaring up with animosity and vexation. In principle, he wasn't averse to the idea of standardisation. But earning the rights to distribute Microsoft computers – which had been selected as the standard – was something he could not overlook. Nishi Kazuhiko was shaping up to be a strong rival, and Microsoft holding sway over the industry as they were would also affect Son's global strategy.

Son had been the one to originally herald standardisation, which was something that shouldn't be wielded just for the sake of one company's profits: more broadly speaking it was a matter of great import concerning the fate of Japanese society looking ahead, and Son had been the first person to realise this.

His goals, however, were not entirely altruistic as there was something of Nishi's scheme to rake in all of the money from standardisation for ASCII in Son's outlook as well. Microsoft's proposal revolved around a flat fee for participation in the standardisation scheme ranging between 30 and 60 million yen ($300,000 to $600,000) and several thousand yen per computer sold in royalties – steep amounts.

To counter this, SoftBank Japan set its own flat participation fee in the order of several million yen and a per-unit royalty of several hundred yen.

Son was furious at Nishi's way of doing business – it just wasn't fair – but thinking more broadly about the future of the personal computer he would do whatever it took to stymie Nishi's plan for a monopoly.

He would have to take on Nishi head-on whilst bedridden.

The first time Nishi and Son had met was the summer of 1977 at Matsushita Electric Industrial in Osaka, whilst Son was still studying at Berkeley. Introducing the two to each other was Maeda Hirokazu, Matsushita's Head of Technology R&D, who for whatever reason did so in English.

Son was at Matsushita as, having concluded his deal with Sharp for the pocket translator, he was going to be signing other agreements for similar hand-held learning devices. Nishi was introduced to Son by Maeda with the words, 'This fella's quite an interesting character.' Nishi and Son exchanged pleasantries and that was that. The next time the two met was four years later, in 1981.

Son had only just got SoftBank Japan up and running, whilst Nishi had already found tremendous success with ASCII. Son, for whatever reason, called him over to greet him, to which Nishi responded by asking whether he was that kid who had started speaking to him in English that one time.

In Nishi's mind Son was apparently little more than some funny Korean who was over-enthusiastic about the pocket translator he had come up with. Son's recollection of his encounters with Nishi is clearer, as the latter has only stated he thought he was clever after meeting him.

Afterwards SoftBank Japan gradually started to do well for itself and the two would start clashing with each other.

With this latest news, Son felt absolutely disgraced.

Things were ticking along on the software distribution front, but SoftBank Japan were now looking into opening retail stores and establishing their own software companies, so advertising and publicity would assume the greatest importance. Being subjected to an advertising boycott could have been the death knell for the company, had the unexpected setback not inspired Son to go one better and set up his own publishing company – about which more later – a tipping point for his own career.

But ultimately wasn't what had got Son so riled up just cut-throat big business?

When he found about the advertising boycott and that people wouldn't let him distribute their software, Son took it personally and was never able to completely stomach this underhand way of doing things. Son was soon to be the subject of more widespread bashing, however, and in 1983, Nishi and Son collided head-on over the MSX matter.

Nishi was a proponent of MSX, passing off his attempt at creating a monopoly as a push for standardisation, once again offending the truth and righteousness within Son which were his namesake. Son's main bone of contention was that said standardisation wasn't open to all.

Day and night, Nishi was frantically developing new software and charging competing developers and manufacturers ever higher royalties: this wasn't business egoism, it was bullying everyone else around.

Further fuelling Son's sense of humiliation was the fact that Nishi had made all of his moves without Son knowing about it.

*　　*　　*

It was 21 June 1983 and rain was falling. Son sneaked out of hospital again to make a business announcement, not giving one thought to his own condition.

On this occasion, at least, Son outwardly looked to be in rude health, having gathered together 21 computer manufacturers. In a loud voice, he announced that SoftBank Japan were going to offer their own standard.

A large din reverberated about the room in response to this. Not one person in attendance could have guessed that Son was suffering from a chronic disease based on this performance.

The previous evening, Son and Nishi had met in a hotel for a chat, Nishi wanting his counterpart to come on board and offering him reduced royalty fees. He gave him until 10 o'clock the next morning to ring him up with his decision. It was a declaration of war. The negotiations behind closed doors were over.

After his round table, Son returned to hospital and collapsed on his bed. It didn't matter if he was going to spew blood every step of the way. He was absolutely going to knock the living daylights out of MSX.

Nishi was just as adamant too, at which point Matsushita's senior manager had to step in to mediate between the two. Son's quarrel wasn't with Nishi in particular – it was about future prospects for the computer industry.

Son was determined: 'Nishi getting behind the MSX and charging developers high royalty rates, whether for hardware or software – the only standard there is for the benefit of ASCII and Microsoft. They need to be more open about this. If they aren't, then tell Nishi we'll just do our own standard in response.'

After the attempt at mediation, Son and Nishi met once again for a tête-à-tête lasting from late at night till the early hours of the morning, concerning making hardware specifications publicly available to developers. It ended with Nishi's concession that information concerning the development of software would be freely available and open.

Computer sales for 1983 totalled over 1 million units, and Son's vision of the future was fast becoming a reality.

Chapter 19 **Resigned to fate**

As 1983 drew to a close, Son's hepatitis showed no signs of abating and his physical condition was a constant cycle of ups and downs. Laid up in his hospital bed, the future looked bleak.

Whilst Son devoured whatever articles he could find written by liver specialists, desperately searching for doctors or new treatment methods, his salvation would come from a very unexpected source.

His father Mitsunori – perhaps heaven heard the prayer of a father in anguish – came across a newspaper article describing a ground-breaking new way of treating hepatitis. Dr Kumada Hiromitsu, a physician at Tora-no-mon Hospital, had gained considerable attention for a completely new form of liver treatment – corticosteroid withdrawal therapy – that he had presented at a liver health academic conference. There was nothing in the article about the treatment efficacy rate, but he promptly rang up his son, urging him to go and see Dr Kumada.

Masayoshi was so happy at having this new lead from his father, he could have cried tears of joy.

Son's first consultation with Dr Kumada at Tora-no-mon was at the start of the year in 1984. Son mentioned how he had read about the new therapy in the newspaper and asked whether he could be treated.

His words had a desperate edge to them. Sitting opposite him in the examination room was a portly man of 37 years, who had yet to make a name for himself as a doctor, but had more than enough self-belief and passion to make up for it.

Dr Kumada spoke in quiet, hushed tones, but he agreed that it was worth a shot.

It is worth repeating once again that, at the time, there was no prescribed method for treating chronic hepatitis: there were no effective therapies so once a patient was diagnosed with the condition, it was only a matter of waiting for the cirrhosis – and then cancer – to set in.

Kumada had a look through Son's medical chart.

The zero hepatitis B antigen (HBeAg) count aside, he was perfectly healthy, which meant the hepatitis virus was still raging inside him, gobbling up his liver.

When looking at lab work, defined ranges are set: low, mid and high. In Son's case, he was over 200 points on the high end of the scale – having developed a clearly advanced case of hepatitis, on the brink of developing cirrhosis – with the general progression of the disease being mild to moderate, moderate to advanced, then cirrhosis of the liver followed by cancer. He was headed towards full-blown cirrhosis of the liver within five years, which was characterised by ascites, or the abnormal build-up of liquids in the abdomen.

Kumada promised Son that as his doctor he would do whatever it took to get him back on his feet again. At the time, he had no idea Son was a promising up-and-coming entrepreneur – all he saw in front of him was a young patient suffering from an incurable disease, albeit one who was determined with all his might not to lose his battle to it.

The traditional treatment method in treating hepatitis – accepted worldwide – had been to keep patients on a corticosteroid regime to slow the progression of the condition. Kumada had intentionally sought out a break from tradition and the results had been staggering. Son listened to all of this intently, impressed by how dedicated Kumada was in coming to grips with and dealing with the problem, and was more convinced than ever that he had come to the right person.

In 1981, Kumada announced his innovative corticosteroid withdrawal therapy method at an academic conference. Far from being applauded and accepted, however, his findings were rounded on with criticism from all sides. The main bone of contention was that temporarily suspending treatment and allowing the affected part of the body to grow worse should under no circumstances be deemed therapy.

A small number of doctors expressed some interest in Kumada's method, but the Japan Society of Hepatology largely rejected the approach. The ensuing controversy concerning Kumada's approach was picked up on by the newspapers, which is how Mitsunori found out about it.

However tempted Masayoshi was, however, he was reluctant to change hospitals: it wasn't as if the medical staff at the one he had been admitted to weren't frantically trying to hit on an effective treatment formula either. His life was in their hands and he had developed a relationship of trust with the medical staff there; and besides, changing doctors offered no guarantee at all he would be cured.

Son sat up straight and asked Kumada point blank whether the therapy would work.

Kumada decisively replied that there was a 70 to 80 per cent chance of success.

Hearing these words moved Son to his very core: his untreatable chronic hepatitis could be cured. He may have been in the hands of a famous university hospital, but the treatment he was on was a stop-gap measure, nothing decisive. Effectively they were doing everything they could to preserve his condition, and not necessarily heal it.

Son gave his response to Kumada. It didn't matter how long it would take, he wanted to be rid of the disease. Kumada smiled and nodded.

It was at this point that Son felt truly alive.

The full therapy would begin on 17 January, with Son being given a short course of corticosteroids and then being taken off them. His HBeAg count quickly shot down, his immune system waking up to rid his body of the antigen.

Son's mood, however, remained dark and when Kumada called in during his rounds, Son voiced his concerns. He wanted to know whether he was getting better and if the therapy was working. Since transferring to Tora-no-mon those were the only words that seemed to come out of his mouth. Kumada, smiling, told him that the count was looking good, but it would take time. That smile was not returned.

On his way out, Kumada pulled the curtains closed and Son was left on his own to stare at the ceiling. He let out an exasperated sigh. How long would this take? Once again, he was plunged back down into the depths of darkness and despair.

Day would finally break for Son and his condition on 5 May (in the middle of Golden Week, when several Japanese public holidays follow one another), when his HBeAg levels dropped to below 50 – near baseline levels.

Unlike his stay at the university hospital, this time Son didn't try to sneak out occasionally to get work done – he was focused on doing whatever he could for his treatment to work. He spent his time reading instead: from manga to history books, all manner of texts, burning through hundreds of books. Day in, day out, he read one book after the other on his bed next to a south-facing window. The one book he was utterly captivated by was *Ryoma Goes His Way* by Shiba Ryotaro, which he had loved so much during his middle school years, taking inspiration from Ryoma's insistence on living his life on his own terms, going so far as to leave his clan.

Rereading *Ryoma Goes His Way*, Son began to pick up on things he had missed the first several times around. Ryoma had tremendous ambitions and his life had been cut short aged 33 by a gang of assassins – his life-span wasn't what was important, though. Whether a person lived intensely or not was what mattered and, once again, Son took great strength from the way his historical hero had lived his life.

Bathed in the afternoon sunlight pouring through his window in hospital, Son felt invigorated. Devoting yourself to what you feel is your calling, he realised, is important.

Chapter 20   **Bouncing back**

May 1984, near the start of summer. South-facing Room 5030 at Tora-no-mon Hospital in Kawasaki was bathed in light, Son having dozed off on his bed whilst reading. He jolted awake to his usual surroundings – showing some relief he was still alive – and took in the warm sunlight.

He felt grateful to be alive.

When Son had been admitted to Tora-no-mon, he had told Kumada Hiromitsu, his doctor, that he was going to give treatment his undivided attention so he could properly get over his chronic hepatitis, effectively retiring and leaving the running of his company to Omori Yasuhiko.

'I'm absolutely going to get better,' became a mantra Son would repeat over and over again to himself.

Dr Kumada would call in for a visit once a week during his rounds, Son inevitably asking him whether or not he was getting any better, a dour look on his face. Kumada in turn would always smile back at him, reassuring him that he was getting better.

Whenever Son would hear those words his faith in Kumada would deepen. All things aside, the experience had taught him to simply enjoy living, viewing each new day as a gift. If – when – he made a complete recovery he was going to take the world by storm, and it was at this point in time he began dreaming up his most ambitious business plan for the future yet: he was going to go public, investing the money his business needed to achieve this goal. This time he had his sights trained on America, wanting to develop a business in the country where he had spent his youth.

All Americans dream of success and compete fairly amongst themselves to achieve this, so this was no pipe dream for Son. If anything, he stood a clearer chance of success there, but ultimately making it in America was only just one part of his master plan: he had a global strategy he was looking forward to implementing, moving on from SoftBank Japan to SoftBank World.

Son would soon be able to put his long period of health problems to rest, but when he did return to work he was faced with a massive conundrum, something that may have proved too much of a mental strain for him to deal with whilst he was focusing on getting over his disease: in his absence the wheels had effectively come off SoftBank Japan.

Naturally, whilst in hospital he was still receiving reports on the state of the company, and those close to Son – particularly those executives who had endured the hard times by his side – were being handed their pink slips in rapid succession. Tateishi Katsuyoshi – who had been a major player in the company ever since its founding – had been transferred to the Osaka office and when Son came back he barely recognised the faces of the executives sat round his boardroom.

Son had originally got SoftBank Japan up and running all by himself and then it went through a period of rapid growth, meaning that organisationally speaking contradictions were inevitable and the company was a bit chaotic. That chaos, however, also served as a source of energy within the organisation.

During Son's absence Tateishi had kept his mouth shut and gone along with Omori's personnel changes, strongly believing this was for Son's sake. Tateishi looks back on this turbulent time. 'I think Omori thought Son a bit beneath him. He brought in a lot of outside specialists and decided he was going to show us all how a "proper" company was run, and in doing so caused a lot of people to quit. For better or for worse after Omori came in we started to resemble a proper company, but it wasn't the same as before.'

Hashimoto Goro, who headed up the publishing department, recalls being asked the following from a client: 'What's been going on at SoftBank Japan recently? Things seem a little off. The reason we got on board with SoftBank in the first place was because it was Son's company.'

Sasaki Tadashi had also noticed that the company was in a state at the time, feeling they should have done whatever it took to stop the rot, recalling: 'Son was getting all manner of company reports whilst in hospital and he was getting really down about what he was reading.' Sasaki didn't think it was his place to tell Son what he thought of the situation whilst the latter was battling an incurable disease, but it was likely he heard about it from his executives who had gone to visit him in hospital.

SoftBank Japan had experienced its rapid rise by everyone putting in an almighty shift and keeping expenses down as much as they could. Furthermore, everyone had been on the same page about what needed doing. Son, however, painfully came to realise his executives were in a miserable state during his time away from the company.

Omori had only worked for major corporations. SoftBank Japan was, to all intents and purposes, a company in name only and he wanted to recast it as a corporation in his own image. Those executives who had been around when the company was founded were confounded by the direction Omori was trying to steer the company in.

The situation was giving Son no end of grief.

Son, tenacious as ever, decided to confront the crisis head on. A fire was lit inside him and he felt the exact same level of enthusiasm he had felt when he was at Berkeley and had started up a company with Hong Lu, or when he'd just come back to Japan and founded SoftBank Japan.

He observes, 'Back then I couldn't really understand the things Omori was trying to tell me, although looking back now I realise I actually learnt a number of things from him, and the more time goes by the more grateful I am for that.'

After being discharged from hospital in May 1984, Son considered working three- or four-day weeks, but no one privy to the reality on the ground would say he was working a leisurely schedule.

The problems SoftBank Japan were facing weren't just ones that were part and parcel of being a smaller company: the times were changing, undergoing a tectonic shift, and Son's digital information society was just around the bend. During the executive shareholders' meeting, Son set out his stall, placing great emphasis on the fact that they had to do something to usher this new era in. 'Moving forward, content will be king. Databases in particularly are going to be key in this respect. If we don't act now then this new era will completely pass us by.'

The executives in attendance, however, voiced their strong opposition to Son's plan for SoftBank Japan, stating this was outside of the company's business domain. No matter how much Son tried to convince them of his vision, they would not change their stance.

Chapter 21   **Holding his nerve**

In 1982, the Second Provisional Administrative Investigation Council established by the Nakasone Yasuhiro government issued a report containing the findings of its remit, the most impactful of which would be its recommendations for the partial privatisation of Japanese National Railways (JNR) and the full privatisation of the Nippon Telegraph and Telephone Public Corporation.

This occurred for the latter on 1 April 1985, the company being renamed the Nippon Telegraph and Telephone Corporation, or NTT for short. Son must have felt like this was the start of something huge and sprang into action – this was no time for hesitation. In 1984, and despite the vehement opposition of his board members, Son invested 100 million yen in getting a data network up and running – in anticipation of the coming digital information society, of course – and launched TAG, a shopping catalogue.

Despite expectations, however, the magazine floundered, opening up a 100m-yen sinkhole in that year's accounts. An advertising campaign on both television and on trains could not turn the magazine's fortunes around, nor did trying to analyse the reason it wasn't selling produce any real findings.

Son had always promised that if the magazine didn't sell he would wind it up and, six months on and with no real results to speak of, he made good on his word, taking full responsibility for its failure.

Within the space of six months he had opened up a 600m-yen deficit on the company's statement of profits and losses and, taking into account the further 400 million yen incurred in winding the magazine up, the company had a whopping 1bn-yen debt on its hands.

Returning home to Nandomachi in Shinjuku, Son unusually confided in his wife, revealing SoftBank Japan only had 100 million yen in the bank. Masami couldn't believe her ears and Son couldn't forgive himself for having placed such a burden on the company. He would have to sell off the shares he held in his own company.

Even more so than what his extended hospitalisation had cost, this time he had incurred a debt so massive he would most likely spend the rest of his life paying it off. Anyone else would have collapsed in a heap of despair at this point – but not Son. Whenever a new challenge presented itself, he was ready to rise to the occasion, actively taking it on and refusing to back down.

He'd just earn the 1 billion yen back.

Despite spending the next two or three days thinking of ways to do this, however, he had come up against a brick wall. He needed to change his perspective and what ended up being the touchpaper for his big idea was the rebellion against NTT and the creation of new common carriers such as DDI (now KDDI), Japan Telecom (now part of SoftBank) and the Teleway Corporation (now also KDDI).

It all began with a meeting with Okubo Hideo from Shin Nihon Kohon (now FORVAL), who would later became one of Son's closest allies.

Aged 26, Okubo had set up his own company specialising in the sale of communication devices, mainly telephones and fax machines.

Later on, in 1988 (now aged 34) he would be named the recipient of the very first Entrepreneur Award from the Tokyo New Business Conference, given to rising entrepreneurs whose companies were publicly listed and offered over-the-counter shares. He was only three years older than Son. Although he had initially wanted to become a lawyer, the worldly Okubo had twice failed the national legal examination (to no end of frustration).

Shin Nihon Kohon purchased software from SoftBank and had a positive trading relationship, but other than that the two had no real history together. Shin Nihon Kohon had its head office in Shibuya in Tokyo, where Son and Okubo had agreed to meet.

On the day of the meeting, however, Son was nowhere to be found at the appointed time; 20 minutes turned to 30 and finally word got through to Okubo that Son was stuck in traffic. Son finally turned up, 40 minutes late. Okubo was an extremely busy man and in his mind someone who wasn't punctual simply couldn't be trusted.

After exchanging formalities and taking his seat, Son immediately started on his spiel, telling Okubo that if he wanted to work with SoftBank Japan then it would have to be an all-in deal. Okubo was somewhat exasperated; on top of being late, Son had the cheek to make demands straight off the bat. Son continued, giving the reason behind his rationale.

'A business relationship is the same as a relationship with a woman: if you're trying to woo two at the same time you'll end up losing both because you can't devote yourself to the one. Mr Okubo, with all due respect, this is the best chance you're ever going to get. We should go into business together.'

Son, having said what he wanted to say, then promptly left. For some reason, however, Okubo found their meeting refreshing. Son may have been small, but he was tough as nails, a truly impressive man.

A few days later Son rang up Okubo out of the blue wanting to know whether he was free that day, as he had something he desperately wanted to speak about. Okubo responded, saying that he was about to head into an appointment but was free that evening. The two eventually settled on a meeting time.

It was close to midnight when the two met in Nagata-cho in Tokyo and, as soon as Son saw Okubo, he promptly asked him point blank again to go into business with him with the words, 'Want to get married?' Okubo looked into Son's eyes. He was deadly serious. Little wonder then that Okubo, a battle-hardened entrepreneur, was caught off-guard for a moment.

'The hell's wrong with you, man?'

Okubo would later recall his impression of this meeting in an interview for this book.

'Anyone else I would have told them to do one right then and then but . . . Son has got a strange charm about him, hasn't he?'

Those who have met Son – and particularly those who have had business dealings – are all unanimous in mentioning that 'strange charm'.

'Have you heard of the concept of C&C (computers and communications)?' Son asked. 'Right now I'd say SoftBank Japan are probably the top computer company in Japan, but in terms of communications Shin Nihon Kohon are second only to NTT. And shouldn't top companies go into business together? Hence my asking you whether or not you'd be interested in wedding your company to mine.'

Son could talk a mile a minute.

'Have you heard about the new common carriers? They've very much to do with your field of business, after all. The thing is, however, if you haven't got computers involved then you may as well not get into the field – so what do you do about that problem? Well, I've got a really good idea in this respect, but what do you say?'

At the time the new common-carrier framework had just been launched and was in the process of being implemented. With NTT being broken up everyone was scrambling to acquire new customers.

The trouble for new entrants, however, was there were a number of hurdles left over from the old system that had to be cleared first. NTT's My Line fixed landline service now seems like ancient history, but at the start if you wanted to ring someone up cheaply you had to dial a four-digit code followed by the actual number of the person you wanted to ring. Depending on the region as well, there were some cases where calls simply wouldn't go through or it would have been cheaper to stick with NTT as opposed to switching to one of the new common carriers (NCCs). Customers were placed in a quandary: despite knowing there were benefits to using the new common carriers, if they wanted the cheapest rate they would have to manually look up the rates offered by NTT and the three NCC companies for the call they wanted to make. All of which is to say it was a major hassle for users and one that was detrimental to business.

The matter at hand then was how resolve this issue.

An adapter capable of automatically finding the best rate for customers without their having to dial the additional four digits first could be one solution: no one had thought of this before, but whilst this idea looked good on paper, rolling it out presented a major logistical headache.

Son and Okubo started seeing each other every evening, just like any other couple slowly inching towards tying the knot. They would meet up after they had finished their respective day jobs, at around eight or nine in the evening – occasionally even later – and they would debate sticking points until one or two in the morning – or occasionally even later.

An outsider observing their conversations – using the term loosely here – could easily have mistaken them for massive rows. The two were completely incapable of finding any sort of middle ground. Son wouldn't give an inch to Okubo and whenever Okubo suggested something, Son looked like he was about to recoil in horror at the thought. It was a highly charged relationship between a pair of rivals and one that couldn't easily be resolved by getting a third party in to mediate.

Okubo understood the situation, however, and would graciously bring coffee for the two to drink during their butting-heads sessions. Once the two had finalised their plans, Son – with Okubo's permission – contacted the patent office. All of Son's experiences to date had been leading up to this moment and the first thing to do was check whether the adapter was already in existence or otherwise.

The very same day Son completed the patent application; elsewhere he got in touch with the management of the new common-carrier companies and had them sign non-disclosure agreements before explaining his plan.

Inevitably, those who heard him out were startled by the adapter and even more so when Son told them he'd have a prototype to show off in just a few months' time. True to his word, he had an adapter ready by the deadline quoted.

On Christmas Eve 1986, Son and Okubo went to see Inamori Kazuo, the Kyocera chief executive and de facto owner of DDI, to pitch their new NCC Box.

In addition to manufacturing a wide range of products – from semiconductors and electronic components to finished goods – he also supervised the Seiwa Academy, which sought to help bring on young entrepreneurs and business managers. Later, at the age of 65 and already a tycoon due to the success of Kyocera and KDDI, he retired and became a Rinzai Buddhist monk.

On the day Son and Okubo (then 29 and 32, respectively) called in for their pitch, Inamori was 54 and had just been appointed chief executive of Kyocera, overseeing a boardroom of over 20 directors. After listening to Son's presentation, he asked him whether or not he and Okubo would grant him exclusivity if he bought 50,000 of the adapters, his polite way of speaking masking his cut-throat streak.

All things considered, his offer ran contrary to Son and Okubo's own business plan – selling adapters to all of the new common carriers and leveraging a commission on sales – and they initially refused.

Inamori wasn't so quick to give up, however. The two sides were unable to reach a compromise and negotiations lasted for 10 hours, well past nine o'clock in the evening – proof of just how hardened the DDI head was. Inamori pushed and pushed, ultimately offering them 2 billion yen for 500,000 units, the most he had ever offered anyone and enough to future-proof both SoftBank Japan and Shin Nihon Kohon.

Son and Okubo eventually succumbed to Inamori's persistence and signed an exclusivity agreement with DDI. It felt like a crushing defeat for both of them.

As 'Jingle Bells' provided the soundtrack to the cityscape the two headed back to their hotel, Son looking physically defeated and complaining to Okubo what a sorry state of affairs they had themselves into. Neither of the two could sleep that night and the next day they called in at Inamori's home. They said they had thought about the agreement they had signed and wanted to annul it.

The normally resplendent Son was cowering, his voice quivering. The two wanted to hedge their bets with the other new common carriers, and being bullied into signing the exclusivity agreement had left a bad taste in their mouth.

Inamori had a few choice words for the pair, but ultimately agreed to let the two out of the contract.

In the end, however, the pair successfully pitched their idea to Japan Telecom, signing an OEM (original equipment manufacturer) agreement with them for the adapter to be sold under their name.

As might be expected, DDI retaliated for the rescinded exclusivity agreement by promptly developing their own adapter, but the combination of Son's data network and Shin Nihon Kohon's technology netted the two several hundred million yen in royalties alone. Son was able to clear his massive debt, but his experience during negotiations and ultimately his failure to properly deal with Inamori would haunt him.

There was a lot to pick apart there, but ultimately it showed Son just how much he needed to toughen up as a negotiator.

Chapter 22

A pleasure making your acquaintance

R ound of face, baby-faced even. Friendly of expression. Short of stature. Completely boundless in energy. Occasionally explosive of temperament.

Son Masayoshi was passionate about a number of things, so much so he was willing to bet everything on them and toil away to make them a success, not one aspect neglected – qualities any business-man should possess.

For Son, his publishing business was irreplaceable. So when one of SoftBank Japan's directors suggested closing the division during a board meeting, Son looked he had just been shot through the heart.

As part of efforts to expand business, and from a completely corporate mindset, the profits and losses for each individual depart-ment had been rigorously audited. Whilst the software and publish-ing departments were what the company had made its name on, publishing was running a 200m-yen deficit; the board meeting had been called to address the future of the division.

Son and Omori, the company director, were overseeing proceedings.

Omori and the directors suggested closing down publishing, citing that despite every effort having been made results weren't improving, so they'd do well just to get rid of the entire division. Son had to resist the urge to jump out of his seat and give them a raging earful. That division was his very lifeblood and here were his directors sat around talking about gutting it.

He had literally built the division up from nothing, overseeing its development closely, and all of the memories came flooding back, such as single-handedly securing major distribution deals with Tohan and Nippon and haggling with Dentsu and NEC to get them on board.

It's safe to say Son looked at the publishing division the same way he looked at his own children. Japan was on the verge of becoming a digital information society – the reality was not far off. Son then corrected himself. Saying 'not far off' was an understatement – that future was here now, and publishing was going to play a major role within the new era, so therefore rather than view it as traditional publishing they should view it as a means of providing tremendous amounts of information to fuel this society.

SoftBank only stood to benefit in this way and Son could not grasp why Omori and the other directors couldn't understand his vision. Having thought all of this through, Son finally opened his mouth. 'I want to state my opposition to stop publishing. It's not being run as it should be, that's all.'

Up until one year before, publishing had always been in the black, so by shaking the division up a bit, he was certain they could get it back on its feet again. To the board's disbelief, Son announced he himself would take over the role of acting division head. He would get publishing back in the black, but if he wanted to stand any chance of success, he was going to have to completely overhaul the division.

Son's thought process went as follows: firstly, if no one involved had the ambition and conviction required then he wouldn't be able to achieve anything. With this in mind, he immediately called a meeting with his editorial staff and the accountants. Hashimoto Goro was involved as well.

At the time he was head of the editorial department, but was reporting to both an office director and a publishing division head and he felt restricted in terms of what he could do – he couldn't properly do his job.

During the meeting Son asked everyone in attendance why exactly they thought the division was doing poorly, but the expression of those in attendance changed completely when Son announced that those publications which couldn't turn their respective ships around could be axed.

The entire room seemed to be paralysed in shock: Son had always been so kind and friendly towards everyone in the company, but was showing a completely different side here. He explained that expenses had to be aligned with what was coming in, which meant cutting both costs and jobs, and that the editors-in-chief would be responsible for managing profits going forward.

As soon as Son mentioned cutting jobs, Hashimoto and the rest began protesting vehemently, saying that they were doing their best and the fact they weren't turning a profit wasn't for lack of trying. And yet all of a sudden Son was talking about having to cut expenses and staff – it wasn't fair for him not to give them a chance to turn things around.

Hashimoto had always been faithful to Son, but on this occasion he openly opposed him, completely frustrated by what he was hearing. It was his belief that Son had only just come back to the company from hospital so everyone had to come together and do their best for the company. Despite all protestations Son kept his cool, his tone gradually growing more pointed as he told those in attendance – attempting to rouse their spirits – that the publications they oversaw were like his children, and no parent could ever hate their own child.

Son listened to each and every idea his employees had about getting the publishing division back into the black. The editorial staff always took great pains with the content of the magazines, but weren't really bothered about the profit side of things.

This would have to change. Hashimoto and the other editors would crowd around Son to see what the results were during the weekly meetings held, their boss not missing the slightest error in calculations. They may have been weekly meetings, but for Hashimoto and the rest of the staff in attendance they felt entirely too frequent, each editorial department's results being aired out in the open. This effectively meant that editorial staff were no longer responsible just for editing but had also taken on the role of making sure enough money was coming in.

They were now the ones taking the orders for advertising and having to make sure every last piece of stationery was accounted for as a means of keeping costs down. Soon enough, though, these measures began to have a knock-on effect on results and after six months almost all of the publications were showing positive results.

In 1987, Bill Gates and Nishi Kazuhiko had a falling out and the computer industry once again became a Wild West. In an interview Son conducted with Gates (Son had flown out to the States to interview the man for the launch edition of *The Computer* magazine in July of that year), he asked him why he had parted ways with Nishi. Gates's response was as follows:

'What ASCII were after and what I was after were two different things. Here at Microsoft we do software, so I wanted K [Nishi] to develop software with us, but all he was interested in was hardware.'

Up until that time computer magazines had tended to cover PC use, but *The Computer* was the first computer industry publication to shine a spotlight on the business side of things. Son – alongside *The Computer*'s editor-in-chief, Inaba Toshio (who later became deputy general director of SoftBank Publishing) – departed for Seattle without having booked an appointment with Gates, although once they arrived, Son did ring the Microsoft founder from his hotel and they were given the green light.

This interview was actually the first time Son and Gates had ever met face-to-face, and Son had more than a few things he wanted to ask him, writing up the question sheet alongside Inaba, having already prepared the title beforehand: 'Another miracle from the most successful man of the 80s'.

Perhaps with this overly positive title, Son was projecting his own dreams and ambitions on to Gates, as at the time Microsoft were growing by leaps and bounds and emerging as a major player.

Microsoft's head office was located in Redmond, Washington, near Seattle, the premises surrounded by dense, luxuriant forest. Whilst the Pacific Northwest is known for its frequent rainfall, on the day Son called in it was bright and sunny.

Gates – dressed in his usual casual way in a deep-red jumper over a pink and white striped shirt – greeted Son (who was wearing a grey blazer) with a smile and beckoned him to sit down. Gates's working desk was a mess of documents, a globe and three different computers: one running Windows as well as a Macintosh Plus and a Macintosh II.

Commencing the interview, Son dived right into the heavy-hitting questions, asking Gates his views on what the future of the computer industry in America was, and trying to get the story behind the failure of the Microsoft and ASCII partnership in Japan. Just like a veteran journalist would do, Son blitzed Gates with a number of insistent, meticulous questions, to which the Microsoft man would offer his responses, the two clashing swords. Inaba watched on in silence as the whole spectacle played out.

Whenever Gates would get excited about something his body would start to shake a little bit; Son was firing off a volley a questions and Gates was fully up for the exchange, progressively leaning forward when answering.

There were some questions he wasn't quite certain how to answer, though, but suffice it to say the two went well past their allotted one hour of interview time. Gates gave Son a guided tour of the premises and, once they had finished, shook hands for the first time.

Chapter 23   **My American mum and dad**

There is a saying that there are no 'what ifs' in history. It naturally follows on then that in the business world as well, the words 'what if' hold no meaning either.

That being said, however, it would be interesting to present such a scenario and ask the question of whether Son would have become a global success if he hadn't met one person.

This person – a man – had a rounded face and a broad forehead, giving him a resemblance not unlike Dr Elefun, the man who gave life to Astro Boy in the eponymous manga series by Tezuka Osamu or – for a more American equivalent – the mascot for the famous chain of Egghead Software computer stores. He always had a pleasant smile on his face, but his gaze could occasionally be ramped up to piercing. His knowledge was boundless.

The name of the man in question was Ted Dolotta, who would be the driving force behind Son making a name for himself internationally. Had Son not met Ted, the former's global strategy would certainly have been more gradual – if not a completely different trajectory altogether. Ultimately Dolotta would prove a tremendous influence in Son making great strides in this area, such that the latter would refer to the former as 'my

American dad', Dolotta teaching Son all manner of things from the American way of doing business to American table manners.

When Son founded SoftBank America in 1988, Dolotta was the one he would place in charge of the company; however, their first meeting was some two years earlier.

Dolotta was 52 at the time and very much embodied the plucky, rough-and-tumble American spirit. He was born in Poland and had studied engineering, showing himself to be a true talent, receiving his PhD and achieving success in the field. As he entered his fifties, however, a fire still burned inside him and Dolotta had decided he wanted to make a new life for himself – mark a turning point, so to speak. At the time, Dolotta was living in California, working for Interactive Systems – just one more in a pool of small companies that had popped up in response to the growth of the computer industry, albeit one specialising in Unix.

Prior to Interactive, Ted had worked at Bell Laboratories, one of the largest research institutes in the world, having been founded as the engineering department for AT&T and Western Electric. Its existence could be traced as far back as Alexander Graham Bell's Bell Telephone Company. The company had around 30,000 employees in 25 countries and 11 of its scientists had been Nobel Prize winners. A former colleague of Dolotta's had been sent to work in Tokyo, where he had the odd dealing with Son; on one such occasion Son happened to be after someone who was handy with Unix for a project he had in mind. That former colleague in turn told Dolotta about the opportunity, telling him to get in touch with Son if he was interested. Dolotta rang him up straight away, perhaps sensing the possibilities offered by working with someone in such a far-flung place.

Son took the call and got down to brass tacks: he had something important he wanted to talk to Dolotta about – could the two meet in Tokyo tomorrow?

Dolotta must have been taken aback at Son's urgency – and no matter how much he wanted to, being in Tokyo tomorrow was a difficult ask as he was scheduled to be in Australia in the next few days. Son suggested stopping off in Tokyo on his way home from Australia, so Dolotta adjusted his travel plans to accommodate him.

Son made arrangements for the two to meet at the first-class Palace Hotel near the Japanese Imperial Palace. Dolotta was right on time – for American businessmen punctuality was everything, and Son, arriving alone, had expected as much.

On arrival he rang up Dolotta and told him to meet him in the lobby, saying he'd be able to recognise him instantly – he'd be an Asian man in a grey blazer. Of course, on Dolotta coming down from his room the lobby was filled to the brim with Asian men in grey blazers, but a short man with a friendly smile soon met his gaze and approached him.

Son took him downstairs to the second basement where there was a Japanese-style restaurant and whilst feasting on sushi, he spoke to Dolotta of his plans. Dolotta soon knew he wanted to get on board.

From 1987 onwards, Dolotta would start working full-time for Son and the two would frequently travel the length and breadth of America together.

Dolotta was 53 when he first started working for SoftBank – truly old enough to have been Son's father, and the two developed their father–son working dynamic to exquisite effect when dealing with businesspeople all across the globe. Dolotta's job effectively consisted of making a name for SoftBank on the American Unix market and he proved a truly loyal partner, working on one project after another.

He oversaw operations at SRI (SoftBank Research Institute, which mainly dealt in developing software for PC and Unix), also paving the way for dealings with US-funded companies who were gaining ground in Japan. Another large part of his job was securing Japanese publishing rights for American computer magazines, this coming about after Son decided this was a worthwhile endeavour, having been sparked by telling Bill Gates he really should have been reading *PCWeek*.

In March 1990, Son flew out to New York with Hashimoto Goro in tow to sign an agreement in this respect with Ziff-Davis, the leading publishing company for the computer industry and publishers of *PCWeek* – at the time the most widely read in its market segment.

Anyone who was anyone in the computer industry had their eyes on it.

Waiting for the pair at the Ziff-Davis head office on 5th Avenue in New York was William Ziff, and it took the parties all of 10 minutes to formalise proceedings (an hour or more is normally scheduled for this sort of thing).

As of May of that year, 50,000 copies of the Japanese version of *PCWeek* would be published each week. Ziff would later comment to Hashimoto that he had only known three bona fide geniuses in his entire life: Bill Gates, Steve Jobs and Son Masayoshi.

Son in turn would confide in Hashimoto during this trip that he wanted to buy Ziff's company one day – which at the time Hashimoto took as a joke, such was the absurdity of his proposal. And yet, the third genius's eyes were deadly serious: he knew his own American dream was bound to come true sooner or later, which it eventually did in November of 1994, when he acquired Ziff-Davis.

'If Ted was my American dad, then Ron would have to be my

American "mum",' Son has said, referring here to Ronald Fisher Board Director, Corporate Officer and Vice Chairman of SoftBank Group.

'Ted would have been the one to introduce me to Ron. We were still small at the time but I knew I wanted to crack on and get things done within the information revolution happening around us. We were at a point in time where you had to be technologically sound to manage on the Japanese market and we also needed to gain a foothold on the American market. Ted told me that due to his background as a Bell Labs engineer he could oversee proceedings on the technical side of things but, by way of introducing Ron, told me he was someone we couldn't do without from a business standpoint.'

And so, whenever he was meeting people across the length and breadth of the United States Ted was the constant presence at Son's side, someone more technically minded who he could bounce ideas off.

Conversely, when it came to investments, negotiations or acquisitions, Ron was the more business-minded of Son's American associates who he could always count on for sound advice.

'Ron is cool-headed, fair, exceptionally intelligent, good at analysing things and is more than capable of looking at things from both a mathematical and legal point of view. He's also extraordinarily easy to get on with, so people are very much at ease when speaking to him, but he doesn't use that to his own personal advantage. Rather he's completely straightforward and fair whenever dealing with people and knows exactly what to compromise on – and what not to!'

Ron would also prove indispensable whenever negotiations would reach a deadlock by finding workarounds to conditions or simply bringing the other side round to Son's point of view.

Son's trust in him was absolute: 'He's a truly thoughtful and affable individual who is always looking out for the best interests of all parties involved.' Son's 'American mum' was an unassailable presence.

The first time the two had met was at a dinner in Los Angeles in 1986, those present being Son, Dolotta, John White and his wife, and Fisher and his wife.

Fisher can still clearly recall this meeting.

'Ted wanted us to meet this crazy guy from Japan, who had this big vision. We had an amazing dinner. Masa spoke about how he'd started SoftBank, he told us a story about standing on the tangerine box with his two employees, telling them his vision, and the next day they quit. And then he spoke about his vision in terms of why he was interested in possibly working with us. Because, again, he wanted to bring technology to Japan.'

After the dinner, Fisher's wife commented to him that Son had been the most engaging person she had ever met, a statement Fisher completely agreed with.

'Masa has a unique ability to connect with people which is very unusual, because with a lot of successful people it's all about themselves. And Masa has this ability, when he is looking to connect with you in a way to really understand and what's important for you and how together you can achieve something much bigger. That's why he connects so well with entrepreneurs.'

Fisher coolly and precisely goes into further detail about Son's character. 'When he is in a room with entrepreneurs, instead of talking about his success and things like that, he wants to know about them. He wants to know their vision and discusses how we can share that. It's this connection, being able to engage with people, that makes him so different compared to many successful entrepreneurs.'

Fisher comments further: 'Masa is very busy but if you have got a call or video scheduled with him, he is always on time, never late, because he has a respect for other people. I wasn't there, but I think that's the same thing that happened with Jack Ma. Masa and Jack connected, and I have seen this over and over again. I saw it with Jerry Yang (co-founder of Yahoo! Inc). I also saw it when we made our early investments. He focused on understanding what's in their minds and then how they can work together as partners. It's not only the intellectual power, but also the power to engage with people that makes him so effective.'

As part of the SoftBank Group looking for ways to grow and develop in America, the first matter of business would be investing in the Ziff-Davis exhibitions department, as they were responsible for overseeing the COMDEX trade fair, the largest of its kind within the computer industry. As part of Son's focus on making technology the centre of things and how exactly to implement this approach, his attention was initially drawn to COMDEX as a trade show and Ziff-Davis as a publisher, the perfect convergence of key players and the latest information.

During the acquisition process Son had a conversation with Eric Pippo, then managing director of Ziff-Davis, about how he had managed to convince Ted Forstmann (owner of Ziff-Davis) to invest in a California start-up specialising in conducting searches across the whole of the internet. Son immediately loved the idea and stated his interest in meeting everyone involved there.

The company was Yahoo! and his first meeting was with Jerry Yang and David Filo. Son left completely convinced of the fact that Yahoo!'s search engine wasn't just going to revolutionise their industry, but change everything.

His first investment in Yahoo! would be made on 29 November

1995, purchasing roughly 5 per cent of available shares, then acquiring more than 30% per cent of shares later in April 1996.

Fisher sheds some light on what was going on behind the scenes.

'In 1996, investment in internet companies had boomed and we had made dozens of investments in the US. Some of them worked out really well, some of them didn't. But it gave us a sense of what was going to happen on the Internet. If you see a new technology trend, you have to put everything behind it. Then we sold Ziff-Davis and COMDEX, and we focused on the internet. That was in the late 1990s.'

After the dotcom bubble of the noughties burst, Japan were also miles ahead of everyone else with the mobile market. Son's all-in approach to the internet extended to introducing the feature as part of Japanese mobiles, effectively combining the two markets.

Fisher picks the story up from here: 'The next generation of the internet is not going to happen on PC's – it's going to be on mobile devices, just like the change from minicomputers to PC's. He has told you about his famous meeting with Steve Jobs. We thought this was something that was going to change the use of technology forever. And in typical Masa fashion, he said "we have to go for it". It wasn't about being a mobile company, it was about being the next generation of the internet. It was about connecting people together using the underlying technology of mobile and the internet. We had the insight that when you combine these new technologies with the adoption or the rapid adoption of new chip technology it drives costs down and you are going to have an expansion of use, which people could not understand how they were going to use.'

The early 2000s would see this occur in China, with mobile use exploding overnight. Alibaba had initially been set up as a PC-based business with no mobile presence, but the idea soon occurred to Jack

Ma and Son that if mobiles could be used to connect people and business got on board with this then mobiles could be used for shopping. And whenever a new trend would capture Son's imagination he would drop everything to focus on his new endeavour, with his 'American mum' in tow.

Chapter 24　**With a firm aim one can do the impossible**

The year 1990 saw widespread use of the mobile phone for the first time, the manga Chibi Maruko-chan's popularity reach fever pitch and the arrival of the Super Nintendo Entertainment System in shops.

Son turned 33 in August of that year.

In July of that year, the amount of the investments to be made by NEC, Fujitsu, Toshiba, Canon and Sony in the founding of the Japanese subsidiary of US software company Novell were finalised and the joint venture Son had secretly gone about putting together would finally see the light of day.

Son's art of war for business was as follows: regardless of the size of the predicament the first thing to do was not to panic. The second step to take was not to further err and take the wrong course of action.

Perhaps Son's greatest strength of all was, even in the face of imminent failure, rescuing some sort of victory. The key to success is found in the heart of failure, after all.

*　　*　　*

When detailing Son's character what must not be overlooked under any circumstances is the theme of familial love. Just as his father Mitsunori drew great pride from his own distant ancestors in Korea, Masayoshi took great pride in his own family. He had tremendous respect for his own mother and father, warmth and affection for his siblings, confidence in his friends and tender love for his children. In his opinion this was only natural for a human being.

Son has been held up as a role model by young people in Japan, but simply emulating him and casting aside one's feelings is a vain and shallow exercise.

There is one person, however, who has been influenced by Son perhaps more than anyone else, and that is his younger brother, Taizo, 15 years Son's junior. Son may have been the second eldest of four brothers, but despite the age gap he was always closest to Taizo, the youngest of the four, although occasionally he would treat him with the severity of a father. And remember, like his brother, Taizo also changed his surname to Son.

When Taizo was born, the head of Toshiba, Ishizaka Taizo, was a well-respected business figure and so perhaps to bless him with a similar fortune he was named after him. Only, the Chinese characters used for Ishizaka Taizo's name included the number three, and as Son Taizo was the fourth-born this was a bit odd, so that character was changed to a similar-sounding one referring to wealth in the hopes Taizo would amass a good fortune.

In April 1991, Taizo began attending the Sundai Preparatory School in the hopes of passing the Tokyo University entrance examination.

Like Masayoshi before him, Taizo had studied at Kurume University Preparatory High School and, unlike his brother, actually graduated from the school with flying colours. He would end up failing the Tokyo University entrance examination though. A fan of jazz,

Taizo then decided to form a band and lived a carefree life back in Fukuoka for a bit, but after failing the Tokyo University entrance examination a second time he was suddenly struck by a sense of anxiety as to what to do with his life and moved to Tokyo to attend a preparatory school.

Seeking advice from his older brother Masayoshi, what he got instead was a stern ticking-off: Son the elder told him he had to stop viewing his life as a complete and utter failure, otherwise he would never shake the image of the loser he had created for himself.

What little bit of pride Taizo had been narrowly clinging to was completely torn to shreds by this conversation with his brother. Much like Masayoshi, however, he had an indomitable spirit and soon frantically set about creating a plan to swot up for his entrance examinations, even drafting a roadmap for success.

Brimming with pride, he showed this to Masayoshi, who once again laid into him, proceeding to explain to him exactly what was wrong with his thought process: it wasn't about adding things together, it was about dividing things up, but in a way no one else would think of.

Masayoshi went on to explain in detail. Firstly, Taizo had to think about things in the space of one year, but doing the obvious and dividing the year up into 12 months was no good. If he was going to draft some elaborate plan then he had to make sure he was going to be able to see the plan through to completion.

Masayoshi then told Taizo to take the 365 days out of the year and – instead of dividing them up by 12 – divide them up by 14. By doing so, each period of time would end on the 26th of each traditional month, giving him four or five extra days a month. Employing Son's unique division again, this would give him an extra day each week.

The purpose of this process was to create a psychological buffer zone for himself so his efficiency would also go up. Masayoshi also advised Taizo to think of ways of doing in 10 minutes things that would normally take one hour.

Masayoshi was just as meticulous when it came to making sure the plan going ahead was properly implemented. When Taizo got stuck into his books again, without fail he would show his brother the progress he was making compared to what he'd laid out for himself on his roadmap. Bits marked in green were where he'd been able to move ahead as planned, with the parts he was slacking off on marked in red and things under way in yellow. All in all, Taizo would spend 18 hours a day studying, well aware that when he was at Holy Names College and Berkeley Masayoshi had spent all of his waking hours revising – he wasn't about to lose out to his older brother.

At the start, naturally the roadmap was marked up in red and yellow, but gradually the number of green spots began to rise and Taizo was keen to show Masayoshi his progress. The older Son took one glance and was dismissive, telling his younger brother he didn't understand anything about what it meant to revise and study. Taizo – moderately confident in the progress he was making – wasn't necessarily expecting heaps of praise, but certainly wasn't ready for another ticking-off and could only stare at Masayoshi in disbelief, wondering what exactly he had done to deserve such harsh words.

Masayoshi was quick and to the point. The trouble was the existence of the yellow bits.

The red bits where he had been skiving off on because they were difficult weren't any issue at all – no one's perfect, after all, and sometimes, try all you might, you just can't get something done. The green bits came about as the result of Masayoshi's 'extra days', so everything going to plan there was the natural result. The yellow bits

– things under way, but which weren't completed yet – were the most important bits and the question Taizo should ask himself was why they hadn't been completed yet. Exactly how far along was he in each instance?

Revising, if nothing else, is shedding a light on challenges and problems have to be solved no matter what. All of which was to say Taizo needed to create a plan where everything was completed by the end of it.

Taizo nodded his head eagerly as his brother explained what needed doing. Having redrafted his roadmap and then used it to mark his progress, his marks quickly began to rise and he was ultimately admitted to the Tokyo University School of Economics, one of the hardest schools to get into in all of Japan, a testament in its way to the brilliance of Son Masayoshi's unique way of thinking.

Still today, Son's diary is divided up into blocks of five minutes.

His father may have had tremendous business acumen and his mother may have been deeply loving and caring, but the family member Taizo had the most respect for was Masayoshi. He was completely in awe of the sheer size and difference in scale – billions upon billions of yen – his brother was operating at. There was no way he was ever going to be able to get one over his older brother.

That being said, however, whilst at Tokyo University in February 1996 Taizo did start up his own business – Indigo – helping develop companies specialising in sales on the then still-nascent internet. He was 23, the exact same age Masayoshi had been when he started up SoftBank Japan – at least he wasn't going to lose to his older brother on that point.

Masayoshi was quite fond of computer games so whilst playing Super Mario Brothers with his younger brother, he'd lecture him on his business philosophy.

He was always keen to learn the best way to snag the power-up mushroom or the best time to hop over King Koopa (Bowser) or to get people to show him which pipes led to warp zones. What was the easiest way to get to World 4 without having to go through all of Worlds 1, 2 and 3 beforehand?

But does taking the warp actually make the game any more fun? You clear the first world, beat the boss, then proceed to World 2 where things get a little bit harder. After that there's World 3 to deal with.

Masayoshi would explain to Taizo that the business world and Mario were exactly the same, and the most important thing was to carve out your own path one stage at a time.

Another game Masayoshi and Taizo enjoyed playing together was Sekigahara, a simulation game where players took on the roles of historic military commanders Ishida Mitsunari and Tokugawa Ieyasu and battled it out. Masayoshi would attack incessantly, surrounding one unit of Taizo's troops with six of his own units, to the latter's chagrin.

Much like when he would engage in large-scale acquisitions, Son was proactive and aggressive, but also meticulous and thorough. Taizo learnt from his older brother that in such dealings he had to make sure his position was exceptionally solid, and that if he knew he was going to have to cross a bridge he should do it in a tank.

'With a firm aim one can do the impossible.'

This quote is attributed to the Bakumatsu revolutionary Yoshida Sho'in, who taught his students that once they had made up their minds they would be capable of overcoming any hardship that came their way.

In the business world, it was therefore important to think about what one should be aiming for, much like the guiding ambition Son himself had nurtured in himself when he was younger. He possessed an unshakeable belief – high aspirations, then – that all of the work he had done up until this point were tributaries flowing into the river that would be his great contribution to the digital information society.

In a significant move, on 22 July 1994, SoftBank began issuing over-the-counter shares.

Chapter 25   **Boldly meticulous**

There are some events in a person's life which are seared into their memory.

One such day for Son Masayoshi was 15 November 1995, a Wednesday. He was in a suite in the Las Vegas Hilton, surrounded by SoftBank Group executives, including Ted Dolotta, David Blumstein and Ron Fisher, as well as Inoue Masahiro, the head of the chief executive's office (and later head of Yahoo! Japan), who had made the trip over with Son.

That year Son had purchased COMDEX, the Interface Group's division overseeing trade shows and exhibitions, as well as Ziff-Davis.

The suite was located on the 29th floor of the building and had a balcony area attached to it, although Son had never actually gone out on the balcony to have a look – with his fear of heights it was much too scary and regardless he was much too busy planning his own daredevil stunt for the business world.

The rest of his executives were leisurely lounging about the room when Son broke the ice with an announcement: Eric Hippeau, head of Ziff-Davis, had asked him to invest in Yahoo!, an internet company, and he had found this proposal extremely intriguing.

Yahoo! were looking to be publicly listed so required investors. Ziff-Davis had decided to invest in Yahoo! but as this happened shortly before they had been bought out by SoftBank, and due to the fixed term set for assets valuation as part of proceedings in this respect, they had never actually finalised payment.

Hippeau accordingly raised the issue of investment with Son – he was someone the SoftBank chief executive trusted, after all – once the dust had settled but the deadline for investment was looming: Friday, only two days away. Son asked those in attendance – in Japanese – what they thought he should do.

Inoue Masahiro immediately responded, saying he thought it was a good idea.

Inoue had started working at Sord Computer Systems, moving to SoftBank in 1987 to work for their research institute, eventually being transferred to the main office in 1992. He remained by Son's side until his death in 2017. Working as the head of the office of the chief executive and as chief secretary, he was able to pick up on Son's management style – he didn't get to where he was just to hold Son's bags for him.

As soon as Son broached the Yahoo! issue Inoue knew he had to speak up. As an impartial observer of Son he knew how likely the SoftBank founder was to bang his head against a telephone pole or forget to put his shoes on before boarding a jet plane due to getting too lost in his own thoughts.

Within Son's circle of senior executives, Miyauchi Ken was the more likely to get excited by or rapidly lose interest in things alongside his boss, whilst Inoue kept a cool head at all times. This time, however, was different and Inoue's passion got the best of him.

His argument was that they were on the cusp of the internet age and that he was certain Son's judgement in making the investment was the correct one here. The group ultimately decided to take $2 million out of COMDEX for the investment.

The next day – 16 November 1995 – Son flew out to Silicon Valley with Dolotta to meet Yahoo!'s founders, Jerry Yang and David Filo, in their small office in Mountain View.

The original plan at Yahoo!'s end was to greet their potential new investors by taking them out to a French or Chinese restaurant to discuss the finer details; Son's expectations, however, involved sitting down with the two young businessmen and picking their brains, so they opted for pizza delivery instead. Indeed, all Son really wanted was for the three to sit down and speak passionately about their lofty ambitions and the future the internet was capable of providing.

Son recalls, 'When I met Yang and Filo and spoke with them . . . That was all I needed, really. At that time I decided to ante up and throw everything I had behind them.'

SoftBank formalised their initial $2m investment, followed by an additional $100m investment to underwrite the allocation of new shares to a third party when Yahoo! went public on NASDAQ, SoftBank ultimately holding 37 per cent of shares in the American company.

When SoftBank's initial investment was concluded, a number of Japanese companies had already come in with offers saying they wanted to enter into a joint venture with Yahoo! Inoue's meeting with Yang concerning setting up Yahoo! Japan occurred later that year, in December. Inoue can still vividly recall the meeting: '[SoftBank] had been selected as the partner for the joint venture but that wasn't down to us having invested heavily in them. The other companies Yahoo! were dealing with wanted to take things slowly, cautiously – their business sense was far too traditional. Yahoo! on the other hand agreed with our stance that speed was the most important thing for the internet and we told them we could roll it out in three months.'

In Yahoo!'s head office in California Inoue recalls glancing at a pile of papers, which were the other offers that had come in concerning setting up Yahoo! Japan. Jerry Yang – dressed in a polo shirt – asked what they should do about all of them.

Deep down Inoue began to harbour doubts about whether or not he should have brought his own official proposal. That didn't matter now though, the reality was he was completely empty-handed. Nevertheless, Inoue suggested letting SoftBank handle Yahoo! Japan. Yang liked the idea but wanted to know how they would make a start on the project. Inoue followed up by saying they could start small with just two or three people and then if more employees were required they could take it from there.

SoftBank were in the position to do it, so why not just let them handle it? Yang nodded in agreement, adding that the internet was all about speed. Both SoftBank and Yahoo! had technical backgrounds and were on the same wavelength at any rate, so they moved on to discuss the issue of localisation into Japanese. Inoue already had a firm grasp on the principles in play, as there was a tremendous culture gap between Japan and the United States.

There were no real precedents in terms of Japanese localisation in this respect, but on the flip side they weren't bound by anything in that sense either, being free to do their own thing.

At any rate, Inoue and Yang shook hands and agreed to make a start.

On 20 December 1995, in San Jose in the heart of Silicon Valley, the area in front of the Fairmont Hotel had been converted into a large square where a large Christmas tree had been set up for children to decorate, turning it into a shining array of red, yellow and green.

Son's contingent filled their stomachs with sushi and then went outside, admiring the Christmas decorations. Kageyama Takumi, a SoftBank employee who had made the trip over with Inoue, also has very fond and special memories of that day, and says the mood was one of having received the greatest Christmas present one could have hoped for. On the way back to Japan the team drafted reports on the flight and even in the car driving them from Narita Airport directly to SoftBank's (then) head office in Nihonbashi Hama-cho.

Son was beaming ear to ear: the trip had been a success. Yahoo! Japan was incorporated in January 1996.

On 8 January, Son called all his directors together for a meeting and issued his manifesto.

'This year is year one of the internet. As such we're going to be putting everything into getting the internet off the ground and running.'

Jerry Yang flew over from the States on the 12th and a service provision start date was agreed on: 1 April. At the time SoftBank were square in the middle of calculating their daily closing of accounts and, looking at their operating profit-and-loss statement, things were very tight. There was one person within the organisation, however, who needed the project done and dusted as soon as possible and that was Inoue.

He decided to get HR involved, telling them they were in dire straits and they needed to get the project done straight away; HR in turn green-lit the Yahoo! Launch Project, which Kageyama Takumi, editor-in-chief of Unix User, would be a part of.

Kageyama originally joined SoftBank the year after it was founded. He had worked his way through university to study computers and editing. A man of few words, his commitment and sense of duty were truly exemplary. The title on his business card was 'editor-in-chief' and he took pride in making sure the publications he worked on were peerless. Kageyama was completely committed to the cause due to Son's passion and warm consideration for those around him, citing one end-of-the-year do where a SoftBank Group company had to be restructured and redundancies were in order, Son openly weeping as he broke the news.

With the task at hand, however, there were three main things that needed doing: sorting out the Yahoo! directory, getting the search engine up and running in the Japanese language, and compiling all of the sites they would want available for searching.

And then on top of that there were other related issues to be addressed, such as what program to use for the search engine, how best to integrate it for use within Yahoo!'s own system and what to do about advertising.

It was an interminable 'to do' list and one only two or three people had been assigned to, and even then those employees hadn't even been allocated a dedicated room for their activities. There was a corner in Son's executive office that wasn't being used though. And there was the fact that those assigned to the task could work via email without leaving their posts.

The most difficult task at hand was compiling all the sites to be listed under the search engine, as Inoue had earmarked 30,000 individual sites for this purpose. He recalls no one having any idea at the time about how to go about this task and their having to fumble through the entire process.

Kageyama put an almighty shift in and managed to come up with a list of 15,000 sites. They would then have to develop a 24-hour availability framework and registration system for the service, which ultimately Son's younger brother Taizo and his colleagues would work on.

In July 1996, Inoue took over Son's position as the head of Yahoo! Japan, after which there was a tremendous explosion in the number of users: one day in January 1997 would yield 5 million page views, with this number doubling to 10 million by June 1998. By March 2004 the figure was over 700 million due to the development of their search engine, media, community, e-commerce and mobile services.

Chapter 26

Willpower and ambition

J ust like a ship which, having cast out to sea, creates a wake which grows broader and broader as the vessel cuts through the ocean waves, so whenever Son would make a move a new wind always seemed to pick up, propelling him further forwards.

Sometimes these would be winds of revolution and Son himself could only stand in awe at what he had apparently summoned.

In April 1995, Son had acquired COMDEX, the world's largest computer trade fair, and then in November of that same year he acquired Ziff-Davis's publishing arm, which at the time was the largest computer-related publishing company around. To top all that off, in January 1996 he became the largest shareholder in America's largest search engine company.

In June of that year he formed a partnership with JSkyB (now Sky PerfecTV), a digital satellite broadcast company that was part of the Australian media mogul Rupert Murdoch's News Corp Group. He would also announce he was going to purchase shares in TV Asahi, although this transaction eventually fell through.

On 16 January 1998, SoftBank were finally listed on the first section of the Tokyo Stock Exchange, four years after their initial issuance of over-the-counter shares. The first day shares were available for trading saw a massive influx of orders placed, with the final closing price well up on the initial opening price (3,870 yen versus 3,700 yen).

In June 1999, Son would partner with the American National Association of Securities for the launch of NASDAQ Japan and in September 2000 he purchased shares in the Nippon Credit Bank Ltd (now Aozora Bank). Son, ever the revolutionary, was constantly dumbfounding people with the businesses he was acquiring and developing and whenever Son appeared on the scene massive winds of change would blow in from behind him.

That being said, however, no matter how fierce the hurricane there is always a place of calm and quiet at its core, and for Son this was an invitation to the Sohen tea ceremony.

It was a once-in-a-lifetime opportunity.

Son was quite similar in a number of ways to the Sohen school's Sen-no-Rikyu, the first disciple of Sotan, who had founded the school some 350 years ago. In 1701 a samurai and haiku poet of the Ako Domain, Otaka Gengo, having been rendered lordless after the killing of his master by the enemy, was toiling away as a labourer when he was admitted to the school.

Sohen, noticing the hardships Otaka was going through, told him the day a tea ceremony was to be held at the Kira residence.

The present-day head of the school is Yamada Sohen, who due to the untimely death of his predecessor, was appointed the 11th-generation head of the school whilst still a student. In June 1997, the Sohen School would hold its only tea ceremony.

Yamada was an alumnus of Sophia University and whilst living in the traditional manner had also developed a taste for incorporating the modern, maintaining a large personal network and coming up with a new school combining Zen Buddhism and the Japanese tea ceremony in his Dairyu school. The school was the brainchild of

Hitotsubashi University Innovation Research Centre lecturer Yonekura Sei'ichiro, assembling the leaders in a number of fields capable of shaping the future (dubbed the 'Creating tomorrow' group) to pass on the importance of the tea ceremony.

The Sohen tea ceremony was going to be held in the Golden Temple in Kyoto to celebrate its 600th anniversary of construction and, as a singular event, held the highest significance for the Sohen school. For those select few guests who were lucky enough to be invited as well it was a once-in-a-lifetime occurrence and truly an honour. Yamada had sought advice from Yonekura for quite some time, as the latter was a business history expert who was well read on those changes occurring within the computer industry.

Yonekura explains his own personal theory concerning the situation. '[In Japan] we tend to look at bright new companies with a mixture of disdain and envy. However, in the era we live in we shouldn't be hoping for these companies to fail – we should fully embrace and support them otherwise there's no way we'll ever see another Sony or Honda again.'

Indeed, when bashing Son became a popular stance to take, Yonekura proved controversial by advocating for him and using logic to point out what he was doing right. Yonekura also possessed a deep knowledge of the Japanese tea ceremony, so didn't hesitate for one second about thinking to invite Son Masayoshi to the prestigious ceremony.

'For this tea ceremony the only way we could hold it in good faith was to invite people who had proved deeply influential. We also wanted to invite businessmen who did a lot of work overseas to get them to understand the importance of the ceremony.'

And this is how Yamada Sohen and Son Masayoshi, two extraordinary individuals in their own way, met. At the time, Son was extraordinarily busy, but contrary to expectations, he readily accepted the invitation – despite the fact he had never attended a tea ceremony before.

The Shomyo-ji Temple in Kamakura is surrounded by 10,000 square metres of lush greenery, with the stream running through it being designated important cultural property. It was built by Lord Ichijo Akiyoshi (also known as Ekan) and Kanamori Sowa, a tea master from the Edo period. Kanamori had also constructed the tea room in Kinkaku-ji in Kyoto, which proved the connection for getting Sohen involved.

The day of the event, Son drove down from Tokyo and promptly arrived at half past four in the afternoon, the appointed time. He slipped into the kimono and hakama he had been provided for the occasion. He looked nervous, although as he would go on to explain this was not necessarily due to previously having had no interest in the Japanese tea ceremony.

'I was really interested in the fact that the tea ceremony was diametrically opposed to the work I did. Taking a cup of tea out in the middle of nature was truly something else and as busy as I was I needed to stop and reflect on what I was doing. I needed something outside of karaoke and golf to relax.' (Son would frequently go to concerts together with his family but, not possessing a golden voice, he would never get up and sing of his own volition during karaoke sessions.)

However, just as Rikyu and Oribe had long ago become pillars of emotional support for Nobunaga and Hideyoshi, 16th-century figures known as the two 'great unifiers' of Japan, so now did Sohen for Son.

In a small tea room – just large enough to seat two or three people comfortably – known as the Fushinan he was served a cup of dark brown tea by the tea master. Son was sat in the traditional manner – kneeling down with his rear resting on his haunches – and looked slightly uncomfortable.

'You who would become a man like Nobunaga, take this tea and drink it.' Hearing these words from the tea master, Son's face became slightly less strained as he prepared to take the tea.

The core tenet at the heart of the Japanese tea ceremony is the communion of minds in a ceremony lasting the ages. Son, in drinking from the same tea bowl the great military commanders drank from, would symbolically commune with them and take them into himself.

Once the tea ceremony was over, the twilight outside was dim and Son felt a wave of relaxation pour over him as he stared at the faint light of the lanterns on the estate. His nerves began to subside and, sitting alone, Son remarked to himself how calm he felt inside. The seating arrangements were changed and dinner was served.

Rather unusually, Son – who never drank alcohol – took a sip of rice wine and, commenting on how nice it was, then went on to take another swig or two. In homage to Bill Gates, who was rather fond of Coca-Cola, Son also drank the fizzy drink, but he virtually never touched alcohol. Additionally, due to his father's poor health and to get him to give up alcohol, Son had promised him not to take up drinking.

After finishing eating, the tea master asked Son to explain the internet to him. The tea master knew the term as something of a buzzword, but didn't quite understand the actual reality of it. Son quietly explained.

'Japanese politicians are trying to frame the internet as some sort of fad for young people, snidely leering at it. Their approach is flawed from the outset. The internet is something which – despite whatever protestations or misgivings people may have about it – will become commonplace, just like the telephone. It's just another part of the infrastructure of society, so we've got to address the question of how it will be used. After that it's just a question of how happy it makes people.'

There was a certain persuasiveness to Son's words; he was speaking from his heart.

Sohen, who was also focused on fusing tradition and new forms of culture, could perfectly grasp Son's point. He recalls his impression of the SoftBank founder. 'I may experience the same feelings of ambition and possess the same intelligence as Son, but whenever he dreams up something in his head, he pursues it and makes it a reality. But the average person is incapable of seeing whatever future Son has envisioned. Whilst some people have criticised him for always changing his message, one reason for that may be that laymen such as yourself and myself simply just can't follow his chain of thought.'

Sohen's impression is one of Son practising what he preaches, a principle of living sincerely, which lies at the heart of the Japanese tea ceremony. Whilst it may have been his first time in a tea ceremony he had already mastered the philosophy behind it.

Two years later, Son would partake in another tea ceremony on a cold winter's night. During the event someone would slip a one-page memo into the tea room: it was an urgent phone call for Son.

Sohen was reluctant for participants in the tea ceremony to bring in things from the outside world which could distract them. He told Son he knew he had his mobile on him but wanted to know whether he would make the call. Son stated that he felt ashamed but asked Sohen if they could interrupt the ceremony for a minute so he could make the call.

Son apologised and stepped over to the storage area to make the call. It ended up being a long one. By chance, the leading disciple of the tea ceremony school saw the scene, Son frequently bowing his head as he spoke with his counterpart on the phone. Son could only apologise again afterwards, asking the other disciple to believe he was trying to act in good faith. He was only a tea ceremony neophyte, after all.

The disciple, seeing Son practise the humility taught by the Sohen school, became a fast supporter.

Sohen recalls a conversation he had with the Hokkaido University Graduate School lecturer Yamaguchi Jiro (a specialist in British government and politics) on the concepts of willpower and ambition. They may be different words but they possess the same meaning. Politicians these days were void of ambition; without willpower and ambition there can ultimately be no vision. With no vision only turmoil can ensue. The word for willpower in Japanese (*kokorozashi*) may have slight religious connotations in the native tongue but certainly doesn't have any implications of making money – in either Japanese or in English.

Part of possessing ambition means having to endure whatever it is people will say about you. This endurance helps refine one's own character, becoming a person who is more endearing to other people. According to the teachings of Zen, without taking delight in hardship there is no way we can grow as people, and in this respect Son's piercing willpower is what has made him the great personage he is. Perhaps those are the circumstances Son finds himself in today, but he remains unbowed and undaunted.

After each tea ceremony ended, participants were asked to write down a single word, an 'epilogue' of sorts to uncover their true selves. Son drew the symbol 風 [*kaze, fuu*], meaning wind. In doing so he manifested the strong desire he had always had to be like the wind. The tea ceremony reflects the inner self of the individual; Sohen recalls that Son's character was like tea which was crystal clear and free from sediment.

Chapter 27　**To battle**

It was 20 January 2000 and Roppongi in Tokyo was dazzling in the twilight.

An unexpectedly short and ordinary-looking man got out of a luxury car in front of a television studio building.

There was something special about him and he was radiating energy. Despite his friendly demeanour and being all smiles, once inside the studios and exchanging formalities with the studio staff everyone around him suddenly got just a bit more nervous – maybe his aura was just that strong. The man was Son Masayoshi and when it was his turn to introduce himself, he very politely and modestly stated that he didn't really know where to begin.

Son was going to be interviewed by Kume Hiroshi, one of the most famous newsreaders in Japan: 'I guess it's safe to call you the man who's obsessed by the internet.'

Whilst the phrasing was completely ordinary, nothing could have summed up Son's life any better than those words. Internally Son felt like the internet for him was like a theorem being developed by a famous philosopher: something they gradually chipped away at until they finally discover the full weight of their pursuit.

Not missing a beat, Kume probed further. 'Would you say the internet was something you bet your entire fortune on?' Yes, of course, wasn't it completely obvious to do so? Son left his response at that.

SoftBank wanted to be a massive conglomerate with the internet at the core of its business and to this end they had been constantly trying to develop new initiatives. This was why they'd set up an international stock exchange in NASDAQ Japan and why they'd acquired the Nippon Credit Bank.

With the internet as their platform, and aside from their business with Yahoo! Japan, they also sold cars and publications and were getting on board the broadband train, completely disrupting the established Japanese economic order.

At the time Son Masayoshi had the largest net worth in all of Japan. SoftBank's total market value (by the standard procedure of calculating a company's worth by multiplying share prices and the number of shares issued) was roughly 10 trillion yen – enough to land them a spot in the top-five businesses in Japan.

But who – or even what exactly – was Son Masayoshi?

How had he become one of the wealthiest men in the world?

How well SoftBank – and by extent Son – were actually doing was hard to glean: it wasn't like he was manufacturing easily quantifiable things. The main public perception of SoftBank was mainly it repeatedly acquiring other businesses, similar to an investment company, with the company itself not really doing anything on its own, simply holding shares in affiliated companies and telling them what to do.

In 1996, it had been announced that Son was partnering with the media mogul Rupert Murdoch to purchase 21.4 per cent of shares in TV Asahi, but then all of the sudden the deal appeared to be put on ice.

Son shed some light on this as well in his interview with Kume. 'Asahi Shimbun had hoped that TV Asahi would carry on under their auspices and said they wanted a share buyback option, getting quite pushy about it, and I didn't like where it was heading . . .'

Son preferred to invest in new companies, have them go public and then increase profits to earn returns on his initial investment. Kume got stuck in with his next question: 'Are you saying that it doesn't matter to you if you invest in 100 companies and 99 of them fail as long as one does extraordinarily well?'

Son replied, 'I wouldn't go that far but at the same time looking at the actual figures right now the returns are inconsequential.'

Kume then suddenly changed tack, asking Son, 'How much do you earn as chief executive of SoftBank?'

'Five million yen each month, or thereabouts. I don't really know.' Son's expression was unchanging – not even for a second – when asked such a question and his response was equally blasé.

Kume continued with this line of questioning. 'So you don't check to see how much you earn each month?'

'No, I don't.'

Son was indifferent to luxury. The day after SoftBank's initial public offering (IPO) he purchased a 300,000-yen golf club set, but that was all he did with the money. He was the sort who would use a wristwatch until it no longer worked and for lunch at work he would pop down to the convenience store to purchase *bento* packed lunches just like the rest of his employees.

Son's brief, casual response to Kume's questioning must have left the latter reeling, and the SoftBank man was similarly unfazed by his interviewer's provocations that there was no real substance behind his company's high market capitalisation and the bubble would soon burst.

'Firstly, the definition of a bubble is something that gets bigger and bigger, and then suddenly contracts. However, if a company gets bigger and bigger and bigger – that's growth. There's a big difference there, I would have to say.'

Son was insistent that the internet was here to stay. Indeed, in 50 or even 100 years' time it would be considered crucial to the conduct of society, and they were only living through the early stages of that. Son was convincing as he set out his stall.

Quite rightly, he identified the world in the 20th century as having been a largely industrialised society but, approaching the issue from another standpoint and looking back at the matter from however many years' time, the 21st century would see society progress to an internet phase, just as it had done with television, the telephone and the automobile before. The internet age had only just begun and was something everyone was experiencing simultaneously.

The last question Kume asked Son was about his goals going forward, to which Son responded: 'Further pursuing the possibilities offered by the internet.'

Others may ridicule him, calling him a charlatan and a gambler, but Son had no intention of straying from the path he was walking on – a path forged from his own belief and conviction. He was only going to live once and he didn't want to have any regrets, and these feelings were ones he always utilised to galvanise himself to push ahead. Son was possessed of self-confidence and the belief that he was doing the right thing, which meant he could face Kume's questions with a smile on his face.

On 12 November 2000 at seven o'clock in the evening, Bill Gates – the man who controlled the ebb and flow of developments within the computer industry – appeared on the stage set up at Las Vegas's MGM Grand Garden Arena to thunderous applause, wearing a jacket with no necktie. Every pair of eyes present in the arena were trained on the man and a flurry of flashes went off from the press gallery.

Gates's tall figure appeared on the giant screens and the crowd went wild.

The presentation saw Gates, holding a water bottle, reveal the new tablet PC he had developed and run through its performance and online shopping features. This new tablet had all of the features of a tower computer, but was the size of a notebook.

Gates spoke of how computer technology was at a turning point, emphasising that the most important task he had as head of Microsoft was deciding which technology to put his bets on. As Gates gave his keynote speech Son was in the front row, watching the Microsoft founder's every move, occasionally letting out a hearty laugh and applauding. Son had already met with Gates the previous day for a round on Las Vegas's best golf course – an annual occurrence that had been going on for years by that point. Son recalls – accurately and still full of excitement – that he hit par on the day. 'Well, at least I can beat you in golf!' Son declared, overflowing in confidence at the one thing he was better than Gates at.

When Son stood up he was quickly surrounded by a throng of luminaries from the computer industry wishing him well and wanting to shake his hand, chief amongst whom was Steve Ballmer, the chief executive of Microsoft. At this massive convention Son had been given equal billing with Gates as the main attraction, but still felt nothing but respect and tremendous affinity for his American counterpart, whilst marking their rivalry having reached a new level.

Son had only gambled in a casino once – when he was a student at Berkeley he had been to Las Vegas – and he had thrown all of his money away on the night. Ever since then he had resolved not to touch gambling, but the next few days in Las Vegas were equally as thrilling and an utter rush.

Since the age of 19 what Son had wanted more than anything else was to kick-start the digital information revolution – and now it was finally happening. The 21st century and this new era would undoubt-edly be led by Son Masayoshi and Bill Gates.

In June 1998, Son and Gates met with Kim Dae-jung, the then president of South Korea. At the time the country was going through an economic crisis and Kim asked Son what the best way to rebuild the Korean economy would be.

Son glanced at Gates, who was standing beside him, then began speaking.

'Mr Kim, there's three things you're going to need. The first is broadband, the second is broadband and the third is broadband. Nothing else, that is all. South Korea needs to become the best coun-try in the world for broadband. If you do this then the company's economy will rebound.'

In other words, the fundamental piece of the puzzle was the country's online infrastructure, and if they could be the best in the world in that respect all manner of electronics companies would flourish.

Son continued: 'You have got to be the first leader of a country to decide that you want your country to have the best broadband before anyone else.' Kim nodded, but then went on to ask Son what exactly broadband was, which the latter duly explained. Put simply, broad-band was high-speed internet, but it required the proper infrastruc-ture in place for it to work. To this end Kim should issue a presiden-tial decree to ensure its thorough implementation.

Kim – despite not fully grasping the particulars – did at least understand it was something important worth looking into and felt reinvigorated. He then turned to Gates, asking him if he had any other perspectives aside from what Son had mentioned. Gates replied by simply stating he was completely behind what Son had said.

If it was good enough for Son and Gates, then it was good enough for Kim. He issued the order for broadband implementation and a month later it had been enshrined in law. Every school in South Korea was fitted with broadband and all manner of regulations were eased. Kim instituted reforms such that the state budget, human resources and even legislation were all geared to ensure broadband implementation was a success, which ultimately translated to South Korea having the largest broadband diffusion rate (at 75 per cent) in the world.

By comparison, at the time Japan's diffusion rate was 25 per cent, whilst for the USA this was a paltry 5 per cent.

Son would go on to describe Gates's legacy in this way: 'Take all of the great names from history – Edison, Rockefeller, Carnegie. Gates is one rank above them. He is someone whose name will truly go down in history.' Gates's intelligence was singular, he welcomed new challenges and he possessed an extraordinary sensitivity to things. The right brain may well govern emotions with the left governing logic, but Gates managed to use both in tandem to reach new dimensions.

'Luckily, Gates focused more on developing technology, whilst using computers as part of infrastructure was more my thing. The two fields aren't at loggerheads with each other, rather they're complementary. We frequently consult with each other and make sure any new start-ups we're thinking about doing don't end up inadvertently stepping on each other's toes.'

Gates gifted Son with a copy of his first book (*The Road Ahead*) and hand-wrote a message for him in it: 'You are a risk taker as much as I am'. The book has gone on to become one of Son's most treasured possessions. Son broke into a smile as he remembers. 'Personally, I couldn't be happier with the fact he called me a risk taker. It is a great honour and privilege. Gates completely understands me.'

Chapter 28   The genius's genius

Perhaps he had finally gone mad. It was January 2001.

'I won't be coming back to my office this afternoon. Cancel all of my appointments. I won't be seeing any clients – no exceptions. I don't want to meet with any company employees. I want to concentrate solely on broadband.' When Son said this, surely all his secretaries must have thought he had indeed gone mad and the heads of the various companies under the group umbrella wondered the same thing themselves – perhaps he'd just been really good at hiding it all this time.

Son walked out of the office and headed towards a small office building just opposite. He had arranged a meeting with one man – a man who had a reputation for being something of a mad scientist. From his facial expression to his form of speaking, Son looked as leisurely and relaxed as the sunlight on a warm spring day.

That façade quickly dropped as he explosively confronted his 'mad scientist'.

'What's wrong with you, why haven't you made any progress? I don't know how many times I've told you, broadband is our top priority, so why haven't you made any progress?'

The man answered Son back in a quiet voice not unlike a shy and bashful child's. 'I can't finish the approval documents.' His eyes were kind behind his glasses and he had never had to fill in approval documents before, which ultimately meant he couldn't buy the machines required for the task.

Son was seething but he wasn't cross with his researcher. Rather he was furious with the system that was so inflexible his man couldn't carry on with his work because he hadn't submitted the right documents. He was certain he had given orders that the broadband project was to be giving the highest priority at SoftBank.

The name of Son's mad scientist was Tsutsui Takashi – born in Osaka in 1960 and current SoftBank Senior Vice President and Chief Scientist – a man Son would describe as 'a genius, beyond the shadow of a doubt'.

Son continued: 'You don't need to bother with the paperwork. Whatever equipment you need, just order it. If you need assistants I'll have 100 people reporting to you by the end of tomorrow.' Tsutsui told Son he needn't bother going that far and at any rate they would need the bodies for when they started working on building the physical infrastructure.

What Son had decided on was the creation of a network capable of rigging up the entire Japanese archipelago using IP technology only (IP standing for internet protocol, a communications protocol commonly used by devices connected to the internet so they can 'speak' to each other). Son was effectively attempting to do the impossible – no such precedent existed for this sort of network – and Tsutsui was dedicating all his energies to making the impossible a reality. His boss, however, was confident it could be done.

At the time broadband technology everywhere in the world relied on the ATM (asynchronous transfer mode) method to work, which naturally was capable of ensuring a certain degree of technological stability. In contrast, however, there were no prior examples for Tsutsui to rely on in his plan to develop an IP to completely connect the entire country. When comparing ATM to IP, the former's transmission capacity was only 53 bytes. IP was capable of roughly ten times the amount of information at 500 bytes.

Even given Son's history of taking gambles on projects, devoting all of his resources to achieving something no other company had done before was quite possibly the longest shot of them all. Any other businessman would have baulked at his audacious plan, but Son was adamant and the project was assigned the highest level of confidentiality – he couldn't afford anyone finding out about it.

Such was his devotion to this project that he would all but lock himself in the R&D room in the nondescript office building. No one saw him in the head office any more. The internal affairs of the company descended into chaos. At the time SoftBank held investments in around 800 companies all over the world, which effectively meant Son Masayoshi the man was in the position where he controlled the affairs of those 800 companies. It wouldn't be a stretch to say he held their fates in his hands.

Still, his word was law and without exception no one was to bother him, meaning those under him were at a loss as to what exactly to do going forward. If approached, Son would simply snap back that he didn't want to know and they should just deal with whatever problem as they saw fit. He was busy focusing on his top-secret project, effectively cutting himself off from his own company.

Son had any number of broadband network projects up and running and he was completely engrossed in all of them.

To all intents and purposes, he had finally lost the plot. This of course was not the case, and what Son was actually so engrossed in had little to do with broadband as shorthand for high-speed internet: he was going to change media as it was perceived. IP would be delivered via telecommunications networks – telephone lines, effectively – bringing about radical changes in terms of what media was available to people.

Systems enabling television and video on demand could be instantly set up, turning the television, film and video software industries on their heads; the distribution possibilities for music and video games were similarly extraordinary. The network system Son had in mind was capable of revolutionising the software business and even the lives of everyday citizens.

Each individual instance of software could be instantly beamed anywhere in the world thanks to the IP network and supporting this infrastructure would be SoftBank, with its massive depository of titles and applications.

Son was willing to do whatever it took to kick-start the digital information revolution and to this end he was willing to risk it all on the unproven pure IP network configuration, a vision shared by 'mad scientist' Tsutsui.

The two were completely committed to revolutionising society in this sense.

Of course, Son wasn't so completely drunk on ambition he forgot to properly test the technology Tsutsui was developing, but when he sent what the two had been working on to top engineers around the world the feedback they got was unanimously negative.

It couldn't be done. They were going about things the wrong way.

Tsutsui engaged in a ferocious debate with his fellow top-rank Chief Technical Officers (CTOs) from overseas, which eventually lasted for three days.

Whilst Tsutsui's overseas counterparts could understand the core principle to a certain extent, it was still unproven, too much of a risk and at any rate they didn't have the equipment needed to make it happen. Furthermore, SoftBank had no real experience working on this sort of operation – it was extremely reckless and a leap in the dark and something they didn't want to be associated with.

The final say, however, rested with Son.

'You don't want to help with the project – fine. Tsutsui and I are both prepared to fall on our swords here and he has got my full, unconditional support in this.'

On a personal level no one knew Tsutsui better than Son, having first met him 20 years prior when he was still a student at Tokyo University and a member of the home-computer club there.

Son, sensing Unix could be a vital tool for businesses, tasked Tsutsui – a Unix expert – with looking into what was happening on the cutting edge for the OS in America. He would describe Tsutsui in these words: 'He was a genius from the word go. At the time when he was in university and ever since he was already a legend in software development circles, having come up with however many programmes. Bill Gates and Paul Allen may have developed Microsoft BASIC in the 1970s, but at the exact same time Tsutsui had already written his own compiler for C (a code translation program), which was a considerably more difficult coding language. His potential was endless.'

When he was a boy Tsutsui's mother had shown concern for her son's future employment prospects, obsessed as he was with computers. When in university, and heeding his mother's advice, he transferred from the Tokyo University School of Engineering to Kyoto University's School of Medicine. Despite receiving his licence to practise medicine, Tsutsui was still much more interested in the cutting edge of communications than becoming a clinician.

After graduating and whilst working as a doctor, he also managed a small software development company, where he was deeply intrigued by the possibilities afforded by ADSL (Asymmetric Digital Subscriber Line) technology.

When Son initially approached Tsutsui the latter was working as a lecturer at university. Son put the question to him of whether he couldn't touch the lives of more people by signing up for his revolution than working as a doctor. At any rate, he wasn't getting any free time to enjoy himself working at university, and as Son was trying to get his broadband network up and running he should leave academia and come work for him.

In April 2000 Tsutsui accepted his offer and went to work for SoftBank. Things didn't go as smoothly as perhaps Son might have hoped, as internally Tsutsui frequently found himself embroiled in rows due to no one really understanding his real worth or capacity. Tsutsui's way of thinking was on the cutting edge and wasn't something your average person could easily come to grips with.

The culture clash was such that some of Son's employees confronted him over the issue, stating it was either Tsutsui or them. Son remained cool in the face of this revolt, stating he completely disagreed with them and they should all start clearing out their desks – which a number of them actually did. To Son, Tsutsui was irreplaceable.

Around half a year after this incident the engineers who hadn't left the company came around to accept that Tsutsui had been right all along.

Son wasn't about to leave the issue alone, telling them: 'What Tsutsui says is absolute. I couldn't care less what words he uses to express his ideas or what the situation may look like on the surface. None of that matters in the least. Tsutsui grasps the essence of the technology and will always be spot-on in his assessments.'

The global standard for infrastructure company networks at the time was ATM, with Son commenting on the technology, 'There was no way you could stage a revolution on ATM: the technology was effectively restricting the internet to what you could manage on analogue telephone lines. Put another way, it was fake IP. Unless the network was built on the principle behind IP – in the purest definition of the term – then it was no good.'

If Son and Tsutsui couldn't implement a network technology that relied exclusively on IP for communications then they weren't going to revolutionise anything. That much was clear as day.

Son continues, 'What makes Tsutsui so utterly amazing is that he was able to completely disregard the accepted wisdom at the time and work from a purely technology viewpoint. That was the splendour of his way of working: it was pure mathematics. It was simple and yet refined.' ATM technology could hardly be described as so refined, consisting as it did of a bunch of pre-existing analogue technologies stacked one on top of the other.

Looking back on his CV in this respect, Son had been an outside director of Cisco Systems, the world's first IP device provider, and had also been in a joint venture with Novell, the world's first LAN (Local Area Network) OS manufacturer. Both of these companies had entered into separate joint ventures with Son and, as part of a partnership, they had kept their sights trained on network infrastructure. It was this experience which convinced Son the time was ripe for IP.

'My core philosophy has always been about trying to create the era of internet networks. Tsutsui is much more practical, maintaining an interest in the architecture used to design networks. In other words, he's more about structure and configurations, which complements me perfectly.'

Microsoft, Novell and Cisco Systems all did their part to translate Son's ideas into reality with the development of standalone devices and operating systems. Tsutsui's position within this mix was coming up with the plans for the world's first national network and, with that, all of the various tributaries converged into one mighty river.

There was no need for IP to be complicated: simple architecture was the answer.

When Son was 17 or 18 he had been moved to tears at the sight of a microchip. With the impending advent of IP he was moved to tears once again by the splendour of the system.

The completed IP network would be tailored to the principles and fundamentals of the architecture, making it both extremely cheap (the cost was one-tenth of ATM) and extremely powerful (it was capable of handling ten times more information). The cost effectiveness was 100 times greater than what had gone before and the more people who signed up for broadband the greater the cost difference would be.

Tsutsui speaks about Son's role in the development of IP: 'Son is a businessman of course but he also fills the role of CTO and he has got a very deep knowledge of the technology – much more so than myself. I was just the assistant. I knew IP telephony was a techno-logical possibility but it was only thanks to Son that I was able to actually make it a reality. He said we were going to do it, so in the end we had no choice really. That ability to make decisions and stick with them is incredible.'

The immediate future was now ripe with possibilities, such as mobile internet. The next issues to be addressed were things like whether to charge a flat rate for broadband or charge for use, waiving the basic fees.

Tsutsui continues, 'With things like photovoltaic cells, devices capable of capturing electricity are completely connected to the internet. The internet of things was just around the corner, in the very near future.'

The 21st century would see the dawn of the internet of things and the historical turning point in this respect would be the year

2001, the first year that broadband became available. The two geniuses would celebrate the day they created a new era.

On 11 September of that same year, however, the world order would be shaken to the core with the Al-Qaeda terrorist attacks on multiple sites in the United States. The world would be plunged into a turbulent, transformative period.

Chapter 29   # The unification of Japan under one banner

There were no other options: SoftBank were about to be forced into battle with NTT, the Japanese telecoms giant. Only one man, however, would be doing the challenging, and Son would claim that since founding SoftBank he had never experienced anything as painful as this.

SoftBank Japan had originally been founded in 1981, with share prices hitting their peak in February 2000 but being on the decline ever since.

JCR, the Japan Credit Rating Agency, had downgraded SoftBank to BB – a speculative rating – and another means of raising new funds was cut off. Son's company had been backed into a corner from which there appeared to be no escape and the company's total market value had shrunken to one-fortieth of what it had been. On 6 January 2001, the Basic Law on the Formation of Advanced Information and Telecommunications Network Companies (the IT Basic Law) came into effect, introducing competition measures and relaxing current existing regulations.

Son recalls his response to the news. 'Now was the time – I had been waiting for this day all my life. We were going to be able to enter the market.' Son had previously made the decision to pour all the company's available resources into his broadband project, but just as things were starting to progress smoothly NTT would attempt to sabotage everything. Complaints started flooding in from users who had applied for SoftBank's broadband service but still hadn't been able to connect to it.

In the 20 years Son had been in business he had hardly seen anything so absurd. He had always taken an abundance of caution with preparations, and in the event he found himself in adverse circumstances but would do whatever it would take not to get into a squabble.

In this case Son – playing the role of David – was left with no other options but to tackle his own Goliath, NTT, head on. NTT may have been divided up into two companies – NTT East Japan and NTT West Japan – but ultimately the shares in the two companies were all held by the same holding company. The reality was they held a monopoly in the market, just like when they had been Nippon Telegraph and Telephone Public Corporation. Conduits, telephone poles, station premises – NTT had exclusive usage rights for them and SoftBank were beginning to experience the detrimental effects of this on a number of fronts.

NTT were blocking Yahoo! BB's access to connection construction works within their own stations, in a number of ways.

One of these was, for example, if the name listed for a telephone number and the name used to apply for Yahoo! B B access were different, applicants would end up having to wait forever for access. Another was the issue of telephone pole usage – common public property – which was almost exclusively NTT's. The application paperwork required to leave network devices within NTT stations was both overly complicated and took a great deal of time to complete.

It was their way of completely stymieing the competition. The terms for using the co-location services in their stations (to establish network facilities) and the dark-fibre network connecting said stations (dark fibre refers to optical fibre which has been laid but is unused) were both extremely unfair towards third parties.

Despite services having been privatised, NTT still had a monopoly on the infrastructure, meaning there was no way to compete fairly with them. Son could not begin to hide his disgust, admitting to himself there was no way to avoid open hostilities.

The 21st-century equivalent of Nobunaga was headed for his own Okehazama, the first great unifier's famous 1560 victory against the odds. He may have been at a tremendous disadvantage, but nevertheless open battle was the only way out.

On 29 June 2001, Son lodged a formal complaint with the Ministry of Internal Affairs. It was do-or-die time. Son's claim was that NTT were a bunch of liars who said that they had no dark fibre available for use, despite a number of NTT stations being connected via a dark-fibre loop. Should one of these points fail, however, the loop would be broken.

Despite ringing up the Ministry of Internal Affairs and even going in person to make his case, the public official would just listen to his complaint but ultimately not do anything. It was the last straw for Son.

He asked the Internal Affairs official – much to the surprise of his counterpart – to lend him a cheap lighter. When the official asked him why he wanted one Son told him it was because he was going to pour gasoline on the place and burn it to the ground.

He explained that Yahoo! BB had been carrying out testing concerning the practical implementation of a network within the Tokyo metropolitan area. Despite being busy with construction work on NTT stations they had received applications from 500,000 people over the course of a fortnight. However, NTT did not want to make any dark fibre available, so the work was never actually completed;

they would also claim there were no available power sources to set up any third-party equipment in their stations.

Son continued railing against the public official. 'You lot don't necessarily see this is a massive problem because you've got the power of authority on your side with your licences and permits. You've not really taken due care with NTT and now you're stuck with them and can't progress.'

Son leaned in, not even pausing to take a breath between what he was saying.

'Our customers can't wait any longer. As a businessman I would rather die than have to tell them to fill in all of the forms they've done so far again and send them to NTT's broadband department. If things carry on as they stand my business is over and I may as well hold a press conference stating we're winding Yahoo! BB up. And then, on my way home, I'm going to come back here, dowse this place in gasoline and light a match.'

This was no performance, he was deadly serious.

The official, his voice trembling, told Son he would look into NTT.

Sure enough, that evening Son received a phone call from the public official, letting him know that NTT East had managed to free up several lines of dark fibre.

Son was indignant with NTT's bureaucracy that was keeping his customers waiting.

'The hardest thing from our end wasn't developing the technology or running tests to make sure it worked – it was filling in NTT's paperwork. Just one example would be if you made a mistake with a single character then that would be enough for them to justify making you wait two months for a response. They'd tell you they had power sources available, then turn around and say they didn't – which is why we just went ahead and constructed our own facilities in this respect. In the end we had to redesign everything from the bottom up, but two weeks after that our application went through. Even though they'd told us it was going to take three months – completely outrageous!'

There were squabbles with NTT on a daily basis and Son ended up working every day – no weekends or bank holidays off – frequently staying up until three or four in the morning to get everything which needed doing done.

Just like 20 years before when he was trying to start his business up, Son felt completely invigorated, ready to take on all comers.

'The company was something I was willing to bet my life on. I couldn't have cared less about the money – whatever it was, was small potatoes compared to actually being able to deliver the service to our customers who'd waited for so long. We had to get them up and running. The profit-and-loss statement was irrelevant for this project – it didn't matter how much debt I had to accrue. We were going to make it happen.'

In the middle of all of this happening the world was shaken to its core by the 9/11 terror attacks. Airports were locked down and the despatch of parts and components was delayed, forcing Son to once again go back to the drawing board.

The new plans included the use of new equipment, meaning occasionally the network experienced outages. If word came in of the system going down Son would get in his car and rush out to the site, which even meant racing out to relatively far-flung Nagoya once or twice. He always had his mobile on him and it was always on – Son and his corps of engineers were on-call and ready to respond 24 hours a day.

Son would recall his head being in a constant haze the entire time, but he didn't want anyone feeling sorry for him: he was at war with NTT and was actually quite enjoying it.

Of course it was rough going, but it was also fun and Son could clearly see he was making progress in the direction he was trying to go in. Giving it his all to the point he could have spontaneously combusted was enjoyable for him.

Son's battle was not necessarily with NTT – rather he had picked a fight with NTT's majority shareholder, which happened to be the Japanese state.

'Patience – it all boiled down to patience. We were going to chip away at them little by little. We were like the Choshu, Tosa or Satsuma clans during the warring states period: we weren't particularly strong, didn't have much funding and had no vested interests backing us up. What we did have, however, was the state of the art, meaning we were taking on swords and armour with guns and were able to completely turn the tide of battle in the end. Our prospects for victory may not have looked very good but we had the latest IP technology on our side – cutting-edge technology and unbridled enthusiasm for what we were doing.'

Revolutions aren't everyday occurrences: they only happen once a century or so – a rumbling from the underground capable of completely upending life as it previously was.

The NTT Group's consolidated annual profits had been in the order of 1 trillion yen, but for the first time ever in their existence their profits were lower than the previous year. The decrease was only 2 or 3 per cent but suddenly everyone was concerned about the state of NTT.

Not that Son was bothered. 'We should all hold a pity party for NTT, then, because their profits had gone down? Give over. On our end, we were staring down the largest debt we had ever faced: 100 billion yen in the red. Despite being penniless we were giving it everything we had and yes, of course, picking a fight with NTT in our condition was absurd. But you know, just because you've got the upper ground doesn't mean you'll always win.'

Son Masayoshi was hot on the heels of NTT via his services-driven business model – Yahoo! BB – where he had managed to anticipate the needs of broadband users of the era.

'I won't touch a sector if I know I can't be the best on the market. I'm not interested in fighting losing battles – it's more creating the conditions for victory for me.'

On 5 September 2003, SoftBank sold off the shares it held in Aozora Bank, with Son being criticised for the move in some quarters. But Son had a very good reason for disposing of the shares SoftBank held in Aozora Bank.

'It takes ten times more courage to fall back then to press forward and you've also got to be decisive about it. We were pursuing too many things and ended up spreading ourselves thin. My goal with SoftBank from day one had always been to bring about the digital information revolution – that was our starting point, the main axle driving us forward. It's not that I don't regret it but we were fighting a war in winter and we needed to trim as much fat as possible. A real man has got to win his battles no matter what.'

He expands on it. 'It was a fundraising exercise. We were at war and if you've got no war chest then you've lost. You need an arsenal and you need troops to wield that arsenal – that was the logic I was going by. The only hard part about it was emotionally – it was rough having to apologise to our partners.'

Son took great care to ensure the process remained fair.

'The one thing that would upset me more than anything else – the one thing I would hate more than anything else – is feeling like I've compromised my honour and dignity as a man. I always want to feel like I've given something back to people. I feel like it's an obligation to provide some form of fair recompense.'

On 10 May 2002, and despite financial results announcing a massive 88.7bn-yen red spot on the books, Son was all smiles.

'I was waking up every morning and feeling excited and my will-power to get the digital information revolution up and running kept growing and growing. There were a lot of announcements to be made that would turn people's heads but they would have to wait just a little bit longer. We were about to open up Pandora's box.'

Nobunaga's dream had been to unite all of Japan under one banner; Son was pushing ahead with his digital information revolution and his own banner never faltered.

On 8 August 2003, SoftBank released their first quarter financial results. Not counting customer acquisition costs, Yahoo! BB had got their results back on track. Just before his 43rd birthday in the same month, Yahoo! BB likewise announced they had broken the 3-million-subscriber milestone.

Chapter 30

You'll never know if you don't try

The news Son received early in 2004 was enough to shake him to his very core: the personal data of 4.52 million Yahoo! BB ADSL service subscribers had been stolen in an extortion attempt.

When Son heard the news from Miyauchi Ken, the deputy general director and chief operating officer, on 16 January 2004 in his 17th-floor executive suite, he immediately reached for the phone and rang up the Tokyo Metropolitan Police Department's cyber-crime office.

The incident had kicked off on 7 January, when a business partner of a SoftBank sales subsidiary was shown a list containing the personal data of eight individuals by an individual named as 'YT' (who would later be arrested on suspicion of attempted extortion). The data was found to be accurate on the 14th and Miyauchi made his report to Son on the 16th, who then immediately set up an investigation committee to look into the matter. Then the authorities were brought in.

On the 20th YT contacted the SoftBank sales subsidiary by telephone, stating his acquaintance held several million lines' worth of information, and on the 21st a list with information on a further 130 individuals was received. The same day SoftBank also received their first extortion threat, instructing them to invest several dozen billion yen in a foreign joint venture. Acting on the advice of the authorities, on 23 January SoftBank representatives met with YT in a Tokyo hotel to receive a disk containing the personal information of 4.6 million people, which was then handed over to the police.

SoftBank had been working together alongside the police but the *Yomiuri Evening News* covered the scoop in their pages, and by four o'clock on 24 January the incident had been reported to the Ministry of Internal Affairs.

Son was back in Japan, having cut short a trip to Europe. He took a car straight to the SoftBank head office and assembled all of his directors and executives.

They assumed the worst-case scenario: that people within the company would be arrested for leaking the information. There had been similar cases in the past where things had gone wrong with the business and Son had taken a pay cut; this was the most serious of them all, so proportionately he took a salary cut of 50 per cent for a term of six months.

By the end of the month the data collation process had ended, revealing that, inclusive of those users who had gone on to cancel their broadband contracts, the personal data of 4.52 million people had been leaked.

At 10am on 27 January, Son convened all the chief executives of the SoftBank Group companies to discuss compensation for their customers – all 5.4 million of them, which included some 1.4 million who hadn't been affected by the leaks. Some non-Japanese directors deeply protested that there was no reason to offer money as an apology, which would otherwise incentivise future criminals to target the group. Nevertheless, as a token of their apologies, SoftBank would issue those affected 500 yen (roughly $5) postal money orders, totalling 2.5 billion yen.

The thinking behind issuing postal money orders as compensation was to somehow contribute positively to society instead of doing something like issuing vouchers for use with a credit company. SoftBank would receive the money back from those money orders that remained unused past their expiry date, which would be put into a Data Security Fund and earmarked for activities such as increasing data security for society as a whole or promoting broadband use for the disabled.

The same day as the SoftBank executive meeting, a press conference was scheduled for half past five at a local hotel. Son arrived, wearing an uncharacteristically severe expression.

Despite all the troubles SoftBank had had with debt over the years Son had never once publicly apologised; on this occasion he bowed deeply in repentance.

'I have caused a great deal of bother for our customers. I extremely regret this and wish to apologise from the bottom of my heart.' Son himself fielded and responded to questions in the following Q&A session, which lasted almost two hours. Some of the issues raised touched on Son's own liability, to which he categorically replied that he was going to carry on pushing the broadband revolution as much as possible.

Following the major personal-data leak SoftBank did their best to prevent such an occurrence from happening again, and yet Son was still at a loss for how the leak had occurred in the first place. He would have to wait for the results of the investigation to be published.

'It's true that whilst we'd been focusing on customer satisfaction up until that point we'd also got a bit lax with our data management. With respect to people who came into contact with the system I took the side of "all people are inherently good" and didn't really bother to introduce stringent monitoring protocols.'

Going forward, however, Son decided it was best to assume the worst and to impose a stricter data protection policy.

One example of the measures implemented was closer monitoring of those individuals entering and exiting the Advanced Security Floor at the support centre responsible for overseeing customers' personal data. Employees and visitors were asked to wear clothing without any pockets, fingerprints were taken and checked against records, ID numbers were encrypted, 24-hour surveillance cameras were set up alongside metal detectors and note-taking devices – from mobile phones to basic memo pads – were banned.

Naturally, measures such as not allowing the use of outside storage devices or banning copying things outright were implemented as well and the number of people with access to customers' personal data was drastically reduced from 135 to three. Whenever the data was accessed the user ID of the person accessing the information was logged alongside the time and what they did whilst logged on. This automatic logging function was enabled 24 hours, 365 days a year, with logs stored for extended periods of time.

Son was going to create the best security framework in the world to prevent the worst from happening again. The leak had been a lesson learnt and a challenge overcome. At the press conference Son stated he had no plans of deviating from his target of having 10 million Yahoo! BB subscribers by the end of September 2005.

When they finally did reach this number their annual operating income for broadband was in the order of 120 billion yen.

The less-than-heady days when they had just launched Yahoo! BB back in January 2001, where customers would frequently complain of having signed up but not being able to connect to the service, were now banished to memory, survey results revealing they were rated considerably higher than their nearest competitors.

Son would state he was never the type to shy away from a challenge, always keen to face up to it in good faith, and he always found a way to bounce back from any setbacks life would throw at him. This life philosophy has served him well every step of the way. The times had moved on from narrowband to broadband and Son had ushered in his new era.

'We are capable of creating a society where broadband is taken as much for granted as turning on a tap and water coming out.

'I want to change people's lifestyles – I want SoftBank to be a lifestyle company, developing infrastructure for society to allow it to evolve. I want our digital information revolution to transform the way people think and go about their daily lives.'

With the widespread dissemination of broadband – and this includes IP mobile telephony – utility computing will change the way we live, and Son has made it his mission to see this change through.

'Companies are entities which are capable of outliving their founder's lifespan. Even after I've gone I hope SoftBank will continue to grow for another 200 or 300 years and, to that end, my main concern at the minute is ensuring the company is in a position to achieve that goal.'

Son, who is constantly trying to find new challenges to overcome, has occasionally been subjected to criticism from more reserved quarters arguing that: SoftBank don't manufacture actual things; they're too much of a corporate business; they don't actually carry out operations; they just focus on simple digital activities; Son is just a gambler who got lucky . . . the list goes on.

Son responds to these accusations: 'So if I set up a factory and started making things – an endeavour I think is completely noble and worthwhile, by the way – that would be acceptable business? I'd be a fantastic businessman then? My question to someone of that mindset is that over the past 100 or 200 years of Japanese economic history, how many people have changed the way people live, inventing that infrastructure, innovating it and then supplying it to become one of the top companies in the world?

'The automobile and home electrical appliances – amongst a number of other things – may have been invented in the West but now there's a great number of companies doing the exact same thing only cheaper with the same quality or with decent distribution. They're only imitating or rehashing what the originators have done.'

What Son has always wanted is what he has achieved as a businessman. 'For me a businessperson is someone who carves their own path in life, someone who creates electrical networks or develops the infrastructure for society to exist on top of. In other words, a businessperson is someone who sets the standards for society.'

This is Son's entire raison d'être, what gives him the most joy in life, his heart and soul. The joy of creating cutting-edge, revolutionary things is irreplaceable for him.

As a businessman Son sought to overhaul Japan's infrastructure, making sure the country had the most cutting-edge infrastructure in line with its transformation into a digital information society. South Korea were the broadband leaders but Japan eventually overtook them in terms of the sheer number of lines, with 14 million households.

Son was also aware that in future optical fibre may edge out ADSL. 'The technology behind ADSL has been steadily evolving – there's not really any media exclusive to optical. Naturally on our end we're also coming up with strategies for optical but at the moment ADSL is the best – it's the right technology at the right time.'

When asked about what governments should be doing, the smile disappeared from Son's face. 'They've only got one thing they should do, and that's to stay out of the way. The regulations in Japan have proved prohibitive for new entrants – compare this to America where there are anti-monopoly laws, so new entrants stand a fighting chance.'

Whilst subjected to criticism from all sides, Son chooses only to listen to those cheering him on. 'Oh, they've said this, that or the other about me – like I'm cold-blooded or I don't act in good faith. But take a look at things now and then look back on them in a hundred years' time. My mission – my company's mission – was to kick-start the digital information revolution. This was absolutely for the greater good and that is the only thing that matters.'

As the founder of a company Son wants to create a roadmap for growth to reverse Japan's shrinking economy and get it back on the road to expansion. For Son, leadership is about having a clear picture about what the greater good is.

'If we can't get things back on track the future is dark, bleak, miserable. A real leader – a real captain, by way of metaphor – doesn't seek advice from everyone on board his ship about where they should be going. In a life-or-death situation, where it looks like the ship is going to sink, even if it means coming to blows with the crew, even if the masts have been sawed off, even if you've got to tell people who won't listen to you to go jump in the ocean, your duty is still to get those left on your ship – as many as you can do – to shore.'

Following on from this metaphor, once back on dry land Son can always search for wealth and treasure and new fields to cultivate, reclaim what was his, increase the number of people working for him and flourish once again.

'There'll have been ups and downs but these are irrelevant – the important thing is the passengers made it to their destination. The bottom line is we need the power to get back to an era of expansion. I have no interest whatsoever in being perceived as a nice guy – being popular achieves absolutely nothing.'

Bakumatsu revolutionaries were possessed of a singular will, a fighting spirit Son also possesses to – in the words of Sakamoto Ryoma – 'give Japan a thorough rinse yet again'.

This extends to the Japanese state, Japanese society and the whole of its infrastructure, restoring it to an ideal and fair society: a society that is just, free and abundant, where everyone can do what they want to do. Our utopia would be a society without cares or worries, full of fun and where life is glorified.

There are still a considerable number of areas where Japanese society remains unfair, running on systems that are truly faulty. The number of poor people is not negligible and, whilst there may be business start-ups, opportunities are closed off to them in a number of ways: Japan needs to be able to once again compete at the international level.

'I dream up a masterplan, create a framework to make the masterplan a reality and even then, if you don't try you'll never know.'

There is a saying that all roads lead to Rome, and indeed the Roman roads were the first instance of infrastructure in history. The British created their own infrastructure in the form of railway lines and shipping routes, upon which they built their empire. The Americans developed infrastructures for electricity, communications and motorisation, embodying the cutting edge for their time.

In each case – the Romans, the British, the Americans – each was the most powerful in the entire world for a time.

'Up until around 1980 Japan experienced a post-war renaissance – a period of rapid and tremendous growth. What we did not achieve, however, was the top position – we were stuck in second place. Now that Japan has become a digital information society we stand an incredible chance of claiming the top spot with the fastest and cheapest internet anywhere and various developments with our world's first IP technology. In future, historians looking back on the 21st century will say the most important thing about it was the creation of the world's best infrastructure using information technology. A tremendous opportunity has come knocking on Japan's door.

'There are three things which are more important than anything else: the first is having ambition and a solid core concept. The second is possessing vision. The third is having the right tactics.'

Son speaks, his voice full of conviction: 'Japan is absolutely capable of being the best in the world.'

PART THREE

Chapter 31　　**Conviction**

In March 2006 – barely into spring with a chill wind sweeping through Tokyo – SoftBank acquired the Japanese branch of Vodafone.

The press conference had been called for five in the evening but well past this time there was still no sign of Son at the venue. Indeed, Son was not there. Instead he was locked in fierce negotiating combat with Vodafone representatives in the SoftBank president's office in a high-rise in Shiodome in Tokyo. It was a hive of bustling activity and it was a big contract they were signing.

Eagle-eyed solicitors were poring over every word, making sure every T was crossed and I dotted – a laborious and time-consuming process, but nothing unexpected for an agreement in the absolutely staggering amount of 2 trillion yen, which at the time was the second largest buyout in history.

Son, however, was not particularly bothered by the colossal figure. 'My view of it is the price is just a measuring stick for the complete deal. The number of zeroes wasn't important, it was the number of users. Vodafone had around 15 million users, but by buying Vodafone out would I be able to retain that user base? Could I build on that? Would it go down? That was the part I was most interested in.'

Son here is particularly referencing the fact that mobile number portability (MNP – being able to switch companies without having to switch numbers) had been floated as a prospect, meaning there was the possibility the user base would fall off in droves, not to mention a large number of other Vodafone-specific problems that would need resolving, chief amongst which was the poor connection rates for calls. Phone models were unrefined-looking and ill-suited to Japanese tastes, and in terms of content Vodafone were behind both NTT Docomo and au as well. On top of all of that, Vodafone's marketing power and brand presence in Japan was underwhelming and with the mobile number portability issue on the horizon, market research found they could expect to lose over 30 per cent of their customer base. Vodafone may have barely been turning a profit, but in the event this prediction came to pass there was still the matter of their fixed expenses not changing, and they would be in the red in one fell swoop.

Buy-outs are normally conducted in one of two ways: either via a share exchange or payment in cold, hard cash. If the buyer is confident they will be able to expand on business results then a cash buy-out tends to be better value; in the inverse case, where the buyer is not confident they can turn things around, then a share exchange is the safer option as debts will not increase.

Which path to pursue was the choice Son faced and, true to form, he opted for the riskier of the two: payment in cash. Regardless of whether he believed he could do it, the Vodafone rescue operation would entail little room for error.

How many cell sites would they need to be able to compete alongside their third-generation (3G) mobile network rivals? What sort of capital expenditure figures would this entail – 200 billion yen? 600 billion? Should he just throw 1 trillion at it? It was a big decision he was going to have to take, and sooner rather than later: just how much investment was it going to take to firstly get Vodafone – the phone company known in Japan for its calls not connecting – into fighting shape to deal with the competition and then eventually overtake them?

Changing the name of the company would naturally prove a good starting point. 'Carrying on under the Vodafone name would have made things impossible and at any rate I wanted to leave the name behind – the brand had become toxic and we needed to completely change course with them.' Rather surprisingly, up until this point in time SoftBank had rarely dealt with general consumers under its own name – the name being a holdover from the company's origins selling software wholesale.

As SoftBank were virtually completely invested in Yahoo! BB they mainly used their subsidiary as their outward-facing brand image, and Son had no real interest in shifting focus onto the main company – in the worst-case scenario where business suddenly tanked it would mean ruin for his company and he would not be able to start another business again. In his own words: 'I may appear to be foolhardy and rash in a lot of my dealings, in the fact that I take a lot of big, bold risks. However, the truth is regardless of what the situation looks like I would never countenance anything that would sink my company in one go, so I've tirelessly endeavoured to make sure this is never the case.'

A failure here with Vodafone could blow a hole in the side of SoftBank, but nevertheless Son had placed himself in the position where yet again he was going to have to battle to win hearts and minds. He thought long and hard about whether or not to use the flagship brand name, as a sheer sign of his own conviction in the matter. Ordinarily an acquisition of this size would take half a year to conclude, involving countless hours spent in meetings negotiating with legal teams, but Son pulled it off in a month. It goes without saying he was firm in his conviction and his judgement was unerring, but what was behind all of this?

Over the 2006 New Year's holiday Son took a break from his normally busy routine, taking several days to collect his thoughts on the Vodafone deal as he struggled to find a way to steel his resolve. Once the winter holidays were over he threw himself into negotiations although, despite having met with Vodafone representatives however many times during the run-up to the end of 2005, a buy-out had not been tabled, discussions rather focusing on lending facilities out and doing business under their umbrella as a mobile virtual network operation. Negotiations had been carrying on in this way for around four months at this point with no real headway – could this all be part of Son's bold and carefully thought-out war strategy?

With the dawning of the new year Son could not help but feel that they had been beating around the bush for the past four months or so. Anything worth doing should be done to completion, but there were the twin matters of not having enough stations and customers being inconvenienced by calls not going through. There may have been something to Vodafone's plan to make capital investments to increase their number of stations over the course of three years, though – if Son accelerated proceedings from three years to six months then that would be a good inroad to finding a solution. Ultimately there was no other feasible option but acquisition, although major sticking points still remained.

During negotiations the 2tn-yen price came up and, whilst this price was deemed acceptable, ultimately SoftBank did not have such a colossal sum available and an initial proposal was made for a joint investment with another company, SoftBank stumping up around 30 per cent of this amount.

Moans of 'leave it, we simply haven't got the money' would not be enough to deter Son at this point. He was not the sort who, whenever conducting an acquisition or setting up a new company, would think about what was in the coffers at present or whether what he intended to do was within the scope of his present abilities. It was not his way. A life lived tepidly putting one foot in front of the other without making any great strides would be no fun at all, and Son's life story both begins and ends based on his sheer force of will anchored in his desire to see the digital information revolution happen.

This started with the personal computer, followed by these single personal computers connecting to a network, and Son realised before anyone else that the revolution was not about to end there.

From 1998 to 1999 – if not even earlier – Son had already begun formulating a plan to advance the cause of mobile phones.

'The currently available mobile phones are as powerful as the CPU driving PCs several years ago; furthermore, mobile phones three years from now will be even more powerful than the PCs which are coming out now. Thinking along those lines I couldn't call the digital information revolution done and dusted without including mobile phones in it, could I?'

The digital information revolution could not proceed until everyone could access information or contact anyone they wanted to whenever, wherever, and not including mobile phones in the equation meant everything would fall apart. Son had also started making plans to build a 1.7 gigahertz frequency band mobile network completely from scratch and an MVNO (mobile virtual network operator) under the Vodafone banner was also an option.

He was about to take the largest gamble of his entire life.

As we have seen, when he was 19 he had drafted a 50-year life plan for himself, starting up his own business in his twenties and making a name for himself. His thirties would be spent amassing a war chest such that when he reached his forties he would be in a position to take advantage of any critical opportunities that came his way.

In August 2006 Son turned 49 – his forties were almost up. His mind and body were at their pinnacle and he had a fortune most could only dream of. The stars had all aligned and if his life were a film the next scene would be the climax.

It had all been leading up to this moment and his mind was made up: he would go through with the 2tn-yen acquisition of Vodaphone and would spend his fifties making a success of the project he had gambled his entire life on. It was time to see his greatest desire through to its completion.

Confucius came to understand the will of the heavens aged 50; Son was on the threshold aged 48, fully prepared to wage war against all comers over the next 10 years to stand at the pinnacle of his existence on the global market.

And it truly would turn into a 10-year war, as the first step to building a 1.7-gigahertz mobile network would be building cell sites, which on its own would take five years. Son had to question whether he had that luxury of time seeing as the number of users would be low, as would the different types of phone models available – meaning the fight might be meaningless.

'I would gladly pay money to be able to have the energy from times in my life when I felt completely up for things – 2 trillion yen to buy myself a bit of time would be an offer I would take in a heartbeat.'

This was the sentiment behind Son's severe questioning of himself and whether or not he possessed the confidence to see the project through to completion. 'If I could just keep the 15 million Vodafone customers I would effectively inherit from them then from a cashflow standpoint it would be enough to clear our debts. That being said though, if the number fell to 10 million people then things would be very grim, although if we could increase the user base to 20 or 30 million then we'd be raking it in.'

Those were the stakes.

In terms of what to do about phone models Son had several ideas in the offing, with an abundance of approaches to take concerning software too and strategies to draw new users in also on the sales front. He was still somewhat at a loss, however, as what to do with the bothersome cell site issue and the attendant capital investment requirements – how many stations would he need to wage war effectively?

Son ran as lifelike a simulation as possible using pinpoint calculations, examining questions like what would happen if tariffs dropped, what it would cost to win customers over, how much precisely should they invest in capital and how any fixed costs added on would affect everything else. Combining all queries gave a result of 3,000 strategies, all of which Son calculated in detail. It took two months to reach his final conclusion on the matter.

And so, in February 2006, master strategist Son steeled his resolve for the battles which lay in store for him. SoftBank would purchase 100 per cent of the shares in Vodafone. They would bear all the risk. Son had decided to go all-in.

'By the way, how much money have we actually got for this?' Son – bursting out laughing – asked those with him in the war room.

Now as much as any other time the ideas came first, the financial particulars later, and Son had not spared a single thought to budget the entire time. He was a firm believer in the saying 'money comes and goes' and knew they would manage somehow. 'I looked at everything, calculated everything from every angle. If I don't believe in something from the bottom of my heart then there's no way I can convince other people otherwise.' Each sticking point was thoroughly thought out, Son stating that once he has thought things through then he can raise the required funds.

He was as good as his word, preparing 200 billion yen, which left 1.8 trillion outstanding. Son recalls only shelling out this initial amount but retaining a 100 per cent stake in Vodafone – this was not business as usual (or ever) and the word he uses to describe the move now is 'cheeky'.

The crucial caveat to all this was that – were the plan to go bust – SoftBank would be held fully liable. 'If I'm confident about something then I can purchase something worth 2 trillion for 200 billion and even get 100 per cent future upside on it.'

The next obvious question in this respect would be the financial structure of the deal, with SoftBank acquiring 100 per cent of common shares in Vodafone, becoming the sole shareholder. Yahoo! Japan and Vodafone would purchase several hundred billion yen's worth of preference shares (shares where the right to participation in the running of the company is limited in exchange for a preferential dividend rate), the shares being treated like subordinated debentures with the interest equivalent being paid on the condition that, in the event business went extraordinarily well, the upper limit of the dividend would be 6 per cent of the interest equivalent on the principal.

In other words, in the event the upper limit was reached then both companies would be doing the funding, otherwise the bank would be handling the financing. Son breaks it down even further: 'SoftBank contributed 200 billion yen and Yahoo! Japan and Vodafone contributed 120 billion yen and 300 billion yen respectively in preference shares. We took out a 100bn-yen loan and the remainder we got from the bank at a 3 or 4 per cent real interest rate.'

Vodafone already had 15 million users and were making 300 billion yen in earnings before interest, taxes, depreciation and amortisation from business operations.

'We could use the cashflow from the mobile side of the business to pay the bank back so they were all too happy to finance us. To top it all off the loan we took out wasn't classified as debt for SoftBank, rather it was an LBO [leveraged buy-out] with Vodafone Japan's assets value given as the security, meaning it was virtually a non-recourse loan [whilst the term originated on the real estate market, this refers to financing for specific business where financial obligations cannot be retroactively applied to the principal] for SoftBank. In other words the percentage of common shares with voting rights attached was set at 200 billion yen and this would ultimately be what they would pay in own funds. The remainder would be paid from fundraising activities excluding common shares, with funds from loans and investments being paid back and properties and assets and the like never actually changing hands.'

In this way at SoftBank's end no liability was ultimately incurred in raising the massive amount required for the takeover. They had been able to eliminate any risk and additionally any future upside would be received in full.

Son gives his thoughts on the arrangement: 'If you look at it from the point of view of a SoftBank shareholder, they'd have to say they got the best possible deal out of it – provided we were confident we could expand the user base. If we failed then we'd only be out of pocket 200 billion yen but if we succeeded who knows how many trillion yen we'd be pulling in. That being said, and looking it at it from the inverse perspective though, you could say we were only getting Vodafone Japan's 15 million users plus their cashflow in return.'

Ultimately, though, they had managed to raise the funds they needed without actually having the money in the first place – thanks to some characteristically masterful manoeuvring from Son and proof that where there's a will there's a way.

SoftBank had purchased Japan Telecom in May 2004, staking out its corner of the landline communications market. Less than a year later on 28 January 2005 Son purchased the Fukuoka Daiei Hawks (now the Fukuoka SoftBank Hawks) as part of his belief that the world was living in an age where content was king; Son had always had it in his head that baseball was content that could be broadcast over broadband.

At this point SoftBank were no longer content with focusing solely on Japan but rather had the world in their crosshairs, and Son's vision was about to expand even further. 'SoftBank achieved pole position in Japan – and then were ranked the highest in the world. Just like Sony had been, just like Toyota and Honda had been. Going forward, I want people to view us as an international concern, and we'll certainly be doing our best to live up to that image.'

A review of SoftBank's various lines of business at the end of 2006 would therefore be in order. In terms of the number of users they had in Japan, 16 million people were signed up to SoftBank Mobile, there were 5 million households subscribed to Yahoo! BB and 6 million households under contract with SoftBank Telecom. The total number of users on monthly billing contracts came to 27 million people or, to use Son's preferred unit, his '0.27 hundred million people – it's not much fun if you're not measuring things in hundreds of millions'.

The number of Yahoo! users in Japan was 0.42 hundred million people, whilst in China this was 0.34 hundred million people; when adding in users from elsewhere this reached 100 million. In terms of global partners Vodafone boasted 500 million customers, with Yahoo! contributing another 400 million for a total of 900 million people. Add the 100 million from above and the total comes to a clean billion.

Son states, 'We were targeting a massive billion users, offering our own technology, business model and content we developed ourselves. In terms of vision we're only thinking in terms of "massive".'

Son's vision could not have been any more massive when he claimed that 'if we can just hit on the one thing, we can achieve global hegemony in that field'.

By May 2007, SoftBank Mobile had topped the rankings for monthly net increases for mobile telephone contracts ahead of NTT Docomo and AU (Docomo counted 80,000 new phones sold, AU counted 140,000 and SoftBank counted 160,000). Son recalls that 'the only thing was that 160,000 figure in May was tempered by the fact prepaid had dropped by 40,000. Prepaid wasn't profitable so we intentionally under-reported the figure as 160,000. Terminals classified as standard mobiles for general use were actually 200,000.'

And yet despite hitting first place in the mobile sales rankings, this was only the first step in what Son desperately wanted to achieve. During the period when they had been trading as Vodafone Japan they had never once got first in sales, having developed something of a losing mentality from constantly lagging behind everyone else for so many years. The same applies to when they were known as J-PHONE as well, developing a reputation as a perennial loser. And yet, here they were, in first. For Son it was an omen and he was not about to hide his joy.

'That was when I thought we could go on and do this. If you hit first place once – if you get a gold medal in something once – there's always the possibility you'll be able to do it again. Your confidence grows.' Son continues, placing tremendous emphasis on the importance of confidence. 'Think about it. The company employees, the people working in the shops, even the users ... All of us knew we were aboard a sinking ship, but then that sinking ship with all of the passengers and crew on it were carried by the crest of a mighty wave to safety. If you look at it like that the energy you get off of a victory achieved in that way takes on quite a different meaning.'

Around this time would also be the first time SoftBank presented themselves as themselves, i.e. using the SoftBank name, to general consumers, making the formal introduction in a television advert, which also took pole position in the advertising sector rankings. With mobile number portability offered from October to December 2006, the advert was ranked highest for enjoyment for all companies and for all industry segments. As 2006 turned to 2007 the advert was still at the top of the charts, finally falling off in April.

It had been the top-ranked advert for seven consecutive months, a completely unprecedented achievement based on research covering multiple years by advertising research institutes. The heretofore unknown SoftBank were now a fixture in terms of brand awareness amongst general consumers, defeating well-known names such as Matsushita Denki, Sony and Suntory to take the crown. Every month 2,000 companies across Japan ran television adverts but it was SoftBank who had taken the crown.

'This must be a sign as well,' Son said, the corners of his lips edging upwards in a wicked grin, although his eyes were focused on something far off in the distance: his 10-year war and the bloody battles that would ensue.

Alongside the complete overhaul of the brand image and the advertising offensive, Son had designed the new phone models himself, with 'style' the key word at the press conference when they were unveiled. The 'White Family' plan – where phone calls to family members were free for 24 hours – was also tremendously popular, pulling in families.

At the time Son stated that 'looking ahead to the next year, the next two years, the next three years, I want to steadily bring out a variety of products and services and I want all of these to be the best around. I want to offer things which move people, which get them excited. Victory must be comprehensive.'

So was acquiring Vodafone a success in the end?

From a purely financial standpoint, 1.45 trillion yen out of the 2tn-yen loan – which had been loaned on short-term conditions – was refinanced to a longer seven-year repayment term, giving SoftBank a bit more room to manoeuvre. What about profitability then? Just looking at business profits from mobiles reveals an increase of 1.7 times what they had been doing, with the net user base four times what it had been the previous year. Total business profits for SoftBank for 2007 were 270 million yen – not only had the Vodafone ship been refloated and turned completely around but all segments posted a recovery, with the ordinary income graph showing a V-shape over time as well. Their credit rating improved as well.

Following SoftBank's announcement of the Vodafone acquisition the number of signees had jumped by a million over the course of a year, which when extrapolating the 200,000 contracts from May over the course of the year would effectively come to 2 million. In short, 15 million people had become 16 million people and they were on track to add a further 2 million people to that figure by the end of the year.

The internal struggle Son had faced prior to the acquisition – whether or not he was confident he could pull a turnaround off – now had a clear answer looking at the fruits of his labour. However, what looked like smooth sailing ahead turned out to only be a brief moment of respite.

In October 2006, the number of network subscription applications fell sharply and the competition lodged a complaint against SoftBank for their advertising with the Japanese Fair Trade Commission, calling the zero-yen offer an 'immeasurable discount'.

The decision was made to take another approach to advertising, but from there it would prove to be a case of out of the frying pan and into the fire, Son's surprise tactics catching even some of his own employees off guard. The problems started to stack up, Son commenting that 'no matter what there will always be difficulties.'

He continued: 'Think of the top athlete in your sport of choice – they're not invincible, they get injured sometimes. What makes them a top athlete, however, is the fact they've got the wherewithal, mettle and confidence to see it through and make their comeback.' Life is filled with hardships to be overcome and it's not like Son was a stranger to them – recall for example the personal data leak which happened during SoftBank's ADSL phase, for a start.

'If you've ever played the Game of Life board game, even if it's something rotten like a fire or burglary that happens to you, ultimately you're only drawing one unlucky card at a time. It's fair in the sense that regardless of the outcome players are only dealing with one pressing issue at a time. With that in mind, if you look at times when you've felt things haven't gone your way in real life – when you've fallen into complete and utter misfortune – I still think making excuses is utterly reprehensible because if nothing else you've still got the ability to act.'

Occasionally he and his own employees would verbally cross swords and he would have to pull himself together again whilst attempting to plough ahead. Son was caught in the middle of a fierce battle but he had comrades and allies, and that gave him the strength to see the battle through to the end. It was simply a period of trials and tribulations they would have to overcome together. Son would have to show some backbone, telling himself (and others), 'here we go again', 'leave it to me, I'll sort it out' and 'we'll get through this, that'll show 'em'.

Using a relay race as an analogy here, Son says the whole process is 'exciting', like when the runner in last place hands over the baton to the next person on their team. This new runner takes off sprinting, trying to overtake each and every one ahead of them. It's not a queue, their chance will not come if they remain idle – they've got to somehow overtake those ahead. And so they do, overtaking all the other runners one at a time . . . and that same thrill is one Son has experienced many times in his life.

Could SoftBank find themselves in similar circumstances again now?

'It's not a position you can achieve in just two or three years. It's something you've got to have done for around 20 years, for your partners' sakes. That said, however, if you spend 10 years doing something and it's still not working out, it's a bit embarrassing.'

SoftBank didn't have enough stations. Their own customers didn't understand them. There was no brand penetration. There weren't enough shops in the sales network. Given all these things, Son would still not make excuses.

'It's not like I could just snap my fingers and all of these problems would go away. But I'm not exactly powerless before them either.' Conviction means sticking to your beliefs and not backing down when faced with the reality of the consequences of doing so. Under Buddhism, strength of mind and a 'no retreat' mentality is achieved through discipline and training.

Of all the battles Son had faced so far in all of the other industries he had traded in, the battle in the mobile industry was shaping up to be the largest. The competitors were large companies as well, with enormous amounts of money, customers and pull within society. And that was precisely why Son was going to place all of his bets on pushing forward and fighting wholeheartedly, until he had won the war.

'No way I'd let myself give up if I were still in third place in something – I'd have to be first, and by a country mile.'

Chapter 32   **Making dreams reality**

Who could've imagined the all-out attack SoftBank would launch with their acquisition of the Japanese branch of Vodafone?

Son would turn 50 in August 2007 and – according to his life plan – he was determined to spend his fifties bringing his business aspirations to completion, with preparations in this respect having steadily been made, dating back to two years prior to the Vodafone acquisition and the unveiling of Apple's iPhone. At the time Son had placed a lot of time and thought into what he would do if he entered the mobile phone market, and the conclusion he reached was he would require a secret weapon.

And who did Son think of asking to forge such a technological weapon? None other than Steve Jobs, and he wasted no time in getting the ball rolling, ringing the Apple founder up for a teleconference.

Steve Jobs may have possessed the charisma required to make Apple an international concern, but despite being the company's founder he had occasionally been estranged due to his rather intense personality and verbal clashes. Jobs, after rescuing Apple from the brink and mounting a miraculous comeback, unleashed the innovative iMac and iPod on the world, sparking a complete lifestyle change in users.

Son had envisioned an iPod with mobile phone technology included in it and had sent Jobs a sketch. Jobs replied that Apple already had something like that in the offing, to which Son countered by apologising for his poor artistic talent, but once they'd got this new model of phone ready he wanted exclusivity rights to sell it in Japan.

Jobs replied as follows: 'Masa, you've got to be mad. I've not even told anyone that we've started developing it [the device which would become the iPhone]. That said, you were the first one to ask me about it. so I'll give them to you.'

Son in turn said, 'If you uphold your end of the deal then I'll bring a Japanese carrier on board.' True to his word, he invested $20 billion and bought out Vodafone Japan, fulfilling his promise to Jobs. On 11 July 2008, SoftBank Mobile began overseeing the sales of Apple iPhone 3G phones in Japan. The number of contracts signed shot through the roof, taking poll position in terms of highest number of net subscriptions for six whole years, from 2008 to 2013.

The image most people have of Jobs is someone who was completely devoted to their job, but surprisingly there was also a side of him that was a complete family man and, particularly later in life, he placed great value on time spent together with his family. At his home in Palo Alto, California, he would make time for his children and their school meetings, class visits, fancy-dress parades and school fundraisers alongside his wife, seeing his children off or collecting them from primary school on his bicycle, dressed in his trademark black turtleneck and jeans.

On 5 October 2011, after a long battle with pancreatic cancer, Jobs died. Son shares his impressions of the man. 'He was like some-one out of a history book – a Leonardo da Vinci who was at the forefront of art and technology, and I think future generations will cherish his truly outstanding achievements.' Naturally, Son would have tremendous respect for a genius as rare as the one Jobs possessed, as well as his character.

Two years later on 21 October 2013, and much closer to home, someone irreplaceable to Son would also die: Kasai Kazuhito, aged 67. Son, speaking with profound sadness, solemnly commented, 'I miss him. I well and truly miss him.'

In June 2000, Kasai had retired from his post at Fuji Bank (now Mizuho Bank) and Son had showered him with all manner of special courtesy to get him to join SoftBank, all but begging him to come and support him. Kasai, then aged 63, would eventually accept and became a SoftBank director, although immediately afterwards the dotcom bubble would burst. SoftBank shares would become worth one-hundredth of what they had been and profits tanked as well; looking back, Son can only comment, 'I couldn't apologise enough to him for the rotten timing.' The 13 years Kasai had been at SoftBank saw the company dramatically evolve and would prove a period where they developed by leaps and bounds.

When the Yahoo! BB deal was done, the first year saw the company 100 billion yen in the red, a situation they would not recover from for four years. And yet through it all Kasai would encourage Son, saying, 'It's fine, it'll be all right. We can do this.' After clawing their way back into the black Son would often seek advice from Kasai concerning the best way to move forward, what with internet use migrating mainly from computers to mobile phones.

'The internet was our main source of income. However, to make everything work there was no way we could focus solely on PC inter-net use – by hook or by crook we had to get into the mobile market. I would approach him with my concerns and he would say, "I'm completely with you, let's do this," and it was like we'd ride off into battle together. To that end we had to make the company a brand. If I told him I wanted to buy a professional baseball team, Kasai would always say "OK". Normally – bearing in mind we'd only just got out of the red – I think it's safe to assume your head of treasury would comment on it being beyond the company's means. But Kasai would always reply with a "Let's do it, let's make it happen", and that's how the Hawks ended up in the SoftBank fold.

'After that we set our sights on the mobile phone industry, where it was either build something completely from the ground up or acquire Vodafone Japan. At the time I was something of a *bête noir* in the bank's eyes and we had enough to cover half of the asking price, so I sought Kasai's advice, asking him how many other companies we should try to get on board and minimise risk as much as possible. He completely opposed the 50 per cent plan, saying that if we were going to pursue the plan it would have to be 100 per cent ownership or bust.'

That was the only time he ever vehemently opposed Son's plans.

'Shortly after Lehman Brothers filed for bankruptcy SoftBank's shares tanked and I lost all of my worldly possessions as well. The company was in a bad state but even then Kasai would encourage me, saying things like, "We may be in a bad way in that respect but we're still turning a nice profit so things will work out." And of course they did. After that the world started to recover from the Lehman Brothers bankruptcy and our profits crept up again. Speaking personally, our shares have always bounced up and down, which must be a nightmare for our shareholders. Trying to explain it to analysts and journalists is tedious in more ways than one too. I'd think that maybe I should just have us delisted and take full liability for the company, but whenever I wanted to just be rid of the whole thing I'd speak with Kasai and he would say, "I really have to disagree with that approach." And that would be enough for me to carry on.'

Going into more detail, Kasai responded: 'Business results have been extraordinarily good, so if you wanted to you could delist and go back to being a private company – we can raise the funds to make it happen. I don't know how, but we can manage it. The only thing I've really got to ask, bossman: is it the right thing to do? Is this really what you should be doing? Aren't we in a position where SoftBank can truly spread its wings and soar high? Would it really be worth not fully pursuing our dream over a bit of irritation, over a spot of bother?'

Son reflects on this exchange.

'Looking back now perhaps if Kasai hadn't stopped me then we wouldn't have been able to acquire Sprint – to say nothing of dreaming even bigger and the massive battles that ensued.' Son's sense of loss for one of the few people he could truly speak his mind to was acute, and was a chief factor in placing all of his bets on making his dream a reality with the mobile phone industry.

Goto Yoshimitsu (current SoftBank board director and senior vice president, CFO and CISO), a former banker with Yasuda Trust & Banking (now Mizuho Trust & Banking), joined SoftBank in June 2000, the same time as Kasai. Goto, who looked up to Kasai as a 'teacher about life', was asked about this relationship with Kasai in the 13 March 2014 edition of *PRESIDENT Online*, giving the following response.

The first time I met him was like something out of a film. Fuji Bank had parachuted him – their head – in to sort out the management crisis Yasuda Trust and Banking was embroiled in. The first time we meet he has got all of us lined up and has got his hands behind his back. Then he looks each of us in the eye and offers words of encouragement. When you think about most chief executives of banks in Japan their only real job is reading through draft versions of texts which have been prepared for them – and then Kasai comes along and it did wonders for our morale. He was someone who took a completely bottom-up approach to management. Whether for financing or real estate he'd go along to speak with customers and using his vast network of connections would get the deal done. His leadership was absolutely second to none.

It was Kasai who extended the invitation to Goto to tag along with him and join SoftBank, which he accepted immediately and without any reservations.

The two struck up a conversation in the car on the way to the SoftBank head offices, Goto starting. 'I'm confident I can manage in terms of management strategies and consulting but . . . I can't speak a word of English.'

'I've heard you don't actually need any English,' Kasai responded.

'I'm not really good with the rigid, overly strictly type of office management either,' Goto would go on to confess.

'I'm fairly certain that's not how they do things,' Kasai chuckled.

'So what is it exactly I'm supposed to be doing?'

'Something to do with the president's office.'

The car arriving at its destination (the SoftBank offices were then located in Hakozaki-cho in Nipponbashi in Tokyo), Son greeted the two in his office, took one look at Goto and then spoke. 'This one's got a bright look about his eyes. What do you say, Kasai, shall we adopt him?' And that was the end of job recruitment proceedings. It was all very anti-climactic for Goto but nonetheless it was how he made his start at SoftBank.

He had no staff working for him and would have to build up a treasury department from scratch – which incidentally to date still maintains a reputation as being the most unassailable treasury in all of Japan. Goto was asked about this in the same *PRESIDENT Online* interview cited above.

After Kasai started working for SoftBank I think he saw himself as something of an adviser who was a bit removed from everything. At the board of directors' meetings he didn't really say much, although when he did everyone took note of what he had to say. He was always positive and no matter how boring or tedious whatever you had to say to him was, he would always grin and bear it, which is why on the very rare occasions he had something negative to say it had a tremendous impact. Last year [2013] he turned up to a meeting in a wheelchair but even after all of us imploring him not to push himself too hard he simply shrugged us off, saying there were still things left to do that we stood no chance of managing. It was something only he could do.

With the Vodafone and Sprint acquisitions Goto was referred to as the 'striker', leading teams to success on a significant number of large-scale projects.

There was one thing and one thing only I was tasked with and that was ensuring the Treasury was completely synchronised with management and their decisions. Being part of management at SoftBank is, starting with the company president, all about seeking out golden opportunities. This applies to acquisition projects which aim to increase SoftBank's value as well as start-ups, although even I was surprised by the robotics venture. At any rate, you bring a number of ventures to the table and then you try to seize every opportunity presented.

Looking at each individual opportunity as such, however, there are a number of cases which just look like money sinks.

If we were a normal company then as soon as the price went past X number of zeroes then we would leave it and forget about it, whereas what actually happens at SoftBank is we think about whether or not the company is one we could partner with. We wanted to be a Treasury who were capable of moving in concert with management at any given point in time, completely focused on getting in before anyone else on the chance to increase the company's value.

Goto recalls a famous phrase Kasai used to use. 'Do work commensurate to the result.'

Does 'business as usual' involve putting in effort commensurate to the result? Work is not something a person can just lie their way through, and there is also the message of not being able to get on your high horse about things without the results backing you up. 'Obviously what I think he meant was results aren't everything – it's more that if you do work commensurate to the result, the result is achieved as a part of that. That is something I always have got to ask myself – whether Kasai is watching or not. I hope he is.'

In the summer of 2011, Son called Kasai and Goto into his office for a word, seeking advice concerning the Sprint acquisition. 'I am completely convinced we can win this battle but . . . can we? Really?' Son asked them. Kasai did not answer, nudging Goto instead.

In October 2014 – following Kasai's passing – Goto was named president of the Fukuoka SoftBank Hawks and swore in front of a portrait of his late mentor that 'the Hawks would be top of the league'. The portrait of Kasai hanging at the Fukuoka PayPay Dome shows him quietly smiling in approval, as his student in life has achieved this goal.

The man appointed by Kasai Kazuhito to replace himself was Fujihara Kazuhito (currently executive vice president and CFO), who had moved to SoftBank from Mazda in April 2004 following a public advertisement of an opening. At Mazda he had overseen business administration, where he dedicated himself – alongside individuals from other industries – to business development for companies who were not turning a profit and, demonstrating his ability in this respect, proving himself a true student of the more aggressive American approach to business.

Fujihara was a US-certified public accountant with a TOEIC (English-language examination) score over 900, giving his reasons for moving to SoftBank as wanting to operate on a 'grander stage' within the realm of finance. He was 41 at the time when he made the jump.

At the time SoftBank were recruiting for the purposes of setting up posts that would oversee and unify their various businesses engaging in international development, and the first task Fujihara was given to complete was analysing international investments made and reporting his findings back to Son. Once the recruitment formalities were completed Fujihara was to promptly set about looking into which areas required investment; after preparing his forecast, results showed they were set to incur tremendous losses, even after investing 100 billion yen.

Fujihara's findings concerning the pet projects Son had got him to look him into all pointed to one conclusion: they would do well to step away from them. Son's reaction was an uneasy one. Kasai recommended Fujihara give it to Son straight and he dutifully obliged. It was then Son spoke: 'Yeah – we're bleeding money, aren't we?'

Fujihara was surprised at this. Son had accepted the conclusion he had reached with no fuss, whereas normally – if someone's pet project was incurring a loss – they would do everything they could do to turn it around, getting stuck in even further. Son was not beholden to past mistakes, however, being someone who was always looking to the future. Afterwards, and reporting on SoftBank's business results, Son trotted out one of his favourite lines.

'SoftBank is like a car and I'm the driver. It's all right to glance in the rear-view mirror every now and again to see where you've been, but what's passed is gone. It's better me looking at the road ahead.'

When trying to predict the future Son believed he would have to be prepared for the worst cast scenario. He had to accept the fact that he would not always hit his target, but what was crucial was carving out a roadmap into the future. 'It's frustrating when you miss your mark – you can really get down on yourself wondering why exactly things didn't work out.' In Fujihara's view, a person's mindset starts to change. They start to think they have got to make a success of things, becoming more sensitive to figures they had seen many times a day. Their entire approach to business starts to change.

Son had always been preoccupied with what things would be like in five years' time, in 30 years' time, even. The future was what mattered most, Son frequently imparting advice such as, 'Whenever you think you've lost your way, look far off into the future.' Even when contemplating major acquisitions he would also say past results or the company's current value had no bearing on proceedings.

Fujihara states that 'Son practised kendo so he applies the same principles [when dealing with multiple opponents at once] of gaining ground on his opponents when they're coming at him from all sides. The same applies when dealing with people within his own company. If it's good, he'll take it on board. If he doesn't agree and he dismisses the idea, saying he can't fully get behind it, then run-of-the-mill willpower isn't going to cut it. Which is why there's no greater joy than when Son accepts something you've put forward to him and puts his all behind it. There's no greater motivation for us employees.'

*   *   *

In September 2008, Lehman Brothers announced their bankruptcy and the world's stock markets duly crashed. SoftBank were not unaffected by this either.

On 24 October – 12 days before the date the financial briefing covering second-quarter results was scheduled for – Son called Fujihara into his office alongside Kimiwada Kazuko (current SoftBank executive officer) from Accounting and asked them what they thought of announcing the financial results one week ahead of time, i.e. shifting this from 5 November to 29 October. Additionally Son wanted to postpone announcing the ordinary earnings forecast for the remaining six months of the financial year, releasing consolidated accounts in bulk in March 2010. Son told the two in no uncertain terms to release results ahead of schedule. When Son commanded them to 'anyways just do it', Fujihara declined, saying they could not. 'I don't want to hear about how you can't do it – I'm telling you now to sodding do it,' Son retorted.

Up until that point SoftBank had never publicly released their estimated profit – although this was common practice it was simply something they had never done. Other companies who would regularly publish their earnings forecast would see these hit rock bottom due to the Lehman Brothers bankruptcy, and found themselves in a position where they could not undo their announcement or downwardly revise figures. Son comments on this incident, 'Conversely, we never made a habit of publicly announcing our forecasts so I wanted us to publish our forecasted earnings for once for both the present year as well as the year after.'

It was an unheard-of business practice – announcing two financial years at a time. 'With uncertainty surrounding credit, things had hit rock bottom. And so not only did we announce results early but we also released our forecast for once as well, two years' worth effectively.' And the amount of financial information concerning SoftBank would not end there. Son also released data on free cash-flow projections and the company's debt balance. 'Because we did all of these things we were able to put the financial unrest about us to bed.' Share values that had hit rock bottom on the day prior to the financial results briefing completely rebounded and SoftBank were able to carry on in a stronger position than previously.

Chapter 33

The future 300 years from now

It was proof of Twitter's mass adoption. When Son created his profile on the platform on 24 December 2009 his number of followers went through the roof, and he was buffeted by questions asking about his vision for the company by his own employees via the medium. He frequently referred to the social media network as a 'hive mind'.

By April 2011, Son had more than a million followers on Twitter – the highest number of any Japanese user (at the time of translating in April 2021 this had increased to 2.8 million). When one of his followers suggested organising a 'SoftBank employee canteen experience' Son retweeted this, commenting, 'Hiya Aono, I'll do it. Comments open till Monday' (5 February 2010).

On 25 June 2010, Son unveiled his new 30-year vision for SoftBank on the platform: bringing happiness to everyone by means of the information revolution, being named one of the top 10 companies in the world. Hitting an aggregate market value of 300 trillion yen, expanding the number of companies in the group from 800 to 5,000. Being a company which experiences growth over the course of 300 years.

The 25th floor of SoftBank's head offices in Shiodome, Tokyo – incidentally, where the canteen is located – offers a tremendous view of the Hamarikyu Gardens. It was 28 July 2010 and the date would mark the opening of SoftBank Academia, the school Son had opened for the purposes of identifying and training his successor as company president and chief executive. Son was all smiles as he was welcomed into the room to warm applause by prospective students, the first year seeing the involvement of 200 SoftBank employees.

The second cycle would commence the following year, with 100 SoftBank employees enrolled alongside 300 external students. The 2010 cycle students consisted of 10 per cent of lower-rank employees, the term lasting half a year, although the following year this was changed to 20 per cent lower-rank employees with the term lasting a full year.

Son's appearance on 28 July, however, would be for a special lecture: 'The art of war, by Sun and Son'.

When under treatment for his liver condition in his late twenties Son would take Chinese military commander Sun Tzu's text *The Art of War* and combine it with his own observations to create his own version (incidentally, the character used for 'sun' in the Chinese and Son's own surname in the Japanese is one and the same). These business tactics were broken down into 25 separate characters, each character standing for a different strategy. When making medium- or long-term plans Son would always compare his thoughts against the 26 criteria to gauge feasibility. These have been reproduced below:

Set 1 – Principles – Do-ten-chi-sho-ho
- Commandments taken from *The Art of War* concerning the conditions required to win a battle.
- 'Do', the path – Bring happiness to people via the information revolution.
- 'Ten', the heavens – Timing, the will of the heavens.

- 'Chi', land – The advantage provided by the land where a battle is fought. Internet expertise and implementation has shifted away from being an American phenomenon to an Asian one.
- 'Sho', the general – Become a superb leader.
- 'Ho', methods – Create your own methodology, systems and rules.

Set 2 – Vision – Cho-jo-ryaku-shichi-to
- 'Cho', the apex – Your vision. The view from the top of the mountain you have decided to climb.
- 'Jo', information – Gathering information.
- 'Ryaku', the strategy – Your strategy for achieving your vision.
- 'Shichi', seven – Commencing battle once you are assured of a 70 per cent chance of victory.
- 'To', battle – Entering into battle and eventually achieving your goal.

Set 3 – Strategy – Ichi-ryu-kou-shu-gun
- 'Ichi', one – Not just being the best but being far and away the best.
- 'Ryu', flow, trends – Do not try to resist the trends of the era.
- 'Ko', offence – Go on the offensive.
- 'Shu', protection – Protect what you must.
- 'Gun', the group – Form bonds with your companions.

Set 4 – A general's understanding – Chi-shin-jin-yu-gen
- 'Chi', wisdom – Possess intelligence.
- 'Shin', belief – Possess both confidence and faith.
- 'Jin', benevolence – Possess benevolence, charity.
- 'Yu', courage – Possess courage.
- 'Gen', severity – Be strict in dealings.

Set 5 – Tactics – Fu-rin-ka-san-kai

- 'Fu', the wind – Act swiftly, like the wind.
- 'Rin', forests – Act silently, like a forest.
- 'Ka', fire – Be intense in your actions, like fire.
- 'San', mountains – Be immovable, like a mountain.
- 'Kai', the ocean – Be deep and still, having taken all things in like the ocean, and you will see your battles through.

The ideal leader Son sought to shape with his Academia was someone capable of maintaining a structure such that 300 years of continuous growth would be ensured, someone who had no use for a centralised structure but would instead create and maintain networks. More than anything else, what Son would seek to instil in Academia students was neither a lust for money nor prestige. He wanted their ambition and spirit.

In March 2011, a devastating earthquake struck the Tohoku region of Japan, leaving over 20,000 people dead or missing and destroying over 45,000 buildings. Its effect on Son was immediate and palpable.

'Ever since SoftBank's inception I had never given a single thought to anything outside of our main business. And our main business was the information revolution. But then, on the other hand, you see such a throng of people forced into abject misery and, spending time with them, you have to question whether or not it's all right to keep turning a profit. The incident made me think about a lot of things.'

Son would arrange for a donation of 10 billion yen of his own money to be made to the relief fund.

The earthquake had also caused a colossal disaster at the Fukushima nuclear plan, which concentrated Son's mind on Japan's reliance on these vulnerable sources of power. On the corporate front, and despite vehement opposition from his directors – opposition he would steamroll over – he amended the company's articles of association to allow for the creation of SB Energy. 'Even though an infinite supply of electric power can be generated via other means the main problem faced is one of money. If you're not relying on nuclear power then you can't provide electricity cheaply or stably.'

Over the past century humans have waged war in pursuit of energy and the problem is of such a scale that there is no guarantee humans will not continue waging war in this pursuit over the next 100 years. 'There are still massive problems with nuclear power, which is why we have got to move our systems over to green energy use.' Son is explicit in this respect.

After the 2011 Tohoku earthquake and tsunami the presentation of a SoftBank Academia student – Miwa Shigeki, currently head of the president's office at SoftBank – caught his eye.

The end purpose of SoftBank Academia is identifying a successor to Son; to this end enrolment is accepted from adult students both inside and outside of the SoftBank Group. At the time Miwa was employed at Mitsui Bussan but had enrolled at SoftBank Academia as an external student for a cycle.

Miwa was a talented trading company employee who had worked in the natural resources sector dealing with global mergers and acquisition and had a passion for energy. His ability to get his point across in English also attracted Son, but what moved him more than anything was Miwa's pure passion. He felt Miwa was someone he could entrust the future of his company to and extended an offer to Miwa to shadow him as he went about his business, an offer the SoftBank Academia student gratefully and promptly accepted.

On 31 October 2011, Miwa left his position at Mitsui Bussan and the following day went to work at SoftBank. On 11 March, Miwa had been in a meeting at Mitsui Bussan's head office in Otemachi in

Tokyo and had feared the building was going to collapse on top of them all, describing the effect it had on him.

'That experience is what made me realise the finiteness of being a human, but at the same time it made me reflect on what was important in life and what I should be living for going forwards.'

Son once posed a question to Miwa, asking what was the most outstanding thing about Rockefeller, to which his junior responded 'petroleum'.

'Wrong,' said Son. 'What was most amazing about him was acquiring the land the petroleum came from.' Son had acquired 220,000 hectares of land – the size of the Tokyo Metropolitan Area – in the Gobi Desert with the best aeolian power – the most wind activity on the entire planet.

'Calling it a desert is inaccurate, it's more wilds. There are places where there is soil, where vegetation grows – it's not completely sand.' Son was looking 100, 200, 300 years into the future.

Miwa comments, 'Son is always waiting for the chance to create a new style and set his plans into action. His thought process is that if it's something for the greater good then people will want to get on board.' Miwa would later gain further insight into Son's principles when he received three new messages from his boss – who was in Silicon Valley at the time – at the end of 2012. 'They've got a clean electricity generation system powered by natural gas. It looks interesting so let's look into it.'

Miwa flew out straight away. Silicon Valley proved it was not just fertile ground for the IT industry, reinventing itself by developing different types of next-generation energy options. In May 2013, Bloom Energy Japan was founded, capable of stably generating electrical power 24 hours a day, 365 days a week. They created electricity not by burning gas but rather an electrochemical reaction, an efficient process not releasing any carbon dioxide into the air.

'There is an entire universe inside of Son's head,' Miwa adds. 'I don't know what it is but the neurons firing in there are different to the ones in your head or mine. He adds a little bit of chaos to each and every thing and creates a cosmos out of it, constantly revitalising SoftBank and imbuing and reimbuing it with dynamism. He isn't thinking about things as X product or X field, he's thinking about how he can make SoftBank the next Silicon Valley.'

In January 2013, Son spoke about 'a new type of business model they were creating in Silicon Valley' in an interview with the Japan Broadcasting Corporation. 'Everything converges in Silicon Valley with these inventions, how everything gets redefined. There's the phrase "made in America" which everyone likes so much but the truth is it should be "made in Silicon Valley". You've got all of these extraordinary things on the forefront of technology being created in Silicon Valley which become integrated into societies around the world and which become the most in-demand products. We're talking about next-generation goods and services.'

It had now been six years since Son first began his war in the mobile phone industry. At a point where his fighting style was a known quantity – to a certain degree – and at a point where he could afford to feel confident about the results, he stated, 'Things got to the point where I was doing things by the numbers a bit more than I felt comfortable with, which gave me pause for reflection.'

Chapter 34   # The goose that lays golden eggs

S on has a saying: 'Wherever I may roam, that's where our head
offices are located.'

In any given month Son would be jetting around the world half
of the time – all whilst still assuming a full leadership position. In
2006, SoftBank Group acquired Vodafone Japan (now SoftBank) for
the cost of 1.75 trillion yen and, thanks largely in part to an affordable
billing system and the introduction of the iPhone on the market,
over the course of six years the number of customers under contract
with the company virtually doubled. Then 2012 saw the acquisition
of Sprint Nextel – the third largest mobile provider in America –
announced for the cost of 1.6 trillion yen. The combined sales from
both companies would come to 2.5 trillion yen, with SoftBank rock-
eting up the rankings to be the third largest mobile phone company
in the world.

Son would declare he was ready to take on the world and that *not*
taking a chance and pushing onwards would be too big of a risk.
They had surpassed Docomo and the landscape had changed.

In September 2013, Son was at Sprint's head offices in Overland
Park, Kansas. The company had been long established – its founding
dating back over 100 years – and was a great source of local pride.

The vast company premises – their 'campus', opening up to pictur-esque Midwest fields of soya and maize – consisted of 19 brick build-ings and employed approximately 7,500 people.

'Together we are one, so let's grow together over the next 300 years.' His speech at Sprint received a standing ovation from those directors in attendance. By mid-October Son had moved on to inspect the executive room at the recently built SoftBank offices in Silicon Valley.

'Are all of you daft?'

It was the Sprint monthly management strategy committee meet-ing with 10 of Sprint's top executives in attendance and Son was in shock at their advertising costs. For eight consecutive years SoftBank's television adverts in Japan had shown an outstanding performance, achieving the top spot in popularity, but at Sprint – and despite the fact the outlay for advertising was exponentially higher than for Japan – results were 'exceptionally poor', incurring Son's wrath.

Whilst Son had appeared on American television programmes and taken the time and effort to speak in Washington and engage in lobbying, he was having a hard time achieving his next goal of acquiring T-Mobile, the fourth-largest mobile provider in the States. Son was convinced that if he could form a company capable of standing up to the top two (AT&T and Verizon) he would be able to increase the speed of American communications and bring prices down.

Negotiations for the planned T-Mobile takeover by Sprint were forced back to square one on 6 August 2014, however. As the American administration at the time was not going to depart from their policy of having four main mobile phone companies, gaining the authorities' approval was viewed as an extreme gamble for both Sprint and T-Mobile, and Sprint ultimately failed to receive authorisation in this respect. The problems were starting to stack up for them, chief amongst which was the real danger of slipping down to fourth place.

The number of subscribers being signed were falling and there were connectivity issues to resolve – a situation not too different from when SoftBank acquired Vodafone Japan. Following the effective dismissal of CEO Dan Hesse, Marcelo Claure was appointed to his position by Son on 11 August 2014. Son describes Claure as a street fighter. When I visited the Sprint office in Kansas to conduct an interview with Marcelo it was autumn and a cool breeze was blowing outside.

Claure's schedule was packed. Every day was filled with meetings with people on both the operations and network sides of the business; furthermore, these meetings were open, such that anyone who wanted to attend could do. Up until that point if you'd wanted to access the chief executive's office at Sprint you would have had to pass through four different sets of doors, but Claure had completely done away with that to facilitate access.

'If I were to describe Sprint accurately, it is a company that's slowly approaching its death. It is losing 2.5 percent of its customers every year and if this continues, there is a risk that the company will lose all the customers. Therefore, everything needs to be changed now. There are so many things to be improved, such as customer relationships, sales methods, fee structure, and so on. Otherwise we won't survive.'

Born in Guatemala in 1970, Claure's first business was selling clothing outside his mother's house when he was 10 years old. Whilst studying at Bentley University in Massachusetts he started a business focusing on buying and selling students' frequent flier miles. After finishing university he was in a mobile shop when he was asked whether or not he would be interested in buying the retailer, and he did. After founding Brightstar, a mobile phone trade-in specialist in Miami, he very quickly found tremendous success.

Claure, who is passionate about football, is the owner of the Bolivian football team Club Bolívar and is also a friend of football superstar David Beckham. He was cut from the same cloth as Son, who had also learnt business from his father during middle school and had started up his own business whilst he was attending university – someone not afraid to make their own path in life. Son would even comment that 'I feel like we share the same DNA'. The two would first meet on 10 September 2012, Son emerging from his office in a pair of slippers.

Claure recalls the time: 'He was grinning ear to ear but he didn't bother to say "hello", he didn't ask me how my family were doing, he didn't want to hear about how the flight to Japan had been. He did not waste one second getting down to brass tacks and talking business.'

Looking back, this was the first sign for Claure that Son was not your average chief executive; he started telling him about what he was doing with Brightstar. 'We mainly distribute new and used mobile devices. We have individual trade-in deals with companies like AT&T and Verizon.'

In that moment Son's eyes widened and began to sparkle and he insisted telling him more about it. Claure obliged, drawing on a whiteboard as he explained his company's business model, and by the end of it Son proclaimed he wanted to enter into an exclusivity agreement straight away. Claure politely declined, stating his next flight onwards to China was due to depart in two hours and he absolutely had to be on it. Son's response was blunt. 'Let us get through what will be the fastest contract process of your life. How long did it take you with AT&T?'

'It was about three months, I guess,' replied Claure.

'OK – tell me then, how long did it take to launch?' Son continued with his line of questioning. Trade-in involves a very complicated process. In-store service briefing and price-setting should also be taken care of. 'So, it should at least take nine months to launch (the service),' thought Marcelo.

'Right,' said Son. 'This is going to be the fastest contract-signing you'll ever experience.'

At the time Son was close to launching the iPhone 5 in Japan – the scheduled launch date was only 11 days away on 21 September 2012 and Son wanted his agreement with Claure locked in place by then. Son asked Claure if he could still manage to do it, and Claure responded he might.

Including Claure there were six people in the office at the time and Son had one call for a solicitor straight away. Whilst it was a Monday in Japan it was still Sunday Stateside, but nevertheless Claure got on the line to one of his legal advisers, commenting, 'I met someone who is crazier than me.'

It was three o'clock in the morning in Miami – four in the afternoon in Tokyo – when they finished signing their agreement.

Son told him, 'When I first started up my own business we were doing distribution so I know how you turn a profit and that's why I know I can trust you.' Here Son asked Claure to tell Son's board members about his business.

Son, prompted by Claure, showed him around the giant board room (his war room) and introduced him to the members present. 'There, Masa began to explain that this was the trade-in business to launch as our new product. He also said that this was the fastest deal he has ever sealed.' Then Masa added that from now on, Marcelo will be leading this business. 'So, I explained what trade-in was and shook hands with the people (in the boardroom).'

Claure would miss his flight in the end.

*   *   *

Afterwards business progressed steadily for Claure, being the largest transaction he had been involved in, although the procedure to gain a licence as a second-hand dealer in Japan would prove a tremendous hassle.

Two months later Son met with Claure again, still all smiles, and congratulated him on a job well done. On being reunited, Son stated he had a project in the offing in the States and it was going to be a big surprise.

'December 12, 2012. I remember the date well because it was a repetition of 12. When I suggested that the joint venture be named Buying Group. Masa said "no, something is missing, let's add the word innovation," and we named it BIG, taking the first letter of each word. So far, the integration between SoftBank and Sprint has not been smooth, and I think the only successful case is BIG. In the procurement process, volume discounts are in effect, resulting in cost reductions.'

Claure goes on: 'Even before the launch of BIG, Masa said, "I like the way you do business. SoftBank wants to purchase a large portion of Brightstar business." I told him I didn't want to, because our customers include companies like AT&T and Verizon, and most of all, Brightstar was like a child I raised with utmost care. However, while I was on vacation with my family in France, the phone rang at about four in the morning. It was from Masa.'

Claure recalls their exchange:

'Marcelo, I've made up my mind – I'm going to acquire 80 per cent of Brightstar.'

'But I don't want to sell.'

'I want to pay a fair price for the acquisition, so you name it.'

'I was appointed as CEO of BIG first. After that Masa told me, "I want you to be Board Director of Sprint and SoftBank." I said OK to that. So, I became a Board Director of Sprint. Since I joined the board, I couldn't keep silent. Usually, a board director goes to board meetings, reviews the outline of the business, and gives opinions on what should be or should not be done. That's it. He or she does not give direct support. However, it was very frustrating for me to see Sprint operating at high cost. I told Masa that Sprint had a major cost structure issue. So, I started pointing out, there is something wrong with this and that, Masa heard them and said, "OK then, you can fix it."'

All of this happened during the rumoured T-Mobile acquisition, Claure being named Sprint CEO around the time the picture was starting to form that the relevant authorities were not going to allow the Sprint and T-Mobile merger to go ahead.

Claure had initially refused the position.

'I don't know anything about telecom business operation, and I didn't want to move to Kansas either. I'm happy with the current relationship between Brightstar and Masa.'

Son in return told Claure he was going to purchase the remaining 20 per cent of shares in Brightstar and – just like the last time – he wanted the acquisition price to be fully commensurate to the owner's valuation. Son told Claure that he had spoken with Dan Hesse (then still Sprint chief executive) about naming him as his replacement, saying the company needed new blood and a new perspective, with Hesse conceding this was a good idea.

'At the beginning of Masa's involvement with Sprint, things went by his rules. It looked like it was internally referred to as the "massacre sessions", taken from Masa's name. It came from this impression of Masa summoning people up to his Silicon Valley office and giving sharp criticisms. I asked Masa for his approval to let me handle the meetings with the Sprint employees.' Claure took on the role of Sprint chief executive in August 2014.

'I told Masa that there were people with more suitable career than mine, but Masa said he didn't want to hire someone just because of his or her career, he said he wanted an entrepreneur. Someone who fights like a street fighter.'

Claure then shares his personal insights on Son's character: 'Masa's speed of thinking is much faster than anyone else's. He looked beyond what anyone else could see, and that's why he invested in both Yahoo! and Alibaba. He is better at seeing the future than anyone else. Masa has a gift that no one else has.'

Chapter 35   The artificial intelligence revolution

'Today is the most exciting day for our company since its founding.'

Son was speaking concerning the acquisition in July 2016 of Arm, a company specialising in designing semiconductors possessing core technology for use in smartphone and automobile CPUs. The announcement had been made on the 18th, with the purchase price standing at around 3.3 trillion yen – roughly 43 per cent higher than Arm's aggregate market value at the time.

For Son, companies specialising in semiconductor design were truly a mirror looking into the future. On 23 June of the same year he had held a dinner at the mansion on his 9-acre estate in California. Simon Segars, CEO of Arm, had been invited as the guest of honour but was mystified as to what the invite could be about – perhaps Son wanted to place an order with him. He had imagined that he might win some new business from Masa. Simon had not realized why Ron Fisher was at the dinner. Segars was yet to cotton on to Son's true intentions – if Ron was there then the matter must have been of the utmost importance.

Son quizzed Segars on all manner of things and spoke about what he thought the future would be like, his voice suddenly spiking when speaking about things he was excited about, just like a young boy would do. Even before meeting with Segars and when musing on what the 'internet of things' would be like going forwards, Son realised a new wave was imminent with the technology driving smaller, albeit interconnected, devices. At the present time around 1 billion mobiles were all interconnected but this would soon become 1 trillion devices and Son began thinking that the internet of things could be the next phase of the digital information revolution.

So when Son finally met the Englishman he had already formed an image of what this future would be like in his head. Masa said to Simon: 'You are a public company, if you want to have the same success in that you have gotten in mobile device that's where you got such enormous penetration of mobile device. And what you are doing with the same kind of process of technology moving into Internet of Things, there has to be investments. You have to invest, make these investments to really grow the next generation of devices.'

Simon agreed with him, whilst explaining some of the challenges Arm faced.

'You are right. The problem that we have is we are a public company. So we are very limited in the kinds of investments that we make. So I would say it to shareholders we need to make investments because our technology can be applied to the next generation of devices. When I spend that money, I get penalized because our profits go down.'

It was a problem Son thought he could help solve.

It would be no exaggeration to say that Arm held the mobile industry in the palm of its hand, as they all used their microprocessors. This was at the heart of Son's interconnected device plan and, whilst vast expansion was a possibility, it was not something Arm could do as a single company. However, if they were to become a part of the SoftBank ecosystem, that would be a different matter altogether.

Several days after his dinner with Segars, Son would phone up Stuart Chambers, Arm's then chairman of the board, who at the time was on his summer holiday in Turkey. Son stated his desire to meet Chambers straight away and soon enough was on a private jet out to meet him; on his arrival he cut straight to the chase, stating he wanted to acquire Arm. The deal was sealed in less than a month.

All was not as simple as it appeared to be, however, and the story goes much further back than 2016. Son explains that 'even before starting talks with Segars in June of 2006 when we had just started up SoftBank Mobile (the Vodafone Japan acquisition having taken place in April of that year), Arm's former chief executive, Warren East, called out to pay us a visit. And who else but Segars had tagged along with him.'

At the time there had been discussions about doing something together and Segars had really pushed to see it through to completion, although that was before Apple starting using Arm chips for the iPhone.

'This was before the advent of the smartphone,' continues Son. 'Of course, even then lesser models were already using Arm chips but they weren't ubiquitous – it wasn't like you had to use them. But then the iPhone came out and from our "feature phone" stage onwards mobile phones stopped being just mobile phones. They became smartphones and that's when we realised that we had to use Arm chips, or bust. If we're going to look at the lineage of computing and the internet, the internet used to be the preserve of PCs but then the iPhone came out and that was the point where mobile devices became the main internet platform.

'iPhones used Arm chips so, as a result, if Google for example wanted to realistically compete with the Android their choices on the microchip front were limited to Arm and Arm alone. So there's a war going on between Apple and Google with the iPhone and the

Android and there was only ever going to be one winner and that was Arm, because both sides were using their chips.'

Arm processors barely used up any battery power compared to Intel chips – not an issue for PCs as these are powered by mains. Son continues: 'From a user's perspective the fact a PC requires loads of power doesn't really matter but for mobile phones – and smartphones in particular – you haven't got a mains, they're running off batteries. If your mobile loses all of its charge over the course of a day then they're not fit for purpose, really. Which is why if you're planning on designing a battery-powered device and moreover you want all of the benefits provided by internet connectivity, you've really got no other choice but Arm.

'That was the instant I realised that SoftBank trying to acquire Arm was simply a question of time, although we didn't have any money then. I had always wanted to buy them out but after the Sprint deal, the drain on resources it became, I was forced to give up on that particular dream – at that time. So in other words when SoftBank started offering mobile services in Japan I had my dream of us being the best in the sector and the Arm deal came secondary to that in terms of priority. Even if I had managed to buy out both Sprint and T-Mobile I still wouldn't have been interested in being the number one mobile company in America, but that's the path I pursued regardless. If I hadn't bought Sprint then I would have gone for Arm – I'm certain I could have got them for a lot less at that point in time.'

Roughly three months after announcing SoftBank's acquisition of Arm, on 20 October Son invited Jensen Huang, founder and chief executive of Nvidia, to his California home for a private meal between just the two of them. Son explains his mindset at the time.

'Speaking frankly, me considering whether to purchase Arm, Nvidia or pursue a business alliance of some sort with them all happened at around the same time. The end result was SoftBank buying out Arm, which actually included a small holding in Nvidia. At any rate, when thinking about an AI-augmented world my vision for making that a reality was based on system-on-a-chip technology incorporating Nvidia's GPU and Arm's CPU design capacity. We had to force advances in what the AI chips could do.'

At his meeting with the SoftBank chief executive, Huang called in at around five in the evening and the two sat on Son's terrace whilst drinking wine and batting ideas back and forth under the California night sky. 'Huang had been close to Steve Jobs, just like myself. We reminisced about Steve whilst also discussing the future of the computer industry. At that point I had already purchased Arm and I spoke passionately about how I wanted to merge Arm and Nvidia together to revolutionise the industry by means of an AI computing platform. That's not unrelated to the sale of Arm to Nvidia happening at present, by the way.'

In September 2020, the SoftBank Group announced its intent to sell Arm to Nvidia, with the British company valued at a maximum of $40 billion.

'There's a lot of people out there who think that I've been forced into selling Arm off because of the impact Covid has had on business, but at the press conference I called it a "purchase kind of sale, a sale kind of purchase", and I stand by that statement.'

As part of the transaction the SoftBank Group would receive both cash and shares in Nvidia which – once the deal is approved – would make them the largest shareholder in Nvidia. 'If anything I want to hold more shares in Nvidia – which is why I've described the deal as a purchase kind of sale, a sale kind of purchase. Whatever happens these two companies are intrinsically linked and together they're going to give birth to an AI computer platform. I absolutely think they'll be able to make it happen, which is why I couldn't care less whenever people assume we're just some run-of-the-mill investment company. I'm completely convinced of the industry shifting towards AI. The AI revolution is the fourth part of the information revolution and I am going to get stuck in this time.'

Ron Fisher offers his comments on the deal as well: 'Arm and Nvidia combining their individual areas of expertise is going to usher in a new generation of performance and I think it was a very good decision. The solution they've come up with by combining the two types of processing will give rise to next-level platforms. One of the more obvious next-level applications is autonomous transportation (such as self-driving cars) but when combining the CPU and GPU pairing with robotics, AI, central processing and cloud computing, there is no doubt in my mind completely new technological platforms will start springing up, much like when the Intel 8088 and 8086 came out, sparking the creation of platforms which were used over decades. When you have this combination of CPU and GPU, it creates a different kind of technology platform more than a company could do on their own. I'm convinced Masa's decision will in future be looked back on as a historical event. He's been following goings-on very closely at Nvidia for years now and believes they're the "next frontier in computing".'

For the online edition of SoftBank World held on 29 October 2020, Huang was interviewed by Son and took the occasion to speak about what made Arm so appealing to him.

'Looking at it from a computer architecture perspective, from a computer systems perspective, the cloud and AI is x86 and Nvidia. In the end, it's Arm. That's the reason why combining Arm and Nvidia makes so much sense, because we can then bring Nvidia's AI and the popular edge CPU to the world. The energy-saving design can be implemented in edge devices and the performance is extraordinarily powerful. But really, the true value of Arm is in the ecosystem of Arm – the 500 companies that use Arm today. Our dream is to bring Nvidia's AI to Arm's ecosystem. The only way to bring it into the ecosystem is through all of the existing customers, licensees and partners. We would like to offer the licensee more, even more. And so of course we will honour them with everything that they currently buy, [but] we would like them to buy even more. So there's a business reason, of course, but the vision is to combine the most popular CPU in the world that is in every single edge device on the planet and it's diversifying into so many different types of systems, whether it's cars or delivery drones or cell towers – all kinds of systems all over the world. We would like to bring that.'

The deal requires the approval of British, Chinese, EU and American regulators but is expected to be concluded in March 2022.

The SoftBank Group announced on 8 February 2021 that its third-quarter net income for the previous year had been around 6.4 times that of the same period for year before that, standing at 3.55 trillion yen. Son would go on to comment that 'I was born a businessman, I got this company up and running, but even still I cannot remain satisfied with results so far,' speaking about what he felt was more important than the highest net income SoftBank had recorded in its history: NAV (net asset value) increasing by 1.2 trillion yen over nine months. Son declared NAV to be of the greatest importance for the company and that this figure would continue to grow going forwards.

He would also comment further on the value of the ecosystem created by the fusion between Arm and Nvidia, stating the two would be capable of creating the types of chips required to jump-start the AI revolution, leading to AI being capable of solving problems faced by humanity, such as AI-led drug development or self-driving cars, or robots with access to the cloud and AI. It would even be capable of developing its own computing platforms. Son would comment that the most important thing with these advances was their capacity for making major contributions to the future of humankind.

Elsewhere in his comments he would state that the seeds sown with the SoftBank Vision Fund were starting to sprout and bear fruit. As much as Son had previously stated the SoftBank Group was his goose laying golden eggs, by December 2020 this was undoubtedly the case.

The SoftBank Vision Fund 1 counted 92 companies in its portfolio (inclusive of companies disposed of), the SoftBank Vision Fund 2 counted 39 companies in its portfolio (including companies where investments were in the pipeline but had not been completed) and the Latin American Fund counted 33 companies in its portfolio (including limited partnership investments), giving a total of 164 companies.

It was a turbo-charged golden-egg-laying strategy and everything was running at a brisk pace. A promotional video showing golden eggs being laid one after the other after the other whilst a track from Tchaikovsky's *Nutcracker Suite* played in the background was eloquent and convincing, the process energising the synergy required for the AI revolution around the corner. Furthermore, with its 'Beyond Carrier' scheme launching, SoftBank were creating even more synergy. PayPay, a smartphone payment service and SoftBank Vision Fund portfolio company, entered into a partnership with Paytm, the largest payment service in India, for the purposes of using its technology to help develop its own smartphone payment services in Japan and expand its service offering.

There was only one thought in Son's mind, however: 'AI is the most incredible thing humans have ever made and I am fully prepared to throw everything I've got behind it.'

Chapter 36   Vision Fund

The SoftBank Group announced their settlement of accounts for March 2017 on 10 May of the same year; operating profit had increased by 12.9 per cent compared to the previous period to 1.26 trillion yen. It was the first time the SoftBank Group had posted profits in excess of 1 trillion yen since the 2013 financial year and, commenting on the achievement, Son may have surprised some with his words. 'We hit the 1 trillion mark this time but we had to do it by force. I feel confident we can continuously repeat the trick going forward. It may sound odd given the achievement but I don't feel particularly relieved or excited – I think we'll hit the 1 or 2 trillion milestone again.'

May 2017 was also the first time the SoftBank Vision Fund was included in closing accounts.

'"What did Son Masayoshi invent?" I want future generations to ask that question and I want the answer to be I invented an organisational structure which has shown growth over 300 years, for one. I say this because the information revolution will occur over the course of 300 years, and for the SoftBank Group to remain at the epicentre of the information industry we've got to adopt a "cluster of number ones" strategy. It's not about just me doing things, we act as a group.

If you acquire [shares in] a company, you don't always have to acquire the controlling interest of 51 per cent – sometimes 20 or 30 is all it takes, enough to make you the largest shareholder.

'There is only one thing I really want from the SoftBank Vision Fund. SoftBank was originally founded at the very start of the PC revolution and the critics said we were only ever going to be a software company. Then there was the internet revolution and even though we got in at the ground level and regardless of the amount of money we invested, we were still just an internet company to them. After that came mobile internet and again we realised it was going to change everything – we were Stateside before anyone else, meeting with Steve Jobs even before he had announced the iPhone. In China and the rest of Asia we scouted Jack Ma well before anyone else, although that – if you want my opinion – was only a half-success at best and we could have done better.

'So three times on the trot I've noted exactly when a new chapter is about to begin in terms of epoch-making changes in society, and that is why we have been able to get on board with new trends before anyone else. You cannot say I wasn't there leading the way when the revolution started, but I still feel I haven't been able to achieve anything.'

Son saying he was quick to pick up on the way the winds were blowing but then adding he feels he still has not achieved anything reveals that in his own life, on a personal level and as a businessman, there are still things he is not completely satisfied with.

'Going forward there'll be no excuses. I've realised that up until now the problem has always been we never had the money. We were always just that little bit short.' Son laughs. 'We always had loans to repay. I'll tell you a story about Jeff Bezos, before Amazon went public. The two of us met in private and I told him I wanted to invest in the company – we actually ended up going back and forth with negotiations for about four hours. But SoftBank were just that little bit short on the financial front.'

Son is speaking frankly, honestly, absent of any affect. Going forward he does not want to have to resort to the excuse of coming up a bit short. 'So then I asked myself how much money would it take for me to say I've got enough – absolutely, unequivocally, so I couldn't make excuses to myself any more? The answer was 10 trillion yen, and that 10 trillion became the Vision Fund.'

In other words, this time – the start of the AI revolution, the fourth chapter in the information revolution – there would be no more excuses. Son had a 10tn-yen fund set up and he would catch his unicorn start-up, no expense spared. Or rather, he would catch his unicorn start-ups (in the plural), as each segment promised something different: AI could be used to develop medical care, transportation, financial technology; the list could go on and on. There was any number of categories and the goal was to achieve pole position within each one – his aforementioned 'cluster of number ones' strategy.

To resource these number ones he would need a system in place for a small army of fund managers to identify suitable candidates and then, once found, all of the money in the world to pour into his cluster. 'SoftBank, as a business, has to juggle customer care, its own expenses and the needs of its employees as part of its daily operations. As the chief executive and president all of that rests on my shoulders so day in, day out, sunrise to sunset, I've got to make all of the decisions. There's two main roles required to kick-start the AI revolution: a team of people who can really get stuck into the nitty-gritty of things – the micro level – and then another team of people to identify potential entrepreneurs and then properly invest in and develop them. Pursuing both paths would entail time and human resources that we simply haven't got – that no one has got. That being the case, the option I went for was to leave daily business operations to Miyauchi and his staff whilst I would concentrate full-time on the AI revolution. And that's how the SoftBank Vision Fund came into existence.'

Son continues speaking, revealing his true motivations for setting up his fund. 'There are 5,000 venture capital companies in Silicon Valley. When looking at the size of the funds at their disposal the larger ones tend to be in the order of 50 billion yen, with the average amount estimated to be 10 to 20 billion yen or so. Investment horizons for funds are largely seven years – so for example, 30 billion yen invested over the course of seven years. Then, looking at investments as part of a single deal, these are normally in the amount of 500 million to 1 billion yen. Then on top of all of that there's series A and B rounds, which are only made just after a company starts up.

'In this case you need someone to make all of the decisions there, providing support immediately after the company gets up and running. By way of analogy, if you had to say whether the education you received in kindergarten is crucial, everyone would say the education you get in kindergarten is crucial, as is primary education, as is secondary education, as is a university education. So all of the various stages of education are vital and valuable, but with venture capitalism there aren't any funds which would deal with the stage in a company's development right before it gets launched – the part that corresponds to the university or latter part of secondary education. By all means we need to see series D and E rounds whenever considerable investments are made – the amount for a single project should be huge.'

To summarise, in Son's estimation if companies only receive investment when they are still small and starting out they will never survive.

'The AI revolution is my own personal unicorn start-up, so we are looking at a valuation scale of over 100 billion yen. We would be investing in units of 100 billion yen at the scale of 100, 200, 500 billion yen, and there's no other investment fund out there doing the same thing. Setting 100 billion yen as our base unit of doing business is enough to guarantee victory, so with that in mind you can understand why we'd need the 10 trillion yen. Rather than worry about how much we had and making plans based on that I calculated everything in reverse, from the endpoint I wanted to achieve.'

As Son finds his star unicorn start-up, that platform capable of shouldering the AI revolution, that game-changer, he is prepared to throw the full weight of the Vision Fund behind the project in a heartbeat. Anything less would simply not be worth the trouble, as he explains that 'there's 100 companies in the SoftBank Vision Fund 1 portfolio, with 100 billion yen earmarked for each, on average. At the very start we only had 30 billion yen for investment – the 100-billion-yen figure each was beyond our dreams. Classically trained Silicon Valley capitalists may have looked at what we were doing and been puzzled. It may look like we've taken a very scattershot approach to investment, but the aim has never been to disrupt, rather it is all part of our AI revolution strategy.'

The man at the heart of Son's Vision Fund with whom he shares his dream for the future is Rajeev Misra (SoftBank Group Corporate Officer, Executive Vice President). 'Misra is incredibly sharp. He can look at the figures and see what's going on and he's flexible. He's also just a lovely person – very kind and pleasant to be around. But a banker's job naturally entails lending money to people and that involves having to be realistic about things and assume the worst. As this pessimistic tendency is normally quite strong in bankers it made sense to put someone like him – who only sees the risk involved – in charge of the fund. That side of him is very much fully formed but in the end he's a dreamer like myself and can also see the positive side of things.'

Son first met Misra in 2003, whilst he was working for Deutsche Bank, in charge of fixed-income securities and lending; Misra assisted with financial arrangements as part of the Japan Telecom landline and Yahoo! BB projects. Mirsa looks back at that time. 'Back then, I had an enjoyable time in SoftBank's Tokyo office. Good food. It was good times.'

On one such trip Son gave a presentation on what he wanted to achieve with SoftBank over the next 10 years and, whilst Misra was somewhat sceptical – hedging risks for his employer – in the end he signed off on the loan. The next time the two met would be a year later, in 2004, this time Son urged Misra to take him on a trip to India. Misra obliged and the two spent four days on the subcontinent, split evenly between Delhi and Mumbai.

Prior to the trip, the thought had first occurred to Son to purchase content for the purposes of streaming it over broadband – anticipating the popularity of Netflix by over a decade – and he was introduced to people in the sector in India. During this trip, Rajeev began to feel that there was something indescribable and special about Son. Smartphones had yet to be invented and even still Son was making deals to purchase content, intent on beaming it directly into people's homes and personal devices – truly the actions of a visionary and daring risk-taker. 'Masa is a visionary who can see the future, and a bold risk taker,' recalls Rajeev.

In the first week of January 2006 Son received a phone call from Misra, concerning securing funding for the acquisition of Vodafone Japan. At the time Misra's wife was heavily pregnant with their third child and could give birth at any time – her due date was the 20th. 'Generally speaking, if your wife gives birth and you're not there it's not good and it's not something that would be forgotten. So I said no, I cannot come.'

As Misra would not be flying east Son decided he would fly west to meet him in London instead. He needed $20 billion in cash but could only contribute $2 billion from his own money; his market value on 4 January 2006 was approximately 5.1 trillion yen. He would have to ask Misra for the remaining $18 billion, who in turn responded by saying, 'I'll have to think about it. It is not my bank. I am an employee. You are asking for 18 billion dollars and that will require approval from senior management.'

Apparently not leaving anything to chance during the meeting itself, Son said that Deutsche Bank would be providing them with a loan of $18 billion, with SoftBank stumping up 2 billion, prompting Vodafone to seek confirmation from Misra. 'It's subject to conditions,' he replied.

Two days after the meeting Misra received a phone call from Deutsche Bank chief executive Josef Ackermann, who was also on the board at Mannesmann, a company held by Deutsche Telekom. Ackermann was apoplectic. 'I just got a call from Vodafone saying some Indian guy came and said they are financing the acquisition for 18 billion of this other crazy guy in Japan. Is it true? Rajeev, did you say that?'

'Not really. I just said we will look at it.'

To get the deal to go through, Misra effectively invented the concept of whole business securitisation, and Son got his way and his funding. As for the conditions, however, SoftBank Group's $2 billion investment went on to create $80 billion of value for SoftBank.

Misra and Son would see each other one more time in 2007, although after that it would be quite a while before they met again: in June 2014 at the wedding of Nikesh Arora, who would join SoftBank as Vice Chairman later that year. The day after the wedding Son was due to give a presentation at eight o'clock in the morning on the future of the SoftBank Group so had to make his excuses early on in the evening, but nevertheless he invited Misra to come to Tokyo sometime so they could speak, with ideas concerning the SoftBank Group's international expansion percolating in the back of his mind.

Alibaba had applied for their initial public offering. Son set out his stall: for the SoftBank Group to do business at the international level they needed someone like Misra who had a strong grasp of international finance and investment working for them. Misra found the offer enticing. It could be the start of a new chapter for him and, regardless of whether it was Deutsche Bank or the SoftBank Vision Fund, he had a passion for getting companies off the ground.

Misra would prove to be a useful person to know with his knowledge of strategies for raising funds as well as international tax law. He would add considerable value to the Vision Fund and in exchange for his knowledge of the money market he would be able to learn about technology from Son.

Misra thought for a while. 'There is always the right time and right place in life. Do you believe in destiny? I do.' Misra accepted.

In August 2016 Misra took a week or so out of his summer holiday with his family in Greece to prepare a 20-page presentation he was going to give Son about his plans for the Vision Fund going forward. The first thing he did was to contact someone who had worked under him at Deutsche Bank who handled affairs for Saudi Arabia, Qatar and the UAE to see if he would be interested in the project.

Back in Tokyo a month later, Misra approached Son with the results of his endeavour. 'Look, there might be some money from sovereign funds of Abu Dhabi and Saudi Arabia, maybe to raise 10 to 30 billion dollars.' Large venture capital funds such as Sequoia and Benchmark had been awarded a billion dollars from them so it would not hurt for SoftBank to have a go as well. If they could get $10–20 billion in investments alongside $5–10 billion of SoftBank's own money then Misra was confident his plan would yield results.

At the time there were only a handful of people at best overseeing investments at the SoftBank Group. A meeting with the various sovereign funds had been arranged in the Middle East, with Son flying in from Tokyo and Misra arriving from London. Son was going through Misra's presentation on the flight and making changes where he deemed fit; it was only after the meeting had started that Misra realised his Japanese partner had changed the amount they were asking for from $30 billion to $100 billion – he could hardly believe his eyes. Eventually they were given $60 billion.

Fast-forward a bit and the SoftBank Vision Fund now has offices in Abu Dhabi, Hong Kong, London, Mumbai, Riyadh, Shanghai, Silicon Valley and Singapore, counting over 400 full-time employees around the world.

Born in 1962 to an upper-middle-class Indian family, Rajeev Misra won a scholarship to Pennsylvania University and then worked as a computer programmer before taking an MBA at Massachusetts Institute of Technology. When he graduated from MIT it was the start of the credit boom and for the next 20-odd years – initially at Merrill-Lynch, later at Deutsche Bank – he would ride the crest of that wave, conducting derivative and interest-rate swaps and dealing in foreign exchange and credit derivatives, eventually being named Global Head of Credit at Deutsche Bank and leading a team of 3,000 around the world.

When Son asked him how he had managed such an impeccable track record, Misra replied that 'performance is absolutely crucial in finance but it's not just about making money – you had to be entrepreneurial: build businesses, hire and manage well, develop strong relationships with clients.'

Misra would also comment on his golden rule for investments. 'Investments are a long-term business. Especially when you invest in private companies, you have to experiment, you have to try new products, new geography. And it takes years. SoftBank invested in Alibaba in 2000 and Alibaba went public in 2014. So, it takes five to seven years. You cannot decide one quarter to the next quarter how it is doing.'

Private investing is a completely different animal to putting money in publicly held shares, which can be disposed of on the market at any time – it requires a long-term strategy. Even in the event an investment manager quits after two or three years, someone else has got to take over from them and keep on course.

At the end of February 2021 the combined number of companies who were receiving investment from SoftBank Vision Funds 1 and 2 was 128.

'Say you take 100 companies,' says Misra. 'Fifty will do well, thirty will do very well, twenty would not do well. And the ones who do very well, you do not need to help them, they do very well. You do not need to spend a lot of time on them. The ones who are going well, you have to spend some time on them to make them do better. The ones who are not doing well is where you end up spending all most of your time. Just imagine, 100 companies, how much time it takes. Imagine you had 100 children. The smart children of yours do not need your time. Only the ones who are not doing well will need your time.'

Misra is commenting on how the AI revolution will generate value around the world. In response to criticism of the SoftBank Vision Fund, Misra had previously stated that criticism for SVF would be proved wrong.

He hasn't changed his mind. 'This was in the January or December before Covid hit but it's a statement I still believe to be true. As of February 19, 2021, the Vision Fund has not only recovered all its losses, but is up $40 billion on $84 billion invested in less than four years. All Covid has done is expedite the trend of every-thing moving online – in America, for example, the e-commerce penetration rate increased by the same amount over three months in 2020 as it had done the previous decade. Many SVF portfolio compa-nies are related to online education, online medicine, online cars, online sale of insurance, online sale of glasses, e-commerce, food delivery, dark kitchen, real estate broking through online.'

Misra's analysis is that whilst the travel and hospitality sectors have taken a hit there are signs they are recovering. For the third and fourth quarters of the 2021 financial year SoftBank Vision Fund companies showed a combined 2.7tn-yen return on investment. Out of the 128 companies at least 15 to 20 are thought to be truly revolu-tionary, and their emergence and mass popularity will change people's lives: companies specialising in new medicines to prevent cancer, businesses focusing on online education to completely change the way people learn, virtual kitchens, self-driving cars, driv-erless delivery vehicles.

Misra also makes his expectations concerning the scope of the Vision Fund perfectly clear. 'Where venture capitalists invest early, SVF will invest later, mid-stage and help those companies in a number of ways. SVF helps them in bank financing. SVF helps them hire people. SVF helps them with business. SVF helps them grow in countries. Automation Anywhere going to Japan and Paytm going to Japan are two good examples. Original investors and venture capital-ists get helped a lot. We stepped in to assist the people who had initially invested in the companies, but in any event the Vision Fund operates at such a large scale we were able to accelerate growth. I think it was just too big and we went from 0 to 500 people in the Vision Fund very quickly. We went from 0 to $100 billion very quickly, too, and it was a bit too rapid for them. They invest 10 million, 20 million, 50 million, and the company said, "I want 100 million." We said take 200 million and grow. The existing investors would get diluted. But at the end of the day, they are realizing that we are helping them because we are making companies they invested in grow.'

Another criticism Misra and his colleagues receive is their practice of simultaneously investing in competing businesses – such as the DoorDash and Uber Eats investments. He explains the rationale behind this. 'But, you know, I think it's a very close club which has been built over 40 years. Somebody comes in three years ago and starts, you have to earn their respect. And you have to have humility because they exceed in professionalism. So our objective is to be partners with them.'

The governments of Saudi Arabia and the UAE have committed to provide a combined total of $60 billion to Vision Fund 1 via their Public Investment Fund and the Mubadala Development Company. Were it not for these sovereign funds the Vision Fund would not be able to operate on the scale it does, with the PIF and Mubadala making this investment for two main reasons: turning a profit and strategic purposes, enticing the companies they have invested in to set up shop in Saudi Arabia and the UAE.

This strategy seems to be paying off as Oyo, FirstCry, Lenskart and OSIsoft have all established companies there, leading to business development and the creation of new jobs following large investments. 'We have a commitment of 10 billion dollars from SoftBank in SVF2 and we have invested close to 5 billion already,' Rajeev explains. 'The 5 billion has doubled to 10 billion. Investing is a long-term process. Some of these companies take four, five years to grow and to go public. We started in 2017. We are only three-and-a-half years old.' From the SoftBank side, the SoftBank Group have committed to $10 billion and by December 2020 had turned a fair value of $9.3 billion on investments of $4.3 billion.

As Misra stated before, investing in businesses is a long-term process and, regardless of the amount of money poured into companies, they may still require four to five years to show growth or make an IPO. Looking at one case in particular, DoorDash went public in December 2020 and on 5 February 2021 the return on the initial investment (the sum of realised and unrealised value divided by total investment) was 16.8 times the original amount. The company was only launched in May 2017, so at the time was only three and a half years old.

Due to the Covid-19 epidemic the trend of the world conducting all of its business online has only been speeded up: it is a sure bet to say not many people had heard of Zoom before the novel coronavirus dictated they would live their daily lives indoors, but now it has become an important part of life.

People who may not have thought of ordering food online before have had to reconsider their stance and those who did not previously use Netflix are now watching films on their mobile phones; many more companies have had to expedite their plans to move the majority of their business online. E-commerce has also expanded, with it now being possible to purchase a new car online in China and in Europe. The same goes for the insurance industry and even the purchase and sale of homes – normally one's greatest asset – is now being conducted online. The so-called 'American dream' more practically translates to ownership of a home and a motor car – these can be purchased online now.

The past six months have only seen this trend accelerate, but it is not as if this is a new phenomenon. With the sudden normalisation of everything happening online the rate of acceleration will only continue to speed up. Online sales cut out the middleman as well as unnecessary costs, so prices are driven downwards. With the digital revolution continuing to march forward and the adoption of AI, the 'inconveniences' within the process will be eliminated.

The world has suddenly become a much smaller place and

another fine example of the changes taking place would be within the education sector, with secondary and higher education forced to change their way of doing things. Online education is a massive industry with extraordinary growth expectations. Zuoyebang, a Chinese online education service, may have 1.3 million students signed up for its service; the implementation of bespoke services to fit learners' needs is achieved by AI by making adjustments to examinations and homework assignments.

Finance is another massive sector that has been transformed. From the smallest credit unions to megabanks, a large majority of transactions can now be performed online. It used to take foreign exchange students in America a considerable amount of time to open a bank account, but now this can be done the very same day.

Industries across the board have seen their business models disrupted by the information technology, and the next in line are life sciences and healthcare. When looking at US GDP broken down by segment, healthcare is the highest. Across the pond in the United Kingdom the largest employer is the NHS, with one million employees. The most immediate effect of ageing populations is the increased medical fees, but the old model will soon be completely disrupted with the emergence of telemedicine and the development of new drugs via companies such as Alto Pharmacy, which provide home delivery of prescription medicine. Thanks to AI the development of therapies for Alzheimer's and cancer is now remarkably cheaper as well.

And then there is the small matter of self-driving cars – from Nuro, an American robotics company – destined to become a common part of everyday life in five years' time. These are already a reality in some American cities, delivering food and prescription drugs and eliminating one of the major cost barriers in transport and delivery: the driver.

Chapter 37 **Street fighter**

'Mission complete!', Marcelo Braure was pleased to announce.

When Braure was named CEO in August 2014, he sat down with Son to define the goals they should pursue going forward: turning Sprint into a 'winning company' and then setting them up for a merger with T-Mobile US.

The reason the Braure was selected to head up Sprint was due to the saga that had unfolded with the ultimately rejected (at the time) acquisition of T-Mobile US and the subsequent merger. It was left to Braure to pick up the pieces of the company and put them back together.

Son has labelled Braure a street fighter in the past. 'But a street fighter with brains. He knows how to get results. He's the sort who thrives off being thrown in the deep end; someone who comes alive on the field of battle and no matter the cuts or bruises he's got, he's always ready to get stuck in with the next scrap. Normally, if you know you're heading into a fight you've got no chance of winning; no-one will put their hand up to lead the charge – most will have run away by that point. There's no-one who wants to draw the short straw, no-one who wants to try to win an uphill battle. No-one but Marcelo, that is'.

Braure is the sort who will always fancy his chances, someone who – when all others would be writhing about in the agony of defeat – will be working sun up, sun down to see the project through. He is willing to clean up even the messiest of situations. He embodies the popular phrase 'it's a tough job but somebody's got to do it' and possesses the absolute belief that no matter how difficult the problem, he will be able to find a solution. In that sense, Son labelling him a street fighter hits the nail on the head.

Sprint may have lost many contracts, but Braure was going to transform the telecommunications giant into one capable of winning the same number, and more, back. He had a plan to turn the Sprint brand around from a toxic one into one everyone wanted to be involved with. And by large, he did. Sprint would record their largest operating income under his watch and would create a free cash flow. He would also achieve the impossible (even for Son) by finally seeing the merger with T-Mobile US through and reversing the fortune of the company, whose shares had bottomed out to two dollars in 2016.

In 2014, SoftBank Group's future hinged greatly on their rehabilitation of Sprint and, suffice to say, Braure played an integral role in ensuring the project was a success, completely overhauling the corporate culture there. It used to be that if anyone wanted to see the chief executive of Sprint they would have go through however many doors before they could meet him. That meant having to go through security on each floor and then dealing with the chief executive's assistants and then finally there he would be. It was a symbol of how far removed the chief executive was from the actual running of the company. Braure did away with all of that, installing an open plan layout instead and got rid of all the private, detached rooms. Now anyone could stop by the chief executive's cubicle to give their opinion on how things were being done.

Braure was able to learn quite a lot from the direct feedback from his employees as well as listening on calls from customers. The information he gleaned would serve him (and Sprint) well during the rebuilding process. When Son first told Braure he wanted him to head up Sprint he would have none of it, telling Son he was 'crazy'.

Braure told Son he was a just a businessman, with no experience on the technical side of things. He had no clue how networks worked. Son, in turn, responded by saying 'I'll cover for you on the technical side of things – I just want you to oversee sales'. It may have been enough to convince Braure to take the position at the time, but ultimately Son never reported for duty as he was too busy elsewhere. Chief operating officer Miyakawa Jun'ichi (SoftBank representative director, president and chief executive as of 12 April 2021) appearing in his stead a week later, interpreter in tow.

Miyakawa met with the local network team first, detailing the possibilities of small cells, 2.5 GHz frequencies and 5G networks. At the time – 2014 – everyone thought Miyakawa had lost the plot and no-one could understand what he was on about. Fast forward six years, however, and T-Mobile US owes its success to those very same 2.5 GHz, small cell and 5G networks – everything Son or Miyakawa suggested then became the foundation for the present.

Braure is certain they are poised to become one of the most important communications companies in the entire world, citing Son's extraordinary capacity to correctly anticipate what the future holds better than anyone else as his greatest strength. He had a clear vision in 2014 for where the telecommunications industry would be in the future and things in 2020 came to pass just as he had foreseen.

Having successfully resurrected Sprint, the next lost cause Son parachuted Marcelo Claure in to rescue was WeWork. WeWork was originally founded in 2010 as a co-working space by Adam Neumann, with SoftBank making its first investments in the company in 2017. At the start of 2019 an additional investment was made in the order of $2 billion and plans were afoot for WeWork to go public, but after a number of major issues with Neumann the company was plunged into a crisis.

Claure comments on his brief from Son when everything started to kick off with Neumann. 'Masa gave me the task of basically making sure that a new WeWork was to be formed with the right capital structure, with the right shareholders, and with the right management.' Neumann may have had the right vision in place for WeWork but the practical implementation of that vision posed serious problems for the company.

The business model in place is a winning one and the sector is in good health as well. The available market is worth $3 trillion and the market scale is gigantic. The property market is ripe for revolutionising and the customary practice of 20-year contracts is not suited to the pace at which changes have occurred and continue to occur within society. Add to this the fact that demand for a more flexible form of acquiring and managing office space is huge – even with the scourge of Covid afoot – with the potential to become even greater.

When the trouble with Neumann started in 2019 Son and his team considered all of the options on the table, including selling their shares in the company. Ultimately they took measures to change the person at the head of the company and Neumann resigned; Son was and is eternally supportive of entrepreneurs so it could not have been an easy decision to make.

And so once again Son found himself on the line to Claure, history repeating itself. 'Masa said: "I have a good idea. Why don't you become the new CEO of WeWork?"' Once again, Claure rejected the idea outright, once again Claure told Son he was mad as a hatter for suggesting it – he knew nothing about real estate, after all. Son told him not to worry about it; everyone at the time thought WeWork was going to go under.

The picture Claure paints, however, is considerably tempered: 'Next year [2021] we should break-even, and a year after [2022], WeWork makes money.' Possibly the most critical point of rehabilitating WeWork is restoring its reputation: within the investment industry the phrases 'before WeWork and after WeWork' have even been coined, although this has only served to strengthen Claure's resolve.

Of course, it is vital investors get a return on their investment but Claure also believes that on top of that it is important to prove wrong those people who have written off WeWork. It was the exact same thing as happened with Sprint.

Would it help then to view WeWork as a key platform? There are two kinds of networks – the digital type and the physical – but WeWork is an actual physical platform. One of the major parts of working is having a physical space where people can gather together to get that work done. To date there has been no readily available solution for small businesses in terms of high-quality office space that can be accessed any time day or night – except for WeWork. Booking can be easily done online as well.

The first step towards WeWork's rehabilitation was cutting expenses and that in practical terms translated to trimming the workforce, from 16,000 people to 5,000. Over the course of six months expenses fell from $6.4 billion to $4 billion, which was in line with a usage rate of 65 per cent. Prior to the pandemic this rate had risen from 85% to 90%, and with expenses kept low this resulted in a profit of $1.5 billion.

The '1.5' in WeWork 1.5 refers to the current 'access' phase of its reboot, with contracts available for use on an hourly basis and flexible terms; with the All Access membership model, you have unlimited access to any WeWork in the world. WeWork 2.0 refers to the phase where the brand becomes a business solutions provider, offering marketing, accounting and insurance services to companies, providing users with an environment where all they have to do is focus on their core business. WeWork continues to evolve, with 70 per cent of the world's largest companies – such as ByteDance, Google, Facebook and Goldman Sachs – having accessed its services.

In any sector or business, being at the right place at the right time – random acts of fate, essentially – plays an important role in success and with the Covid-19 pandemic and social-distancing requirements companies have been forced into a rethink of population density within the workplace, with some concluding agreements with WeWork to accommodate their employees. It also presents a solution in terms of new trends in reducing the distance between the workplace and employees' places of residence, such as with Facebook telling its employees they can work from any WeWork they please. Furthermore, a large number of companies have adopted a hub-and-spoke model approach to business, with a head office and then a number of satellite offices, including WeWork spaces.

Son certainly took a large gamble when he asked Marcelo Claure to take over at Sprint, given the latter knew nothing about the technology – it actually ended up taking him three years to get his head around it, although Claure is adamant that 'when you get older, you get smarter and you get wiser'. Accordingly, and so as not to waste any precious time, Claure told Son he wanted Sandeep Mathrani – an experienced hand in the real estate business – to come in to act as CEO of WeWork whilst he spearheaded the rebuilding project as chairman of the board. Mathrani was well-versed in the property market and Claure was adept at dealing with consumers and the more business-oriented end of things.

Claure comments further on the division of labour at the top of WeWork. 'Because I also do all the Latin-American investments and other businesses, I dedicate one-third of my time to WeWork and Sandeep Mathrani dedicates 100%. It's my evolution of working with leaders to help them turn around business.'

WeWork operates spaces in 650 buildings in 150 cities in 38 countries and is developing office spaces to meet the needs of customers supporting larger companies such as Amazon as well as SMEs, within both urban and rural areas.

Why is WeWork so appealing to these segments?

Small business owners may for example contemplate opening an office in Manhattan but find the number of good-quality, nice-looking buildings quite limited as these are usually the preserve of larger companies. WeWork becomes an option then, giving them an office with an appealing address (location is everything for a new business). Furthermore, anyone looking to lease office space in New York City is looking at a 10-year agreement – if not longer – and even if a company could afford the contract they would still have to access the services of an architect, designer or a solicitor as well as someone to provide security for the property once everything was done. The timespan between concluding the agreement for the space and actually being able to use it would most likely take a year, whereas with WeWork a space would be available for use immediately.

Ten years may also be too much of a commitment for companies, so whilst WeWork are perfectly capable of accommodating this type of customer, they also provide hourly agreements: either way is fine. If the company expands it can always move to a larger WeWork space and if it shrinks it can move to a smaller one as well, with a minimum of fuss and no bickering with estate agents. The whole process is geared towards enabling businesspeople to focus on their business and none of the peripheral matters.

In other words, WeWork's value proposition is incredibly strong and robust from a flexibility standpoint and this will be the reason the company should pull through any temporary turbulence. There are also the communal and networking benefits to be taken into account, making it easier for businesses to win customers or find mentors who can advise on growth and expansion, and without the bother of having to go out and buy a coffee. The possibilities in this sense are tremendous.

WeWork currently provide three types of services: 'on demand', or hourly rentals; 'all access' (which includes membership and passport services) allows use of WeWork facilities anywhere in the world; and 'dedicated space', which is more akin to traditional property letting services but more flexible.

Due to the Covid-19 pandemic the world has changed and working from home has rapidly become a widespread practice. People's expectations have changed as well: they may be perfectly happy working from home or they may not want to work from home but would still like to avoid the hassle and time-sink of a commute (the notorious three-hour commutes into Tokyo on crowded trains immediately spring to mind here). The hub-and-spoke model has been adopted by businesses as a means of addressing this, with a smaller head office but a relatively larger number of satellite offices.

In a number of surveys conducted amongst company employees asking whether they would want to go back to working in an office once the pandemic is over, 10 per cent stated they wanted to go back to the old way of working, 20 per cent stated they were happy with work-from-home arrangements, and an overwhelming 70 per cent stated they would prefer a hybrid model where the two systems were mixed.

Furthermore, 45 per cent of survey respondents felt they were 'less productive than they had been in the past', with 36 per cent stating they 'didn't feel positive about their career going forwards'. In other words, arguments against working from home included reduced innovation, reduced chances for collaboration, a lack of company culture and a feeling amongst respondents that it would be harder to get ahead in their career.

Claure views WeWork's situation as one of simple mathematics. WeWork have currently got $4 billion to work with in cash. The current occupancy rate is 50 per cent and if things carry on at this same rate with no change – under pandemic conditions – then they will be able to survive for four years. The world, however, can be expected to go back to how it was pre-pandemic within those four years, with the development and widespread adoption of vaccines and testing, and so office work is never going to completely disappear.

As an example in this respect, the Chinese economy has by and large recovered to pre-pandemic levels, so it has basically become a waiting game; because of its simplicity, the WeWork business model is fool-proof in terms of its stability and soundness.

Claure is convinced that WeWork will a profitable company with a surplus. WeWork is changing the way people work and Claure wants the company to be the first thing people think of when they think of flexible spaces, just like they would do for FedEx for next-day delivery or Google for online searches.

Son speaks about Claure's approach with WeWork. 'The pandemic has made it so people can't turn up to their habitual place of work – they've been told or incentivised not to. Meaning people no longer need an office and in turn WeWork's occupancy rates have also fallen. That being said, however, they've already developed vaccines and within six months to a year of everyone getting vaccinated the world is inevitably going to open up again and then the whole Covid thing will disappear, like waking up from a bad dream. That'll be a year or two from now. The question to ask then is what sort of lifestyle and working style will people have once Covid's gone – how will they feel about work? I think that's where the new normal will come from, rather than things just going back to how they were. Even if it doesn't necessarily mean everyone in a company working together from sun-up to sundown in the same office building I think people are questioning whether there's a more efficient way of doing things than before.

'With Zoom, for example, you can see the other person's face and get your point across. I'd much rather everyone work from home until it's safe to go back to the office but with your family around it's hard to be productive sometimes. That's where WeWork comes in, where you can hold Zoom meetings from the nearest WeWork office or even call face-to-face meetings with a select number of colleagues. I think it's giving rise to a new way of working as well as creating new communities. WeWork represents the dawning of something new – something outside of a fixed office and desk, something more efficient, more community-based. In that sense I think it stands a big chance of doing well in the post-Covid-19 era.'

Marcelo Claure is obviously someone Son rates very highly as well. 'In a certain sense Marcelo is a lot like Miyauchi in that he's cautious. If you tell him to go out there and take a chance on a project that 10 years from now will be a big deal, he'll simply reply, "Yeah, but how much money is it going to make in the meantime?" That being said, when it comes to the present or the very near future he's very good at making a success of things. He'll fight tooth and nail to get things done in that sense. He knows all about risky endeavours because before he came to us he had his own company, he has got that business background. He's had to be very clever in his time and he's got a strong sense of justice. He's a natural-born leader as well, so in short he knows how to get a result, how to win a fight, how to track and capture his prey. He's a hunter, and if you've not got that sort of hunter in your ranks you'll never grow as a company.'

Son never tires of speaking about Claure and how he reflects his own philosophy about business. 'In any company you certainly need your hunters, but by the same stroke you also need your chefs. However much an art form preparing food may be, though, if you've not got hunters going out there and bringing the raw ingredients in then your chefs are going to have a lot of time on their hands and there won't be much in anyone's stomach! But then again, someone has got to prepare and dress what your hunters catch and both roles are important. But if you had to choose one it all starts with the hunters, and hunting is an eternally risky business.

'There'll be times where a hunter will find himself out in the fields in the hunt and nothing will come along or they won't be able to capture their prey and it will be a year, having only set off with their rifle and enough food for three days. If they can't catch something within those three days then they won't be eating and under those conditions they're forced to do everything it takes to track and capture their prey. It takes courage to do that, it takes extraordinary decision-making skills to survive under those conditions. It's a risky business, it's a duel to the death almost.

'Put another way, a street fighter isn't someone like a boxer, who's doing their fighting in a ring with the laws of the sport governing what they can and can't do. There's quite a vast difference between someone like a professional boxer or a *judoka* at the Olympics where the fights are all lit up, and someone in a brawl in a back alley somewhere, where the fight isn't confined to a ring. In that sort of fight you don't know what the other person's going to resort to, so everything's fair game in that sense. I'm not saying we don't care about playing by the rules, just that the business world is like one giant bar brawl in that you constantly have to deal with the unexpected, either in terms of who you're squaring up against or what weapons they've brought to the fight. Whenever something unexpected like this comes up you've got to decide right then and there how you're going to deal with the matter and then leave every-thing to your own reflexes. There's no time for parleying or reaching a consensus – what good would that be in a bar brawl?

'This is precisely why people from administration don't make good chief executives, why companies never experience any growth under them. Using the analogy from before, administrators are the chefs. In business you've got to go on the attack. If you look at conservative companies in the mould of the Japanese Business Federation and why they've got zero growth potential it's because the heads of the planning department and senior administrators have all become the decision-makers.

'These sorts are only good at managing internal affairs and in terms of promotion as long as you don't actively fail you could be promoted to chief executive as long as you stick around. You can't afford to take that approach in business any more. They're only good at renovating the same old ways of turning a profit, they aren't look-ing ahead to the next big thing and investing in it – because they're the last of their kind. They're a hopeless case – all they can really do is brag about how great they once were.'

So how was Son able to completely misjudge Adam Neumann's character? He is frank in his response.

'Well, sometimes an apple I bite happens to be a poisoned one. It was a poisoned apple, Adam,' Son laughs.

'Adam's concept was good, and his passion as an entrepreneur and his enthusiasm for stepping up to get something were extremely great. He had good taste and insights. However, as a whole, his balance was lost.

'After all, it's about adrenaline. You cannot go hunting without exceptional adrenaline. Without serotonin, you can't keep your balance, right? You have to have both, but out there in the world where reason is dominant in so many people, adrenaline is regarded as personal gain/desire. It's a very powerful component, but still, you need to hold onto reason until the end, or you will lose your balance and fall. In that sense, there were a series of unfortunate events, I think.

'There is always a certain balance at the end that everyone is convinced. There is always common ground, being well-balanced, where many people out there are happy with, you know. You have to survive when going hunting. If you feel that a snowstorm is coming, you need to be brave enough to decide to go down the mountain. However, I still appreciate a lot of wonderful things about Adam. And I think there is still a good chance for him to get back on his feet and get the next opportunity by taking this as a meaningful experience. I think it was a good lesson or hardship in a positive way for him.'

Ron Fisher gives his own take. 'Masa trusts the entrepreneurs, really trust them, and 95% of the time that works and 5% of the time it doesn't work. WeWork was the situation that where it was one of the 5%, but I think the business model of WeWork will be proven to be right. I think that, especially in the COVID environment, where COVID has changed the way enterprises work, they realized that that they don't have to have everybody in the same building, every day of a week. This flexible way of working is going to be part of our business life and WeWork allows the enterprises to create these flexible working arrangements, so in the long term, Masa is going to be right.'

Son has his own thoughts. 'Right now, it's a lockdown situation, stay-at-home, as you are well aware. People are not supposed to go to their offices. So, I think businesses in real estate, hotels, and airlines right now are in a state of collapse, no matter who is running them. However, if vaccines are widely available, I understand enough vaccines and antibodies will be distributed by the end of next year.

When that happens, I wonder if the lifestyle in the post-pandemic era would go back to the way it was before the pandemic. Is it really the right thing to sign a 20-year contract for a huge office? With a short-term and flexible contract, you can work from a place close to your house, you know you can not concentrate on your work at home when your family members and children are making noise, that's tough. You have to have Zoom meetings so often, too. In this sense, the new sharing-economy, such as WeWork, shared offices, shared cars, shared travel, or gig-workers, food delivery, Zoom as well, brings about a new lifestyle and work style, and the pandemic is accelerating the penetration of the new styles for sure. So, in post-COVID, that (implying the lifestyle and working style before the pandemic) will be reviewed as a matter of fact.'

Son himself is confident, citing the T-Mobile and Sprint merger as an example of America leading in the technology sector going forward as T-Mobile has become the world leader in 5G, with a successfully rehabilitated and rebranded Sprint becoming the pride of America.

According to Marcelo Claure, however, the real story lies elsewhere, as there were voices saying that getting permission from the US authorities for the merger to go ahead would be a tall order. By the econometric model employed by the American government there was no reason for them to authorise the merger; furthermore, there were thought to be problems with respect to competition and the amount agreed.

It has been reported that the actual reason the US authorities viewed the merger more favourably in 2019 was because of the strong standing they would have in terms of winning the global struggle for 5G supremacy, as 5G will be the technology that underpins almost everything going forward. Extraordinarily, the decision appears to have been made not by looking at past events but rather by looking ahead to the future; by Son refusing to back down, the technology he would introduce will change America's future.

Going forwards, it will not just be in the mobile sector where the world realises the technology nurtured and developed by Son is life-changing, but across multiple sectors with investments made by the Vision Fund, with his contributions in this respect more widely recognised.

In 2018, Son introduced Claure to a 35-year-old Chinese entrepreneur by the name of Zhang Yiming, the CEO of ByteDance, although Claure could not really grasp what Son meant when he described Zhang as the head of a 'new media company'.

ByteDance operated TikTok, a service where hundreds of thousands of people could record and upload video content, with the algorithm showing users those it thinks they would like to see. Users would spend all day watching videos, and the products featured in the adverts between videos were selling quite well. Son told Claure that TikTok was the future of media and e-commerce, to which his counterpart chuckled, 'Masa, you are always dreaming.'

'Bytedance and TikTok, in my opinion, will be one of the world's most valuable companies' Marcelo recalls. 'But again, that is Masa's incredible ability to be able to see the future better than anyone else.

'The new platforms that are disrupting transportation via apps like Uber, DiDi, Rappi, Grab. So, these are applications that basically allow you to utilize one application, to do a lot of your daily tasks. So, on any normal day, you just Uber to go to the office. You use UberEats to bring your food. And that's what Uber does, but if you are in Grab in Latin America or in Grab in Southeast Asia, you use this application to move, to get your groceries, to make your payments, to book your travel, to order your food.'

At present the market scale for transportation and food-delivery businesses has exploded and is set to expand even further once pandemic restrictions are lifted. With the steady adoption and implementation of driverless vehicles, the most costly part of the model – drivers' payments – will be eliminated and Uber will be able to boast an unparalleled profit margin. Marcelo Claure believes investing in these types of platforms has been a good decision.

'I think it is very unfortunate that the geopolitical wars between the China and the US can somehow potentially damage an incredible company like ByteDance. But, there will always be a solution because the technology, the company and the connectivity with people is so powerful that these are just obstacles that get in the middle. I have no doubt that ByteDance will be an incredibly powerful company, because it has the ability to deliver the news and the content that you want.

'Compare this model to the *New York Times* website where everyone is reading the same type of news – there is an absence of personalisation. TikTok shows you the videos about the news you want to see and the news you are interested in, and the figures speak for themselves, with average viewing times for the *New York Times* website standing at just two minutes per day; for TikTok average viewing times are 90 minutes per day. Looking at these figures from an advertising revenue standpoint TikTok is vastly superior, underscoring the capacity of ByteDance's algorithm to provide users with the content each and every one of them wants to see.'

Claure was in New York during the early stages of the COVID outbreak when the city was locked down, when the local government deemed letting people go to their place of work was too big a risk as they needed to keep the number of infections down. Claure also owns a home in Miami, but the situation there was even more dire. So, to escape the pandemic, he and his family headed off for Aspen, Colorado with its incredibly low infection rates as simply waiting the pandemic out was not an option for him and he wanted to keep everyone safe.

'It hasn't been as wonderful as I make it look on Twitter, I can assure you. I wake up at five every morning and go hiking for a couple of hours but from seven o'clock I'm in the office doing work just like anyone else, spending the entire day in Zoom meetings. Once the New York City lockdown was lifted, I was ready to get back to turning WeWork's fortunes around'.

When asked whether he wants to go back to how he was working in Aspen or whether he had any desire to split his time working from two locations, Claure immediately answers. 'I'm the sort of person who, no matter where I am, wants to keep my activities as local as possible. Aspen is out in the middle of nature and is an incredible place, so I got to do a lot of hiking and biking but I'm back in New York City now, knuckling under along with everyone else busy trying to revive WeWork'.

In Claure's life, a good balance between work and family is important. A quote, written on a yellow board in his office, captures his ethos. It states 'The master in the art of living makes little distinction between his work and his play, his labour and his leisure, his mind and his body, his information and his recreation, his love and his religion. He hardly knows which is which. He simply pursues his vision of excellence at whatever he does, leaving others to decide whether he is working or playing. To him he's always doing both.'

Prior to his retirement, Claure's father worked as head geologist for the United Nations for a number of years – mainly on projects having to do with natural resources – and this saw him despatched to a number of countries including Guatemala, Morocco, Brazil, the Dominican Republic, the United States and Bolivia. Up until the age of 18, the Claure family would have to move to a new country every two or three years. As a result, Marcelo had to learn to adjust to going to a new school, making new friends, learning a new language and adopting a new culture. He had to become both chamaeleonic and resilient.

'My wife is the self-appointed chief executive of our household but I'm the self-appointed chief financial officer,' he laughs. When asked what qualities a leader should possess, he states the first thing is being able to set an example for others. A good example of this would be his work ethic at Sprint, where he spent every day working from six in the morning until nine in the evening. His reasoning being that if he himself did not put in an almighty shift, there was no way he could ask others to do the same. If Claure himself wasn't fully committed to the work he was doing, then he could not in good conscience ask others to put in big hours in as well.

The second quality Claure believes a good leader should possess is surrounding themselves with people who work better than you. 'Getting the right people on board is difficult, but in doing so it creates an environment where the will become better at what they are doing.' Claure explains this further. 'When I was at Sprint, the CFO was Michel Combes. He had more telecom qualities that me. When I'm getting in WeWork, the CEO that I put in is Sandeep Mathrani. Sandeep knew real-estate much, much better than me. He had 20 years of experience in the industry. I always believe that the key to success is basically to surround yourself with people that are more qualified than you.'

The third quality, Claure discusses, is being able to dream big: if you can't dream big then you'll never be able to achieve big things. If Claure had not thought this way during his tenure as head of Sprint, it is likely the company would have gone bankrupt.

The fourth quality is simply loving what you do. A personal rule of Claure is that if you don't like what you're doing, then you'll never excel within that role. I ask him whether this equates to constantly taking on new challenges, to which he responds "that's what you've got to do if you want to achieve big things".

When asked how he views Son as leader, Claure calls him the 'captain of the ship'. If the business is the ship and the company employees are the crew, then if they don't know where the ship is headed there is bound to be mutiny. There is only one captain on the ship and it is his or her duty to make sure everyone understands the route they are on and the path that lies ahead.

'When it comes to a captain, some have got better sight than others. Some can see 100 miles off into the distance, others can see 1,000 miles, but there aren't many like Masa who can see well past the horizon. I'm more of a captain or chief executive who specialises in the short-term: I can manage a five-year plan for any company out there, but Masa would be capable of coming up with a 30-year plan for them.'

For Claure, a mission is a successful once a company is in a good place after five years but Son is always looking 30 years ahead. 'If I'm a boat captain, I can see 500 kilometers ahead, Masa can see 5000 kilometers. That's why we work very well together. He is the strategist, I'm the operator.'

Asked whether he views Son as a boss, father, older brother or friend, Claure answers 'All of the above. We're lifelong partners.' Son would no doubt be grateful to hear these words: he is still Claure boss after all. 'He would be the commanding officer of the ship, but the commanding officer is only human and will need to sleep. During that time, he needs people under him who can take over and make sure the ship doesn't crash on the rocks, and at SoftBank Group that would be myself and Rajeev Misra. But Masa's the commanding officer, he sets the course. Our role is making sure the ship stays that course".

Claure recalls one of his favourite things Son has ever said, which was on the night before the final negotiations concerning the Sprint and T-Mobile merger. At this meeting there were heavy discussions with several billion dollars at stake and so Claure got on the line to Son, asking if he had a minute to chat about goings-on. Son replied, 'I trust you. I know you'll do what's best for the company in the circumstances.' It was the highest possible praise for Braure.

As a response to the Black Lives Matter movement in the United States, Claure has set up his own Opportunity Growth Fund. When the movement first began gathering pace, Claure got on the line to Son, stating they had a duty to do something to help and they had to find a way for Black and Latinx entrepreneurs to access investment and support.

On 3 June 2020, Son would go on to tweet: 'Racism is a lamentable thing. The SoftBank Group will be setting up a 100-million-dollar fund so Black and Latinx entrepreneurs can find their way out of an unjust world and be successful.'

The United States have been very good to both Son and Claure. So, in a time of crisis such as the protests caused by the murder of George Floyd, they were not in a position to follow trends but tp lead by example. Across all the major news networks like CNN, most business leaders regardless of the sector – seemed to trot out the same line: 'we stand with the Black community.'Claure comments on this, stating 'What does it really mean to stand with someone though? It sounds good but that's it, really', and was quickly in discussions with Son, saying now was the time for them to be leaders. 'We weren't going to stand with anyone, we were determined to take the moral lead' he says. Claure rang Son up at eight in the evening, making his case for what would become the Opportunity Growth Fund. 'We should set up a special dedicated fund for Black and Latinx entrepreneurs', at which point Son immediately gave it the green light.

'Masa, you were a Korean, who struggled in Japan. It's hard to be a Korean in Japan. I'm Latino and it was hard for me when I first came to America as well, but it was even harder for Shu Nyatta, a Black partner of ours and that is why we've absolutely got to launch this fund.' Son replied it was a wonderful idea and Claure continued with his pitch. 'The fund won't be for just anyone, it's not going to be first-come first-serve free handouts. I think Black and Latinx entrepreneurs are perfectly capable and it's got to be exclusively for them and their businesses.'

'We have seen 700 businesses. We have invested in 20 businesses. It's a lot of fun. It reminds me when I was starting Brightstar and I had to go ask for money and it was very hard to get money when I was a Latino. I would have loved it, 20 years ago, if there was an Opportunity Fund.'

Claure also oversees the SoftBank Latin America Fund, commenting 'Latin America GDP is half the size of China and two times the size of India-Southeast Asia. Yet VC funding in the region paled in comparison. While China had roughly 100 billion of venture capital funding, Southeast Asia and India each had roughly 10 billion in funding and Latin America is only at roughly 1 billion. Something is wrong with that picture. So I said, "Masa, we have to invest in Latin America" and in Masa's mind, Latin America is very far, like Japan to me was very far. I told Masa 7% of the world's GDP is in Latin America. So I said we should start with 5 billion. Masa said, "Makes sense." It has been two years we have invested 2 billion. We have over 30 investments in amazing companies.

There's Kavak, an online used car sales platform which makes use of both AI and robotics, the first ever unicorn start-up from Mexico. Colombia's largest unicorn start-up is Rappi (a home delivery app in the Uber Eats mould; the name comes from *rápido*, the Spanish word for 'fast'). Both of these unicorns are quite similar to

Chinese companies, with Kavak mirroring Guazi and Rappi mirroring Alibaba's own super app. There are two unicorn start-ups from Brazil which have also benefited from the fund, and momentum has started to grow in terms of Latin America-bound investments and the winners are the entrepreneurs: the ecosystems they had been confined to are now starting to change. Claure is proud to boast that 'Masa's famous in Latin America now – he's on the front cover of all the magazines there!'

Even still with all he has achieved the fight continues for Claure, the street fighter with a clever head on his shoulders.

Chapter 38   **There is always a way forward**

On 10 March 2020 Son tweeted: 'Hi all, it's my first tweet in a while. I'm really concerned about the pandemic'.

He was back on the platform after a three-year absence and the next day he tweeted a thread about PCR testing. With the spread of Covid-19 he wanted to provide free PCR testing to anyone who wanted it. The tweet, 'first we'll order enough for one million people', was followed by, 'we're working on sorting out the application method', but ultimately the SoftBank Group press office stated: 'PCR testing shall remain a strictly personal activity', and that appeared to be the end of that. His first tweet in three years had created a sensation, however, but due to the negative response to his explanation that 'it would cause confusion with medical institutions' he was back two hours later, publicly stating 'it didn't go over that well so we may have to leave it'.

Son's approach was later vindicated as having been the correct one, but at that point in time there were few who could grasp his true intentions. 'It was a rough time for the country and we wanted to attempt to get a conversation going so we could see what we could offer and Twitter was the best platform for doing that,' Son explains. 'I wanted there to be some way to counter the spread of Covid by getting the largest number of people tested as soon as possible during the early stages of the pandemic, before a major outbreak occurred in Tokyo. That way anyone with slight fever – as well as their families, anyone they'd been in contact with – could access testing services without having to go through the bureaucratic rigmarole. You've got to have a sustained fever of 37.5 degrees or higher over the course of four days [before you can access testing]? Who came up with such a stupid rule?'

Whilst this is Son's strictly personal opinion it does reflect the frustration faced by a large number of people.

'An acquaintance of mine was poorly over the course of four days with a temperature of 38, 39 degrees, and even then all they got were excuses as to why they couldn't be treated – just "do your best to hold out and when you can't take it any more ring for the ambulance". So the family are doing their best but in the end they had to be hospitalised, they were in critical condition, all because they were just being shuffled from one department to another then back to the first place. And then of course you finally get to the hospital and it's "well, why didn't you come sooner?" But if you try to explain to people what's actually happened they directly accuse you of having misinterpreted guidelines or outright deny such an exchange could have ever happened.'

With the spread of the Covid-19 pandemic over the course of 2020 stock markets worsened, affecting the fair value of SoftBank Vision Fund recipient companies, with things like the announcement of WeWork withdrawing its planned IPO causing sudden drops in valuation. In the specific case of WeWork both the SoftBank Group and the SoftBank Vision Fund had committed to investment, posting non-operating losses of 500 billion and 300 billion yen respectively.

When the SoftBank Group announced its first-quarter 2020 operating losses on 18 May 2020 the fair value of the companies it had invested in had fallen off dramatically in the order of over 1 trillion yen in losses, with the company in the red for the first time in 15 years. During an online meeting Son stated he would convert 4.5 trillion yen's worth of owned assets into cash to enable share buy-back and debt reduction.

Meanwhile, Son's popularity on Twitter had rebounded, one of the reasons being his announcement that he would be supplying masks on a zero-profit basis, which was met with a chorus of gratitude. In a tweet on 11 April 2020 he followed this up with a brief 'all sorted', announcing, 'SoftBank are partnering with BYD, the largest mask maker in the world, to manufacture a line of masks'.

True to his word, by May he had procured a million sets of protective wear, 800,000 face shields and 230,000 pairs of protective eyewear, which were sold on by the SoftBank Group at purchase cost.

Another reason for this popularity was his frankly and openly admitting the 1tn-yen operating loss. As part of the state of emergency declared by the Japanese state, businesses were unilaterally asked to cease their daily operations, with business owners – particularly restaurants – being negatively affected. A chorus of sympathetic voices encouraged Son with comments such as 'having to close temporarily is still better than being a trillion yen in the red', 'that announcement was encouraging, it's good to know we're not the only ones', or 'even though they're up to their heads in debt he's still selling masks on at purchase value and not skimming anything off the top. It makes my own worries look a whole lot less serious in comparison'.

Son began posting a series of inspirational quotes he adhered to:

- 'I believe that true behaviour is knowing when to batten down the hatches when a storm rolls in, laughing at anyone who would call you a coward.' (15 April 2020)

- 'Giving up is not an option, there is always a way forward.' (30 April 2020)
- 'Can you achieve great things by going about doing them quietly or tastefully? You'll never achieve anything if you're not prepared to be called a hypocrite – or worse.' (12 May 2020)
- 'The source of one's failure is never an external factor, it always lies within oneself. One can never move forward until [one] admit[s] this.' (19 May 2020)

At the financial results briefing on 18 May 2020 Son appeared devoid of his usual drive and ambition. The truth is that at this time Son was more concerned than anyone else about the Covid-19 crisis, even more so than his own company's performance.

'We had to adopt a strategy of no new investments and as part of that some 15 of the 88 companies [as of the end of March 2020] receiving funding from SoftBank Vision Fund had gone bankrupt, although another 15 looked like they were going to be even more successful because of the pandemic. The rest were managing, for better or for worse. However, I choose to focus on those 15 companies which are really taking off who we hold a 90 per cent stake in, and where they'll be in five or ten years' time. We may be staring into the abyss from atop a cliff, but at least we're still on top of that cliff.' It was a singular statement of support.

'When the dotcom bubble burst the post-bubble landscape was largely shaped by a small handful of companies such as Alibaba and Yahoo!, with the rest either [falling] into bankruptcy or surviving, but with their influence greatly curtailed. The exact same thing is likely to happen again this time, I would reckon.' Son is not particularly concerned by SoftBank's current losses, dismissing them outright as the result of 'the shock caused by Covid-19'.

During the 2020 second-quarter financial results briefing, Son repeated the phrase 'I am searching my conscience as to what to do about the WeWork situation' close to 20 times and the fact he referred to himself as an 'information revolutionary' and 'venture investor' was similarly telling.

Commenting on the 1 trillion yen being the largest quarterly loss in the SoftBank Group's history, Son states, 'It's not that big of a deal. What I want to make perfectly clear, however, and what I've always maintained, is that we are an investment company. The consolidated totals concerning the valuation of the companies we invest in is irrelevant when looking at our own valuation.'

Goto Yoshimitsu (SoftBank Group director, senior managing executive officer, chief financial officer, chief information security officer and chief sustainability officer) gives his assessment, his tone calm and measured as ever.

'Take the current situation, for example. Having an operating loss of 1.3 trillion yen is unthinkably bad but you only have to look at the financial results for 2019 where we posted an operating profit of 2.3 trillion yen – an extraordinary good result, second only to Toyota. At the time we posted that profit, however, we tempered the result saying, "Whilst it may be true our operating profit results are more than robust, ultimately that has absolutely nothing to do with our current operating condition".'

Goto also comments on whether there were any lessons learnt from SoftBank having survived the 2001 dotcom bubble bursting and the 2008 financial crisis sparked by Lehman Brothers going bankrupt that could be applied to the Covid shock, and how SoftBank might overcome the setbacks.

'For one, our current balance sheet is considerably more robust than it was in 2001 or 2008 – it's a moot point discussing it. Back then Alibaba wasn't a listed company and SoftBank weren't listed as a communications company either, so this time things are completely different. From a financial point of view in terms of protecting our treasury and other such aspects Covid is not something which poses any sort of risk whatsoever.'

The most important indicator for an investment company is not its net income but rather its net asset value, and SoftBank Group shareholder value actually increased from the end of March 2020 to September 2020, going from 21.7 trillion yen to 27.3 trillion yen.

On the evening of 9 June 2020, the SoftBank Group announced the test results from a novel coronavirus antigen test it was providing in a live broadcast on YouTube featuring Son and a number of medical staff. This test was different to PCR testing as it looked at whether or not an individual had been previously infected, with medical staff and SoftBank Group and subsidiary company employees all being tested. Amongst medical staff the scope covered those working in reception or the back office as well as at the doctors and nurses and even dentists. Regarding SoftBank staff working points of sale, Son stated he 'was concerned the positive rate was higher than what it was thought to be. The PCR testing we had conducted beforehand had given us six positives and I thought that number was suspiciously low. But when we got the antigen test results back there were only two more positives, so suffice it to say I was pleasantly surprised.'

By the 40th annual general SoftBank shareholders meeting, held on 25 June 2020, Son's countenance had brightened considerably.

'Frankly speaking, I'm quite confident. I know I can build up a head of steam and then you will come along and try to put me in my place, saying, "Oh, it's just Son on his high horse as always," but again, if I am completely honest, I'm very confident. I know I can get overconfident at times and it turns into a one-man show but I think it's important to possess a bit of self-belief.'

Son did not mince his words in his address to the company share-holders about what was required going forward.

'That being said, I can make loads of investments and lead a number of companies, but it is not on me alone to push myself to the limit and see us through: I need all of our employees and management to rally everything they've got to show the world we can do even better. I believe we can do that, from the bottom of my heart. With all of our employees' skills and the recent additions we've made to management I believe we will once again be able to expand the scope of our business activities around the world.'

Son then took time to acknowledge several of his key employees.

'I would like to thank Marcelo Claure for the amazing job he has done for us with T-Mobile and Sprint. And I know Rajeev Misra has been criticised in some quarters, but were it not for him I do not think the SoftBank Vision Fund would have ever been set up. I appreciate his hard work.'

SoftBank family companies such as Vir Biotechnology (in the US), Coupang (a Korean e-commerce company), Grab (a delivery app company based out of Singapore) and Uber are all showing signs of growth and none of them would be where they are now had it not been for Vision Fund investment during the early stages of their existence.

'I think the reason why Vision Fund companies have grown as much as they have done is because of the shift Rajeev has put in; furthermore, with respect to raising investment funds and any other number of aspects Vision Fund employees and management have done a good job.'

Son ended by stating that were he to go through the complete list of people deserving of praise it would take 20 hours or so, but he was satisfied with the effort everyone was putting in in the midst of a war on all fronts and the growth they were achieving.

At the briefing session for the first-quarter projections for the 2021 financial year on 11 August 2020, history buff Son's comments were given in the form of an analogy with the Japanese warring states period, where the strongest cavalry corps in the land were completely crushed by an emergent firearms corps.

'As we continue to try to conduct business as usual in the Covid era, we businessmen face a number of hurdles to overcome. Looking to history and what it can teach us, the most important thing needed so as not to lose a battle is a strong defence, and for the SoftBank Group – whose main line of business is investments – that strong defence is cash. At the end of 2020 I said I wanted to monetise 4.5 trillion yen for the year ahead and today, as it stands, we have been able to monetise 4.3 trillion yen – 95 per cent of the way towards our goal. Our defensive shell is growing thicker and thicker.'

The 4.5tn-yen goal from August would be achieved in September, with the programme ending having yielded 5.6 trillion yen. For the embattled SoftBank Group with all of its liabilities Son had amassed a solid line of defence with the amount of cash in hand raised.

The consolidated financial statements prepared on 11 August showed net income having increased by 11.9 per cent compared to the previous year, in the order of 1.26 trillion yen – a wonderful gift for Son on his birthday.

There is a saying that 'men tend to mellow with age', but this cannot be applied to Son; if anything the opposite would appear to hold true in his case. As he tweeted on 1 September 2020, 'There is only forward movement. You only live once and no other option makes any sense. Even if you take the odd roundabout route you're always moving forwards.'

In July the SoftBank Group set up the Novel Coronavirus Testing Centre (now the SB Novel Coronavirus Testing Centre), a fully owned subsidiary. The centre is a registered health testing site where PCR tests are conducted using saliva samples. The premises themselves are exclusive leases based in the Tokyo PCR Testing Centre (in Ichikawa, Chiba) and the Hokkaido PCR Testing Centre (Kita-ku, Sapporo), and tests cost 2,000 yen (roughly $20, exclusive of VAT as well as postage and packing); this is the actual cost of testing, with no profit being made. Both testing sites combined can administer and process approximately 18,000 tests on a daily basis and as of February 2021 had administered 420,000 tests. In addition to be being selected as a 'Partner Company for Testing in Welfare Facilities' under the public offering organised by the Tokyo Metropolitan Government, the SB Novel Coronavirus Testing Centre has also provided PCR tests to Kita-Kyushu, Fukuoka (both Kyushu), Matsudo (Chiba), Sapporo, Ishikari and Kitami (all in Hokkaido) councils as well as corporations such as the Fukuoka SoftBank Hawks, the B.League (the Japanese professional basketball league), the V.League (the Japanese professional volleyball league) and, naturally, SoftBank Group companies and Hotel Okura in Sapporo.

In February 2021, a partnership was concluded with Healthcare Technologies KK to provide HELPO PCR testing packages to private individuals.

The SoftBank Group has seen its share price continue to record all-time highs as of summer 2021, going from a yearly low on 10 March 2020 at 2,610 yen to an annual high one year later of almost four times that at 10,630 yen and continuing to gain momentum.

Speaking at the 2020 Junior Chamber International World Congress held in Yokohama on 4 November to an audience of young entrepreneurs (who had all received PCR testing and were perfectly observing Covid prevention protocols), Son gave his address on 'Committing to climbing mountains', a process that had dictated half of his entire life.

'Not deciding on the mountain you want to tackle is the equivalent of wandering aimlessly,' he stated, encouraging those in attendance to not make excuses and to see things through once they had set their goal. The future held infinite potential for any young person who was determined enough, and he urged his listeners on to 'pursue your dreams with all of the enthusiasm in the world'.

Life is worth living, he said, and they should live such that they have no regrets later on. Listening to his words, the young people in attendance were visibly filled with hope.

At the second-quarter financial briefing held on 9 November 2020, Son once again placed great emphasis on the fact the SoftBank Group was 'an investment company with its focus squarely on the information revolution', and reiterated his view that net asset value was the most important indicator for an investment company.

'Whoever controls AI controls the future; the future of humankind lies in AI,' Son declared, once again stating his intent to invest in technological advances and that going forward the SoftBank Group would seek to simultaneously both attack as well as defend its position.

Responding to a question put to him by Andrew Ross Sorkin (DealBook editor and CNBC presenter) at the DealBook Online Summit organised by the *New York Times* held on 17 November 2020 concerning his failed stake in Bitcoin, Son stated, 'I was told to look into it, so I did, but now I don't bother with it any more.'

He would also talk about the optimistic outlook he has for ByteDance (TikTok's parent company), as the SoftBank Vision Fund is a major investor. Furthermore, he spoke about the extensive monetisation operation under way, stating the SoftBank Group had '80 billion dollars (approximately 8.32 trillion yen, inclusive of deals such as the sale of ARM, which should be concluded by March 2022) in cash in hand. We're an investment company, so moving forward there's less of a chance of us making large-scale investments like the one we did for Arm.'

He also gave a general financial forecast of 'whilst the situation looks grim over the short-term I remain optimistic', and revealed he had actively engaged in implementing anti-Covid-19 measures in Japan, stating, 'I wear a mask voluntarily, because I want to, and everyone in Japan is keenly aware of how important they are to preventing the spread.'

However, the mass production of vaccines and the practical implementation of a vaccination programme in Japan would take time and it would not be surprising for uncertainty to persist in this respect. 'It feels like a new disaster has happened every two or three months'; 'one major company goes belly-up and it has a knock-on effect on everyone else'; 'there's the possibility of the global market crashing from the crisis, it's up there with Lehman Brothers going bankrupt'. Son sounded a further word of warning going forward.

'Under present circumstances I feel like anything could happen. Obviously it's good news that vaccines are being developed at pace but we should also be preparing for the worst-case scenario. I think it's important to be prepared and have the cash on hand, just in case the worst happens with the crisis.'

In other words, anything can happen at any time, but for any setback there is always a way forward.

Chapter 39 **The bond of like-minded individuals**

'The bond of like-minded individuals is stronger than blood, or collaboration forged of self-interest; were it not for such a bond the revolutionaries of the Bakumatsu period would not have been prepared to lay down their lives and the Meiji Restoration would never have occurred. That sort of bond far exceeds family ties or mere selfish impulse.'

Son was speaking about his values, going on to comment that 'what the world needs the most, more than any superficial measures, is shared ambition'.

The SoftBank Group had originally been founded by just one man in 1981 but by 1982 had 30 employees and was posting 2 billion yen in turnover. By 1983 there were 125 employees and turnover was 4.5 billion yen. 1984 saw further gains with 190 employees and 7 billion yen in turnover and by 1985 SoftBank had finished its initial growth spurt, with 210 employees and over 11 billion yen in turnover. At the time of founding Son had got up on his orange-box lectern, proclaiming to his pair of part-time workers that 'within five years we'll post turnover in the order of 10 billion yen, and within 30 this will be one trillion. I want to form a business that counts profit in the trillions like a tofu factory counts blocks of tofu!' His wish came true in 2006.

SoftBank Japan held its first company information session in the autumn of 1982 which a certain Tsuchihashi Yasunari attended, rapt and hanging on every word as Son spoke about his years of furious study and business development in America. 'I can recall being in awe – I couldn't believe someone as passionate as he was existed. He was intense and full-on, you could tell he was ready to take on all comers.' Despite being only two years older than Tsuchihashi, Son was like a concentrated mass of boundless energy, reeling off such bold statements as, 'We're on the verge of a new era, the era of software!'; 'We'll surpass IBM!'; 'Growth will be explosive!'

By this point Son had already left high school in Japan after one year, gone to America to study, studied like a fiend and completely skipped American high school. Tsuchihashi by contrast had graduated from the Keio University School of Economics and, whilst this naturally involved a fair bit of swotting up, Son was on a completely different level. Rather, and more broadly, his approach to dealing with things was completely different and it left an indelible impression on Tsuchihashi.

Tsuchihashi Yasunari (current director of SB Creative) was born on 13 August 1959, joining SoftBank Japan in April 1983, immediately after having graduated from university. Since joining the company as its 71st employee he has overseen management, human resources and general administrative duties, frequently being told by Son to 'find work you can fully dedicate yourself to'.

Starting in 1983, Son was mostly confined to his hospital room, undergoing radical treatment to completely cure his condition with Dr Kumada at Tora-no-mon Hospital and returning triumphantly to lead SoftBank once again in 1986. During this stay in hospital 20 of his subordinates left SoftBank to set up a competing PC software sales company – a complete and utter betrayal by Tsuchihashi's colleagues, although he comments, 'Even still, Son never stopped treating them fairly, not for a second.'

During his time as head of the president's office Tsuchihashi saw Son's frustration at the matter first-hand and he was frequently the one who would give business briefings to his boss whilst he was on his sickbed.

'Son's desire to shake up the way society is structured has been a constant throughout his life. There has always been a consistent desire there to contribute to the infrastructure underpinning our society,' Tsuchihashi states, going on to say how he will never forget how happy Son looked when he was given Japanese nationality.

Tsuchihashi, Hashimoto Goro, Miyauchi Ken – all of these men have worked incredibly hard for Son and his vision. Son leads the way at work and so it is only natural to follow, and it has been a fun journey.

After Tsuchihashi had been with the company for 20 years he was named head of a subsidiary media company descended from one of the SoftBank publishing branches. Tsuchihashi is quick to state that Son is someone who marches to the beat of his own drum: a 'creator, someone who can see to the heart of matters'. Tsuchihashi explains that Son sees everything through to completion in a way he himself is incapable of emulating, although he possesses the same ambition and drive. He is a comrade, someone who from day one has set out to change the world; this vision has never changed and there are still things left for him to do in line with changes within society. Tsuchihashi is happy Son became a part of his life.

Otsuki Toshiki joined SoftBank Japan after graduating university during its second big employment drive in 1984 and remained with the SoftBank Group until 1999, when he founded SoftBank ZDNet (now ITmedia), which celebrated its 20th anniversary in December 2019, having gone from being listed in the Mothers section (for

start-ups) of the Tokyo Stock Exchange to Section 1 in March of that
year.

ITmedia's founding was also part of Son's vision, so whilst naturally Otsuki was responsible for preparing the business plan he was
acting on orders to make a publication capable of talking about how
technology was changing society, which he believes to be grounded
on information. 'I've got a lot of love and energy for the SoftBank
Group. It's not much but I can be proud of what I've achieved,'
Otsuki says. ITmedia can be proud of the fact it is the future of
publishing.

Otsuki also states that Son does not get emotionally attached to
things, which is why 'my admiration and respect for him never
changes'. Like Tsuchihashi, Otsuki was also named head of the
office of the president, serving for five and a half years starting in
1989. He can recall Son, on his first day on the job, instructing him,
'Going forward and when answering my questions, I want you to
say "yes" 70 per cent of the time and "no" the remaining 30 per
cent.'

Looking back, however, Otsuki states that in practice however
this meant 'only saying "yes" to him' and his role involved acting
variously as a sounding board for all and sundry, passing on messages
from on high to major customers and board members, and being
general minder, housekeeper, minute taker, schedule manager and
personal guard whenever Son was out and about. He was even
responsible for the company budget and managerial accounting
(daily account settlements). Otsuki's claim to being 'the best secretary Son ever had' is a strong one.

One morning during his time as head of the president's office in
1990 Son called him in. At the time his desk was the closest to the
door to Son's office so it took all of two or three seconds to come
when called. The order from on high was an odd one. 'By tomorrow

morning I want you to cover one of the walls in my office with photos of all of my rivals.'

And so Otsuki did as he was told, plastering a wall with faces of technology sector entrepreneurs and giants of the IT sector such as Bill Gates, Scott McNealy, Steve Jobs, Larry Ellison and Philippe Kahn. When Otsuki asked why exactly Son wanted him to do such a thing, he replied, 'Across the Pacific Bill, Scott, Larry and Steve are all putting a mighty shift in, achieving their own visions, and I want to be reminded of that every morning. It's motivation and inspiration for me to go one further.'

Around the same time, Son had started to contemplate SoftBank's existence after he had left the group, wanting to implement a management system capable of ensuring sustainable growth from within (before such a phrase even existed) and ways to automatically reproduce profits, so to this end he was going to approach management with strategies reconciling the viewpoints of both himself as company manager and the shareholders. Put another way, he wanted to create a feedback loop where the more the turnover and net worth of each individual department grew, the more economic value they would gain, and to achieve this goal preparations broadly involved three main approaches.

The first was to look at the company as a whole and then divide this up into teams of around 10 people, with the business conditions for each team made clear: more practically this meant the disclosure of their profit-and-loss statements and their balance sheet. The second was to give team leaders ('presidents') access to share performance-based payments. The third was to be very public and transparent about the whole process so the competition would catch wind of what they were doing.

Having heard his boss out, Otsuki used his rarely exercised right to say 'no' 30 per cent of the time, stating, 'If we do that, internally the company will get too competitive between departments, ruining the atmosphere.' Ignoring Otsuki's protests, Son went ahead with his scheme and the end result was actually successful, with employee motivation shooting up. At the time no stock option system had been implemented so Son, as chief executive and president, transferred his own shares as a sort of pseudo-stock option.

Son – always looking ahead – did not just use this daily accounts system as his compass to guide SoftBank going forward, he also took advantage of it to spark an undeniable motivation revolution with management, where they also became responsible for driving growth forward. Otsuki is proud to say he has worked alongside comrades – not colleagues – Son and Miyauchi.

Shinba Jun (SoftBank Representative Director and Chief Operations Officer) joined SoftBank in its fifth year of existence during its third recruitment drive for new graduates and has been a constant presence within the company's business department through to the present time (2021), with his main roles involving overseeing the sale of home appliances to volume retailers as well as everything to do with Yahoo! BB. Even in 2021 he retains the unshakeable trust of the heads of volume home appliance retailers; but not also mentioning the tremendous contributions Shinba made to the SoftBank Group by getting into the mobile phone sector would be completely remiss.

Shinba was promoted from managing director to vice president in April 2017. In over 35 years at the company, what has impressed him the most about Son has been his passion for 'building a company that counts profits in the trillions of yen' as well as the follow-up required to make this dream a reality, commenting, 'I realised that was always going to be the case.'

Son was not spouting hyperbole, he was deadly serious with his statement, and it was a feeling Shinba could get on board with, awakening his own passion. For the 2014 financial year the SoftBank Group finally broke the 1tn-yen mark (in consolidated operating profit), Son proudly proclaiming, 'It took Toyota 69 years to hit the one trillion yen operating profit milestone, whereas it only took us 33 years.'

When Shinba joined SoftBank in its current iteration in 1985, it only had 210 employees, giving it a family-like atmosphere and making it a very lively place to work. Now employees cannot do such a thing, but back then it wasn't uncommon for them to work well into the night, missing the last train and so laying down a cut of cardboard on the floor and sleeping on top of it. Everyone was young and it was like they had been given a reprieve from entering the workforce proper, their heady days as students simply carrying on. That is not to say they did not put in an almighty shift, however: it was the golden age of the PC, after all.

Shinba was named manager during this time, being responsible for sales of Toshiba's laptop computer, and would frequently go out on sales visits alongside Son and Miyauchi. He would learn quite a lot from the two on these outings, Son simply refusing to take 'no' for an answer – from the opposition or frequently from his own colleagues, for that matter.

'Why not, Shinba? Why not?'

'Do the research and then make up your mind. It's easy as. We're going to get swept up in it either way, so may as well get in whilst we can do.'

There was no avoiding the information revolution so they may as well commit to it every step of the way.

Above all: 'Don't make excuses.'

Shinba learnt a lot from Son. He can recall working on a project that resulted in the company taking a huge loss and he was completely beside himself with remorse, fully prepared to be handed his pink slip. When Son found out about it, however, his response inspired even greater dedication from Shinba, telling him, 'I'll take full responsibility for this. You've always done such a good job for us.'

When Yamagami Yuhiko – the outstanding head of the distribution department who had joined the company at the same time as Shinba – suddenly died aged 42 Son completely cleared his schedule to mourn alongside the rest of the company employees, bawling as he carried the coffin with the other bearers. Shinba would carry on using Yamagami's chair to honour his legacy following his passing.

Shinba and Son are now inseparable at the new SoftBank Group head office in Takeshiba in Tokyo. At work, though, in the thick of it, Son remains as strict and exacting towards Shinba as he always has been.

'Do whatever it takes – try anything and everything.'

'Don't say, "I can't". Find something you can do and do it.'

Shinba comments on their relationship: 'It's not entirely all about work – I like Son Masayoshi as a person. He's the type of person who shows an interest in other people, gets caught up in their affairs and becomes a true companion.'

At Kakegawa-nishi High School in Shizuoka Shinba had played on the baseball team as a second baseman, who along with the catcher is the most important player in terms of watching what goes on on the field. Playing baseball had tempered Shinba both physically and mentally, giving him the skills to view situations from a bird's-eye view and win over the other side; this sensibility would be further honed in the business world and from Son he would inherit a certain competitiveness and willingness to take on new challenges. Indeed, Shinba states that 'Son is like a father to me.'

In all his years at SoftBank the most lasting memories he retains are the period when they were setting up the Yahoo! BB ADSL service. 'Our main line of business when I started with the company was the distribution of software packages. We would negotiate directly with volume retailers under a B2B2C [business to business to consumer] model. Our line of products would change and we broke into the publishing business, but Yahoo! BB was the first time we were dealing directly with end users.'

This was the most devoted Shinba had ever been to the company, overcoming the various difficulties and conflicts as part of the development of this line of business, which in turn gave him tremendous self-confidence, and the end result was a breakthrough for SoftBank and the laying of a solid foundation for what was to come.

'I think at SoftBank we strive to be the fastest around in terms of incorporating the latest technology and business models, and we also give customers what they want.' As Shinba says, SoftBank have invested in many companies and established many joint ventures and strategic alliances to bring the latest technology to Japan; furthermore, via the SoftBank Vision Fund the number of allies around the world at the cutting edge of their various fields has also increased. He also states that SoftBank cannot afford to rest on their laurels, as this is at odds with their pursuit of innovation and taking on new challenges.

'Innovation and pursuing new challenges is something we want to see happen, so we'll carry on blazing a trail in that sense.'

Chapter 40   Even higher still

Turning points – there have been many.

For Ron Fisher, a core ally of Son's for close to 30 years now, each phase of the SoftBank Group story brings its own set of memories. In 1995, at the point in time where the SoftBank Group invested in Yahoo! prior to their going public, everything suddenly changed for the company.

In 2000, China's GDP was still only $1 trillion, not even a quarter of that of Japan's. Son had met with Jack Ma, who had just set up Alibaba, telling Fisher not long afterwards, 'Over the next five to seven years the Chinese economy is going to experience rapid growth, to the point it eclipses Japan's own. This is an economy we have to be invested in.'

Jack Ma and Alibaba, which originally operated exclusively on a B2B model, began opening up B2C and C2C channels and diversifying their business model, on Son's advice. Alibaba's aggregate market value was valued at $713 billion as of 19 February 2021. 'It was just amazing insight in terms of understanding what you could do with the application of technology because Masa saw what was happening,' Fisher explains. 'The insight in terms of when you apply technology to emerging situations, you have enormous results, you have results way beyond what you could expect.'

Fisher states he has spoken with Son about retiring but concludes – cracking a wry smile – 'He's not going anywhere any time soon.'

Nikesh Arora had been named a potential successor for Son but that was in 2015. When Nikesh joined Masa was 58. Fisher, who is 10 years older than Son, says he has advised him on ageing, telling him, 'Masa, 60s seems old when you're in your 50s because look, I'm gonna be 60. But now, as I'm looking to be in my 70s, I'm telling you, you're not going anywhere. There's no way you're going to step back.'

In 2020 Son still works like a man possessed, operating at breakneck speed, with Fisher explaining 'he keeps the craziest, craziest pace I have ever seen. Almost every day he is on calls after midnight. And you are still hearing from him, we are getting emails from him when we are on the phone with him.'

Of course, Son will take into account the long-term needs of his company before deciding when to retire. At present the SoftBank group have become a strategic investment company after they went through a number of organizational/structural changes. Now they are at a stage of fostering their employees of the next generation by giving them opportunities to gain experience in various fields. It may take 20 years until they have gained enough knowledge and expertise to make their presence felt in this global company as the new generation.

Son has talked at length about the information revolution, which he says can be divided into four chapters: Chapter 1 is the PC Revolution; Chapter 2 is Internet Revolution; Chapter 3 is the Mobile Internet Revolution; Chapter 4 is the AI Revoution. Together, he calls this the Information Revolution. 'Intel came up with the hardware CPU and Bill Gates gave the world software – if the Windows OS had never come along the PC wouldn't be as widely used as it is today. There is no doubt that it was Gates that opened the first chapter of the Information Revolution. He is the real superstar of that period.

The second chapter is the birth of the internet. 'Jerry Yang founded Yahoo! in the States, which paved way for Amazon, Google and Facebook. Each company has played a major role in the Internet in its unique way.'

It follows on that the third chapter would be mobile internet. 'What was amazing about Steve Jobs was that he had invented the Apple II and opened up the first chapter of the information revolution along with Bill Gates but eventually he got fired by Apple and had a hard time. But – true genius that he was – he picked himself up, dusted himself off and once again completely redefined the future of humankind.'

Like Son says, there is no doubt that Steve Jobs was a bona fide genius, creating the platform during his second coming for each mobile service provider to accelerate and expand their own products' growth.

The fourth chapter, which has only just begun, will be AI. 'Within the realm of AI I believe Nvidia's Jensen Huang holds the key to the hardware aspects,' Son says. Huang in turn commented on the possibilities of AI in his video interview with Son at SoftBank World.

'Arm is truly one of the world's rarest, most valuable treasures – a treasure for all humankind – and I am truly grateful they have entrusted me with their business. Nvidia will become global market leaders with their fusion of AI computing and CPU power and will only grow as the era of AI comes into full swing. Our acquiring Arm marks an exciting start.'

AI service providers will require a platform to create their services on, at which point use will become even more widespread, with category killers undoubtedly popping up for each market segment, a whole new world emerging and expanding before our very eyes.

Son says, 'More than anything else I would say I was incredibly lucky to get close to each of the key players in the information revolution so far and develop a friendship with them. They have proved an endless source of inspiration and I've been able to learn so much from then. What I want to do is present their ideas but from my own angle.'

Each of the aforementioned key players pioneered technology from an inventor's point of view, with global expansion inherent to their genius and platform. Unfortunately, the Japanese market is small, and even if an inventor were to be successful, unless the product or service they had come up with became big enough on the domestic market then global expansion would be a tall order. By comparison, the key players in the information revolution were fortunate to have a marketplace as large as the American one almost as a birthright. The Chinese market is huge as well.

'Recently Alibaba and Tencent have made huge strides and experienced massive growth as the top runners of the internet revolution in China. In this sense as well I was more than lucky to have developed an alliance with Jack Ma at such an early stage. I think the fact I don't actually manufacture anything is actually a strength, as it means I can partner with anyone.'

Indeed, it is Son's partners who do the manufacturing or provide services, creating a beneficial relationship, as normally if these partners wanted to broaden their horizons it would have to be by forming alliances with other manufacturers – frequently a tall task.

'As we don't actually make anything our prospective partners are less wary of us so ultimately it's easier for us to form partnerships – it's the classic case our weakness being our strength. In the information revolution there are those who take risks as inventors and those who provide inventors with capital. It is my view that when these two elements are in place then the revolution can begin in earnest.

'In accordance with the times, SoftBank Group is the most readily available partner for those people developing the most crucial new technologies. I think with the founding of the SoftBank Vision Fund, we can partner with unicorn start-ups and rookie companies to create a large number of business chances.'

The current frictions between the United States and China has been increasing the risks of politics intervening economic activities. Big questions remain about how the two countries will reconcile their differences, and then there is also the rise of India and South American countries to take into account.

Son looks higher up and beyond the present international situations. 'The governments of various countries are doing everything they can do to protect their interests. But what if you look at the world in future in much larger units of time, like centuries? What if you approach things from a mindset of looking 100, 200 or 300 years into the future? Are all of these decisions taken to protect minuscule interests bound by geography with a small-scale sense of justice and a short-term mindset really for the greater good of humanity?'

In times past Japan was divided up into a number of domains (fiefdoms) and so, for the purposes of protecting their own interests, they would occasionally go to war with each other. Japanese national interests were, up until 150 years ago, very small indeed. But then the Meiji Restoration occurred, major developments within the fields of transportation and communications happened, and people's worldview was no longer limited to the boundaries of their domain.

150 years have passed since the abolition of domains and the establishment of the current prefectural system in Japan in 1871. The changes to come in the next century will make even bigger impacts on us than the changes made since this landmark event occurred. Communications will develop even further. The whole world can be accessed in less than a second with a single click. People

will benefit as a single group of human beings, above the considerations of nationality, religion and ethnicity, and Son views this as intrinsic to achieving world peace.

'In my opinion national governments going to war over negligible interests, people killing each other . . . Where's the benefit in any of that? Politicians are to negotiate and find a way out at the last minute before people cross blades. I also think heads of state are doing their best to bring happiness to their people, for the greater good. During transitional periods there may be a temporary phase of political gamesmanship concerning interests, a political tug-of-war, but I believe, in the end, our society will be a more peaceful and beautiful one. I believe in the inherent goodness of humankind. I am optimistic.'

Miyauchi comments, 'Son is a true leader, in that he is insightful and can see the path we have to take. As the owner of the company I hope he does everything within his power to carry us along that path.'

Ron Fisher takes this further, arguing that Son has three core strengths. 'I'd say, vision, combined with commitment, and then relentless pursuit. So, it's just kind of three tiers, you have to have the vision. You then have to have the courage to commit. And then you have to have the relentless nature to pursue it in a way that will make it successful. Masa has those three tiers. The relentless execution.'

When Son focuses on something, he commits all his energy to it, aiming to take it to the top and then even higher still. The boy born on an unregistered plot of land has climbed the ranks and become a man of unshakeable belief in the power of the information to bring happiness to all.

To end on his own words: 'The AI revolution has only just begun.'